# INBOUND MARKETING AND SEO

# INBOUND MARKETING AND SEO

## INSIGHTS FROM THE MOZ BLOG

Rand Fishkin and

Thomas Høgenhaven

**WILEY**

This edition first published 2013
© 2013 SEOMoz

*Registered office*

John Wiley & Sons Ltd, The Atrium, Southern Gate, Chichester, West Sussex, PO19 8SQ, United Kingdom

For details of our global editorial offices, for customer services and for information about how to apply for permission to reuse the copyright material in this book please see our website at www.wiley.com.

A catalogue record for this book is available from the British Library.

ISBN 978-1-118-55155-4 (pbk); ISBN 978-1-118-55156-1 (ebk);
ISBN 978-1-118-55157-8 (ebk); ISBN 978-1-118-55158-5 (ebk)

Set in 10 pt. Minion Pro by Indianapolis Composition Services

Printed in the United States by Bind-Rite

To the Moz community—You rock! Thank you for helping to build an extraordinary organization.

To the remarkable writers and marketers who helped make this book possible—Thank you for your generous contributions.

Special thanks to Ashley Tate and Christy Correll—You made this book possible.

*—Rand and Thomas*

To the Moz team—My thanks; I feel lucky, thrilled, and humbled to share this journey with you.

To Geraldine—I'm sorry for all the nights blogging and writing have kept me away from you; your love and support means the world to me.

*—Rand*

To Marie—For making everything look brighter, day after day.

*—Thomas*

## PUBLISHER'S ACKNOWLEDGEMENTS

Some of the people who helped bring this book to market include the following:

*Editorial and Production*
VP Consumer and Technology Publishing Director: Michelle Leete
Associate Director–Book Content Management: Martin Tribe
Associate Publisher: Chris Webb
Executive Commissioning Editor: Craig Smith
Associate Commissioning Editor: Ellie Scott
Editorial Manager: Jodi Jensen
Senior Project Editor: Sara Shlaer
Moz Content Editor: Christy Correll
Moz Project Manager: Ashley Tate
Editorial Assistant: Annie Sullivan

*Marketing*
Associate Marketing Director: Louise Breinholt
Marketing Manager: Lorna Mein
Senior Marketing Executive: Kate Parrett
Marketing Assistant: Tash Lee

*Composition Services*
Senior Project Coordinator: Kristie Rees
Compositor: Erin Zeltner
Proofreaders: Melissa Cossell, Wordsmith Editorial
Indexer: BIM Indexing & Proofreading Services

# PROCEEDS

All proceeds of this book will be donated to Vittana (www.vittana.org).

Vittana's mission is to graduate a generation beyond poverty through the power of education. Vitanna enables anyone with $25 to lend directly to ambitious students in the developing world. 100 percent of lender money goes directly to the students, and more than 99 percent of students repay their loans upon graduation.

# CONTENTS

# INTRODUCTION

*By Rand Fishkin and Thomas Høgenhaven*

THE TERM *INBOUND MARKETING* was first used by Brian Halligan and Dharmesh Shah in their seminal 2009 book, but the concept has been around much longer. As far back as 1999, Seth Godin referred to the same concept under a different name in his blog: "*Permission marketing* is the privilege (not the right) of delivering anticipated, personal, and relevant messages to people who actually want to get them."

Over the past few years, many marketers who focus on organic channels like search engine optimization (SEO), social media, and content marketing have started using the phrase *inbound marketing* to describe the combination of these channels in their roles and responsibilities.

So why are marketers now turning to inbound marketing? Reasons abound, but two in particular are both timely and relevant. First, Google—the world leader in search, with more than 90 percent of the global market share—has evolved its algorithmic considerations massively in the past five years. Google has rolled out new types of search results, cracked down on spam, upgraded its ability to detect and remove low-quality content, become faster and fresher, dramatically dampened many historic SEO factors, and renewed its focus on promoting great brands that produce superlative web content.

Second, practitioners of SEO have evolved. We realize that SEO is a tactic, not a strategy. We realize SEO needs to be used as part of a broader set of marketing tools. In order to succeed in SEO, a multichannel approach is necessary. This book is all about how to perform in a new era of inbound marketing.

# SEO IS CHANGING

Search and SEO are changing. Google is hitting suspicious-looking link networks, devaluing directories, and increasingly penalizing sites with highly dubious link profiles. Underhanded tactics to rank well in the search engine results pages (SERPs) no longer work.

Optimizing a site used to be about getting to the number one spot in a SERP and staying there. Ranking number one is no longer the only important factor. Click distribution is different than it used to be; it's influenced by rich snippets like star ratings, number of reviews, price, author photo, video preview, publication date, and social annotations. Optimizing your author photo might increase click-through rate (CTR) more than moving up one or two places in the search results will.

Moreover, Google wants the "fat head" keywords—the small group of keywords that typically drive the most traffic—to themselves. Try searching for credit card offers, flight tickets, and new movie titles. The SERPs are filled with other Google-owned products, which makes sense for its business. This makes it more important than ever before for you to have keywords in the "chunky middle" (more descriptive terms that drive fewer visits individually, but large amounts of traffic overall) and the "long tail" (the many, more specific terms that may only drive a few visits each, but can drive a lot of traffic in aggregate).

In many ways, though, SEO is still SEO. Search engines still need accessibility help in order to crawl, index, and rank the content in the correct way. This requires logical information architecture, correct use of meta tags, implementation of relevant schema markup, and use of sitemaps, as well as correct use of Google Webmaster Tools and Bing Webmaster Center. You still need links to rank for competitive keywords. You still need to conduct proper keyword research. And you still need to produce content that can be understood by humans *and* robots. Delighting users has always worked pretty well, and will become increasingly more important as the search engines get smarter.

# FROM SEO TO INBOUND MARKETING

SEO is often declared "dead"—but that concept is just silly. People will always need to retrieve information online, and search is a powerful way to do this. Search and SEO are very much alive, and it's much more fruitful to see search as a part of a bigger marketing mix.

Many of us have suffered SEO tunnel vision, but SEO does not exist in a vacuum. It's increasingly difficult to succeed in SEO when using this channel in isolation. That's where the multichannel approach comes in: Google constantly rewards companies who provide good products, user experience (UI), branding, content, and conversion rate optimization (CRO).

Some SEOs are skeptical of the conceptual expansion of SEO to inbound marketing. We hope to reduce some of this skepticism by briefly addressing two of these critiques:

*Critique 1: Inbound marketing is just a new name for SEO*. No, it is not. SEO is a tactic. Inbound marketing is a strategy. Inbound marketing is an umbrella term for many marketing channels, whereas SEO is a channel in itself. Some consider social media, content, analytics, and CRO to be part of SEO, but the majority of social media and analytics professionals will hardly characterize themselves as SEOs. In fact, you can do inbound marketing without doing SEO. Inbound marketing is not a new name for SEO, but a name for organic, earned marketing.

*Critique 2: Inbound marketing is a branded term used to market the likes of HubSpot and Moz.* The term is used and evangelized by companies such as HubSpot and Moz, but we'd be just as happy using terms like organic marketing, permission marketing, and earned media. But marketers are not using any single one of these terms, making it harder to use them broadly. Inbound marketing is rapidly becoming the accepted industry term to sum up all the channels that bring in customers organically.

## INBOUND MARKETING

So, what is inbound marketing? In a general sense, we see it as *things you can do on the web that earn traffic and attention, but don't directly cost money.*

Don't buy. Don't beg. Don't bludgeon. Inbound marketing is all about *earning* attention and love. This is often a superior way of marketing, simply because people prefer inbound channels to outbound. According to Google, 82 percent of clicks in the SERPs go to organic results and 18 percent go to pay-per-click (PPC) ads. Less than 1 percent of clicks on Twitter go to promoted tweets. The best and brightest Facebook ads are lucky to amass a 2 percent CTR.

There is no single way to do inbound marketing, and it's not about being everywhere. Your goal should not be to have a presence on all channels, but to really be present where your audience exists. For example, if your target audience is 55+ year-old men, Pinterest might not be the right channel to invest in. It's ultimately about selecting the channels that fulfill your strategic goals the best, and selecting the channels that give the highest ROI.

The channels with the highest ROI are often those others don't invest in—there is so much potential there! This is what Rand calls the *short men, tall women* rationale: most men are interested in short women, while most women are interested in tall men. Consequently, there are many single short men and tall women who are very attractive based on other parameters. The smart singles, therefore, pursue those tall women and short men the majority tends to ignore. This rationale is one of the reasons inbound marketing works so well: for each dollar spent on inbound channels, eight dollars are spent on paid channels.

Inbound marketing is not free; it takes time and money to create and distribute phenomenal content. But it's often a more cost-effective marketing strategy than paid marketing. We are not arguing that paid marketing doesn't have its place in the world, but the point of this book is to show you how effective and efficient inbound marketing can be.

## INVESTING IN INBOUND MARKETING FOR THE LONG TERM

The best way to build a brand is to be truly remarkable, recognizable, and authentic—and to provide the world with answers to the question "Why?" Successful inbound marketing plays a pivotal role in branding, but takes time and effort. Don't invest in SEO—or any other inbound channel—for the short term. Like all well-planned strategies, inbound is a long-term investment.

Inbound marketing helps with brand building, and having a brand helps inbound marketing. It is a positive spiral that rewards those who are already successful, as is illustrated in Chapter 11, "The Rich Get Richer: True in SEO, Social + All Organic Marketing." As Eric Schmidt said in 2008, "Brands are the solution, not the problem." If you are a good brand, SEO tends to be the solution, not the problem. Through Google, brands receive preferential treatment. Brands get increased visibility in SERPs, and penalties and filters increasingly target unbranded sites. This makes sense, for familiarity breeds trust. You probably recognize this from your own searches. When looking for that new long blue nightgown, you are probably clicking the link to Amazon or Macy's, not the link to longbluenightgowns.biz.

Building your site and marketing efforts for a long-term ROI also solves the old dilemma between using black hat tactics (deceptive or questionable SEO practices that don't follow search engine guidelines) and white hat tactics (best practices to build an experience that's actually valuable to customers and crawl-able by the search engines). Truly remarkable brands do not take the low road or use aggressive marketing tactics. They don't need to.

## WHY READ THIS BOOK?

SEOs are upgrading their job title to inbound marketer, which comes with responsibilities that include a wide array of channels. New marketers are entering this fast-paced industry all the time. While *The Moz Blog* is a rich resource for inbound marketers, it can be hard to get an overview of the field from its many hundreds of posts. This book curates the best of the blog over the past few years. All of the blog posts have been reassessed and many of them have been updated for relevant content. We hope this book will help you make a steady investment in inbound marketing that gives you good returns over the long run.

## ABOUT MOZ

SEOmoz started as an SEO consulting company in 2004 and later became a leading provider of SEO software. In 2013, SEOmoz transitioned its brand to Moz, expanding its product line to include search, social, and content optimization within a single platform, Moz Analytics. Moz's mission is to create products that streamline the inbound marketing process while staying true to the company's TAGFEE* values, giving marketers everywhere a better way to do inbound.

*The TAGFEE code sets the standard that all work and content produced by Moz is Transparent and Authentic, Generous, Fun, Empathetic, and Exceptional.

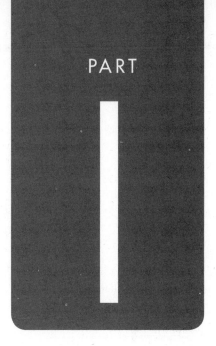

PART

I

# SEARCH ENGINE OPTIMIZATION

*By Ruth Burr*

SEARCH ENGINE OPTIMIZATION has been around for about as long as search engines have. It's hard to imagine SEO before Google with its current market share domination, but as early as the mid-1990s, marketers were thinking about how to make their products as findable as possible on the web.

## THE BIRTH OF SEO

In the early days of search, Yahoo! and its cohorts were run like Yellow Pages services: website owners submitted their sites for indexing, and search engines did their best to match up pages with search queries. Most ranking criteria centered on *keyword density*—did a given keyword show up in prominent places on the page? How many times did it occur in the page's content?

It wasn't long before website owners caught on to search algorithms and began to tailor their sites to meet search engines' criteria. Search engine optimization was born! This meant that the first generation of web marketers had new tools to help get their content in front of the growing consumer base that was the Internet. It also meant that they could, through reverse-engineering the algorithm, easily create hundreds of pages that ranked for search terms without passing much value along to the searcher.

These were the first skirmishes in what would become a battle that continues to this day. Search engines try to create spam-proof algorithms that surface the best content to their users, while marketers struggle to get their sites to the top of the rankings—sometimes, by any means possible.

As weaknesses in their algorithms continued to be exploited, search engines began to look beyond individual web pages to off-page criteria like links. It was around this time that Google came on the scene, and changed everything.

## LIFE AFTER GOOGLE

Google's algorithm was based on a concept called PageRank, which weighed on-page factors against value passed from page to page via links. With PageRank, a link to a webpage becomes a "vote" for that page. It's a form of social proof: the more people who agree that a site is worthwhile, the more credibility that site has.

Google quickly amassed a huge market share, edging out smaller competitors like AltaVista and toppling Yahoo!'s dominion over the search engine space. As more and more people turned to Google to shop, play, and find information, the Google SERPs (search engine results pages) became the place you had to be if you wanted to succeed online. In 2013, comScore reported that Google had 67 percent of the U.S. search engine market share, trailed by Microsoft Bing and Yahoo! with 16.5 percent and 12.1 percent, respectively (http://mz.cm/XOG96n). Eager to reach customers on the web, more and more businesses are turning to SEO as a major revenue stream.

As SEO grew as a practice, Google built Google Webmaster Central and Google Webmaster Tools. Now site owners and SEOs could hear directly from Google about new developments and get some hints about what they should or shouldn't be doing to rank well. The algorithm is still more shrouded in secrecy than not, but Google Webmaster Tools does provide some good diagnostic tools to help site owners maintain search-friendly sites.

The modern SERPs look very different than they did at Google's inception, when the top 10 pages were listed as 10 blue links on a white page. Since then, Google has integrated its News, Video, Images, Local, and other vertical searches into one SERP format called Universal Search. It's started utilizing users' search histories, IP addresses, and social media activity to tailor search results to individuals. Google is also constantly experimenting with different numbers of results, new result and ad formats, and even a Direct Answers service that displays the answer to a question like "How many tablespoons in a cup" directly on the SERP, no click needed. To be successful, it's important for today's SEOs to keep abreast of the latest changes.

## CRACKING DOWN

As Google rose to ascendancy in the search engine market, attempts to exploit the algorithm cropped up as fast as Google could squash them down. With updates to Google's algorithm coming every few months, new ways to game the system had plenty of time to take effect before the next crackdown.

That all changed in 2010 with Google Caffeine, an update that marked the beginning of more frequent updates to the algorithm. Now Google is making slight tweaks to the algorithm almost every day, with frequent larger changes as well.

It had been a long-held axiom in the search world that "Content is King." Without at least some text content on a page, it was very difficult to show search engines what a page was about at all, let alone that it was unique enough to rank. However, this meant that hundreds and thousands of sites on the web were shoehorning small amounts of unnecessary, keyword-stuffed text onto pages that didn't really need it. Additionally, huge content sites sprang up with page upon page of content designed to rank for queries but not provide real answers, instead using content to draw users in to a page full of ads.

In 2011, Google released a major update called Panda. Google Panda targeted this "thin content," looking for more robust signals that content was relevant, unique, and valuable to users. Google has confirmed that Panda is an ongoing algorithmic "check" that is run periodically to target new thin content.

While inbound links have remained a valuable signal for site authority, they were also one of the most frequently manipulated. In 2012, Google released the Penguin update, designed to target "unnatural" links such as links from directories and links that webmasters had surreptitiously paid for.

One major upheaval as a result of Penguin was the changing focus on link anchor text. Google had long named keyword-rich anchor text in inbound links as an indicator of quality, but eventually also found that a high percentage of inbound links with keyword-rich anchor text (as opposed to the name of the website or generic text like "click here") was also a sign of an unnatural link profile. Like Panda, Penguin is a periodic fix that Google runs to catch new offenders.

Panda and Penguin impacted countless websites. Companies who had had search engine success for years suddenly found themselves scrambling. In the wake of these updates, the SEO community has had a renewed focus on "white hat" SEO—that is, implementing solid business practices to create quality websites within search guidelines, rather than resorting to tricks or loopholes. For more on this, see Chapter 1, "White Hat SEO: It F@$#ing Works."

## HOW SEARCH ENGINES MAKE MONEY

When learning how to rank in search engines, it's helpful to remember that search engines aren't public services; they're businesses, out there to make money. Google's market share is an asset that can be used to sell ads. Sixty-seven percent of the available eyeballs in the U.S. are looking at Google when they're searching, and that's an audience advertisers can't afford to ignore. Charging advertisers to get their ads in front of those eyeballs is what drives Google's bottom line.

What this means to search engine marketers is that Google is going to do everything it can to protect its most valuable asset: its market share. That means that Google will consistently do everything in its power to make sure that people who use Google find what they're looking for. Search engines put a great deal of time, talent, and money into discerning what users want when they search, and which pages don't fulfill those needs.

## TACTICS THAT NEVER STOP WORKING

Building an "algorithm-proof" website that won't be hurt by the likes of Panda and Penguin means adopting classic white hat techniques that never stop working. These include building an easily-crawled site; creating content meant to engage users; building relationships and communities to encourage content sharing in order to naturally accrue links; and looking at site performance to consistently improve performance. The benefit of this stance is that SEOs can return to focusing on the user and customer, while still showing search engines that we have quality, rank-worthy sites.

## THE FUTURE OF SEARCH

In addition to a lot of volatility in the SERPs, the last couple of years have brought some really exciting opportunities and resources for search marketers. In 2011, Google, Yahoo!, and Microsoft all agreed to support structured data through `Schema.org`. Now we have a hugely expanded ability to give search engines more information about different types of data on our sites, allowing for faster, more thorough parsing of that data (read Chapter 2, "Schema.org: Why You're Behind if You're Not Using It" for more on the power of structured data).

Structured data has also led to "rich snippets" showing in search results, which may contain information about the page's author, pictures from the page, reviews of a product or service, or more. These snippets can result in higher click-through rates on search results, even if they aren't in the coveted top three positions.

The advent of social media platforms has also fundamentally changed the web, and web marketing along with it. In the early days of SEO, content creation online was limited to people who had their own websites or blogs. Social media changed all of that. Today anyone can create content on the Internet, and everyone is creating it—from Facebook statuses to tweets to Tumblrs to Yelp reviews. People are interacting online all day, not only with each other, but with brands and businesses as well.

Search engines see social media activity as a measure of social proof much like links are (hence the saying "Likes are the new links" among SEOs). Google and company aren't about to ignore this vast buffet of data on what people like, how they interact, and what they're looking for—and neither should web marketers. We have so many new opportunities to get our content and products out there and to really engage with consumers. In the modern world of search, businesses need to be participating in conversations around their brands, because they're happening whether the business participates or not.

The most exciting development in SEO has been how much the industry has grown up over the years. SEO has gone from something only a small group of hackers and cutting-edge marketers were doing to a full, legitimate industry. Businesses who might still have been buying Yellow Pages ads five years ago are investing in inbound marketing instead.

# 1

# WHITE HAT SEO: IT F@$#ING WORKS

*By Rand Fishkin*

> **Editor's Note:** *This article was originally posted on <u>The Moz Blog</u> in April 2011 in response to an off-site post that dismissed the value of white hat SEO. Since then, Google has released many updates to its search algorithm. Most prominent among the updates are Penguin, which devalues spammy back-links and over-optimized sites, and Panda (originally launched February 2011 as Panda/Farmer), which hits sites with thin content and link farms hard.*

I HATE WEB SPAM. I hate what it's done to the reputation of hardworking, honest, smart web marketers who help websites earn search traffic. I hate how it's poisoned the acronym SEO, a title I'm proud to wear. I hate that it makes legitimate marketing tactics less fruitful. And I hate, perhaps most of all, when it works.

Here's a search for "buy propecia," which is a drug I actually take to help prevent hair loss. (My wife doesn't think I'd look very good sans hair.)

**Propecia** without prescription. Cheap **Propecia** online - Propecion ...
**Buy Propecia** online without prescription, get generic Propecia online. Free AirMail Shipping
on big packs. Order cheapest Propecia online and you'll get ...
propecion.com/ - Cached - Similar

**Buy** Generic **Propecia** Online
Buy best quality generic Finasteride with lowest prices guarantee at 4rx.com because
**propecia** is safe and secure, **buy** Finasteride online.
www.4rx.com › Skin & Hair Care - Cached - Similar

**Buy** Brand **Propecia** & Generic **Propecia** Online Without Prescription
Buy Propecia Online. Easy order processing, no prescription required. Lowest price
guaranteed. Customer service worldwide, discount system, round-the-clock ...
www.unitedstatesdiscounts.com/ - Cached

**Propecia**
Merck's official site with information about treatment of male pattern hair loss .
www.propecia.com/ - Cached - Similar

**Buy Propecia**
Buy Propecia Online Without Prescription! Generic Propecia (Finasteride) 1mg & 5mg from a
trusted online pharmacy! No Prescription Needed, Only $0.33 Per ...
buy-propecia.biz/ - Cached - Similar

**buy propecia** price - NMSU Library
In addition to general cataloguing sites, provides resources relating to rare book cataloguing,
medieval manuscripts, and 'history of the book' sites.
lib.nmsu.edu/rarecat/ - Cached - Similar

Like most search results in the pharma sphere, it's polluted by pages that have artificially inflated their rankings. This is obvious to virtually everyone who's even minimally tech-savvy, and it has three terrible results:

1. Marketers and technologists who observe results like this equate SEO with spamming. If you've read a Hacker News (`http://news.ycombinator.com`) or StackOverflow (`http://stackoverflow.com`) thread on the topic, you've undoubtedly seen this perspective.

2. SEOs new to the profession see this and think that whatever these sites are doing is an effective way to earn rankings, and try repeating these tactics (often harming their sites or those of employers/clients in the process).

3. Consumers learn not to trust the search results, killing business value for everyone in the web world.

Spam removes economic and brand value from the search/social/web marketing ecosystem. If you create this kind of junk, at least be honest with yourself—you're directly harming your fellow marketers, online businesses, searchers, and future generations of web users.

In April of 2011, Kris Roadruck wrote a post called "White Hat SEO is a Joke" (`www.krisroadruck.com/rants/whitehat-seo-is-a-joke`). He was upfront about the fact that his post was intentionally provocative, not entirely truthful and more sensational than authentic. Despite these caveats, I think a response and some clarification about my thoughts on black hat in general are in order. I'm responding less because I think Kris believes it and more because of the surprisingly supportive response his post received in parts of the search community.

## SOME POINTS ON KRIS' POST

Kris begins his article with a personal realization:

> *I started realizing there were only really 2 kinds of white-hats. The ones complaining about how they were doing everything by the book and getting their asses handed to them by "unethical tactics", and the ones that were claiming success that didn't belong to them ... because they ... happened to be in a niche that bloggers find interesting or entertaining.*

> *It's easy to preach great content when you have a great subject. But no one gives a shit about non-clog toilets or pulse oximeters or single phase diode bridge rectifiers. Sure you might be able to piece together 1 or 2 bits of link-bait but you can be sure that you aren't going to get the anchor text that you want.*

Kris' premise seems compelling and even has elements of truth. Great content does work better in fields where there's more interest from web-savvy site owners. On the whole, though, his proposition is a lie. That lie—that "great content" doesn't work in boring niches—is one told out of laziness, jealousy and contempt. It's told by spammers to other spammers because it glosses over the fact that white hat, legitimate marketing can work well in ANY field, for any site.

How about some examples, you ask? I am happy to provide them.

> **Editor's Note:** *These examples refer to the status of the sites in 2011, when this post was originally written.*

- Here's Ready for Zero (www.readyforzero.com). It's a Y-Combinator backed startup tackling the horrifically spammy and incredibly boring field of credit card debt relief. They don't rank yet (as they've just launched), but if they invest in SEO, they will. They have the content they need to earn all the links they'll need—a great team, great story, great investors and the right product. If I were an SEO consultant for a company seeking rankings for debt relief type searches, that's exactly the "great content" I'd recommend.

- Here's one that does rank: Oyster Hotel Reviews (www.oyster.com). Today, Oyster is on the first page for nearly every hotel they've covered, and in position five for the massively competitive phrase "hotel reviews." (They're also the best listing in the SERPs.)

- Another that ranks well is Pods Moving Company (www.pods.com). It's not the most exciting site in the world, but it's a good idea with good marketing. It's on the first page for "moving company," another incredibly competitive result. And guess what? I couldn't find any black/gray hat links. No links from bloggers, either.

- Speaking of not exciting, but white hat and "great content," allow me to introduce you to Ron Hazelton's DIY Home Improvement (www.ronhazelton.com). Ron is a mini-celebrity thanks to a home repair-focused TV show. While his site isn't exactly drawing in the Linkerati, he markets it well and his stuff is good. As a result, Ron's site is #1 for searches like "toilet replacement."

- Slightly less boring, but more competitive and equally un-blogger friendly, is the world of business invoicing and bill paying. Yet, the gang at Freshbooks (www.freshbooks.com) is taking Page 1 rankings all over the place.

- Sound effects are another unlikely arena for building a big SEO success story. Despite avoiding every black hat tactic leveraged by the typical ringtone spammers, though, Seattle-based Hark.com has kicked serious butt here. They generate millions of visits from more than 750K keyword phrases each month, and they've built a serious brand in an industry rife with manipulation.

- Kris specifically called out bridge rectifiers as being an impossibly boring industry, yet AllAboutCircuits (www.allaboutcircuits.com) shows up on page one for virtually every diode-related search. There's nothing fancy there, either, just great content. Look at the page on rectifier circuits, (http://mz.cm/Y1hNWg). The illustrations are detailed, the content is awesome and they follow an almost-Wikipedia-like model to get contributors who often link back to them.

I try hard in my writing, my presentations and my other professional contributions to this industry to be warm, generous and understanding. But black hats telling the world that they turned their back on white hat because white hat SEO is impossible is a load of crap, and I'm not feeling very empathetic toward that viewpoint.

Yes, white hat SEO, particularly in boring industries for non-established sites, is a tremendous challenge. It requires immense creativity, huge quantities of elbow grease, and a lot of patience. Black hat SEO sometimes requires creativity. More often, though, it's finding the tactic Google and Bing haven't caught up to, and applying it over and over—until it burns down your site and you have to find another. Black hat is fundamentally interesting, and often amazingly entertaining, in the same way movies and TV shows featuring clever bank robbers are. But a statement like this has no legs to stand on:

> *The longer I practiced and studied greyhat, the more annoyed I got with the poor advice and absolute falsehoods I saw being doled out by so called SEO experts to newbies who had no way of knowing that the advice they were soaking up was going to keep them at the back of the search engine results pages (SERPs) for the foreseeable future. Whitehat isn't just a bit slower. It's wishful thinking. It's irresponsible.*

Thankfully, it's easy to refute Kris' points with hard, substantive examples (something his post doesn't do at all).

Job searches are among the most challenging, competitive keyword phrases to rank well for in the SERPs. Back in 2008, when we still had a consulting practice, we worked with the crew at Simply Hired (www.simplyhired.com) to set up a long-term strategy for beating the odds. It involved creating a syndication strategy with smart linking and anchor text, embeddable widgets, and a search-friendly, crawlable site with a data-rich blog. It included a massive online brand-building campaign, too. After six months, Simply Hired's rankings and traffic had improved, but they certainly weren't #1 across the board for job searches. However, I'm incredibly proud of their progress since then. I stay in touch with their team and help out informally when/where I can do so. They're on Page 1 for "job search" and rank for hundreds of thousands of job title + geo combination searches. Thanks to SEO (and dozens of other successful marketing and sales programs), they're poised to become industry leaders in a massive market.

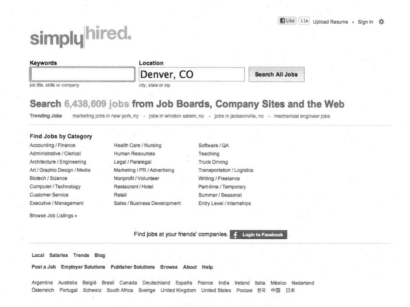

These strategies that worked for Simply Hired (and other former Moz clients like Yelp, Etsy and Zillow) aren't some dark secret, either. I wrote a lengthy blog post explaining the process in depth in a Moz post (`www.moz.org/blog/ranking-for-keyword-cityname-in-multiple-geographies`). I'm not alone, either. Blogs produced by SearchEngineLand, SEOBook, Distilled, and many others give tremendously valuable advice day after day.

I think Kris owes us some examples of "poor advice and absolute falsehoods" being "doled out by so called SEO experts." I'll agree that there's some bad advice floating around the SEO world, and I'll even admit to giving some myself. Regardless, that's a bold statement for Kris to make without any evidence.

Unfortunately, this next statement can't be written off so easily:

> *If you are charging your clients for service and not being competitive then you are ripping off your clients. It's as simple as that. I know you white hats are squirming in your seats right now shaking your little fists and saying, "It's not sustainable. Our strategy is based around long term results!" No, it's not. Your strategy is based around wishful thinking and hoping that someday Google will do your job for you so you don't have to. Until Google starts enforcing the rules, there aren't any. And as long as that is true anyone who is not waiting around for them to be enforced is going to rank. Anyone who does wait around won't. You have an obligation to your clients to do everything in your power to rank their sites using the most effective methods currently available to you.*

He's dead wrong on the false choice between either being black hat or "not using the most effective methods." A tax advisor that recommends quasi-legal, high-risk shelters might be using "the most effective methods" to protect wealth, but that doesn't make his more responsible peers obligation-dodging sissies. Search marketers have an obligation, in my opinion, to know and understand the full spectrum of tactics from white hat to black hat. We also carry the same responsibility that any other professional with specialized knowledge does: to recommend the right strategy for the situation.

Unless your manager/company/client is wholly comfortable with the high-risk variable that comes with black hat SEO, you'd better stay clear. I'm also of the mind that there's almost nothing black hat can accomplish that white hat can't do better while building far more value in the long run. Unless it's "I want to rank in the top five for 'buy viagra' in the next 7 days," you'd better explain that you're recommending black hat primarily because you're not smart, talented and creative enough to find a white hat strategy to do it.

Kris makes a fair point with regards to Google, though (and Bing as well). The engines are not doing enough to stop spam and manipulation from black hat tactics (see `www.moz.org/blog/im-getting-more-worried-about-the-effectiveness-of-webspam`).

And, for as long as they fail on this front, there will be those seduced by Kris' viewpoint (Kris himself used to be quite white hat). To be fair, they've done a good job on several fronts recently—pushing down low-quality content farms in the Panda/Farmer update, making original content rank better, and putting more high quality brands in the SERPs (even if they're not doing perfect SEO).

The biggest problems (IMO) that we are seeing today are manipulative, black hat links obtained through paid sources; automated link drops, reciprocal spam, link rings and article spinning. (Article spinning is probably my least favorite tactic on the rise.) There aren't a lot of truly new types of black hat link manipulation techniques, but the old ones are, tragically, working again in a lot of niches. I hope that's next on Google's and Bing's radar. If it is, a lot of black hats are going to have some painful times. Even if it's rough, I think that's the only way to solve the problems web spam creates. One of my favorite parts of being a white hat is cheering for the search quality teams rather than against them, and getting that little bump in traffic every time they improve the quality of their algorithms.

## BLACK HAT ≠ SEO

The last point of Kris' I'll tackle revolves around the jobs an SEO performs:

> *If your main offering is quality content—YOU ARE NOT AN SEO, you are a writer. If you are billing your client SEO prices for writing services you are ripping them off. If you didn't go to college for or otherwise study writing and literature and you are offering writing services to your client rather than advising them to hire someone who actually specializes and is trained in writing, you are ripping them off.*

> *With the exception of very large sites, most onsite optimization opportunities can be identified and charted in an audit in a matter of a few days. Implementation in most cases won't take very long either and doesn't even really need to be conducted by an SEO if the audit is written up properly. What does that leave: content strategy and off-site SEO. The content strategy is just that … a STRATEGY, which can be handed off to a competent writer. If you are still charging your client after this point and you aren't competing with all the tools available and you aren't advising them of someone else who could or would, then you are doing your client a disservice.*

These are ludicrous statements, but I think Kris realizes it and is simply using them to generate controversy. Anyone who honestly believes that the extent of an SEO's job is to develop content strategies, audit for on-page SEO, and build links has never done the job professionally.

I wrote a blog post back in 2007 highlighting why SEO is so hard (`www.moz.org/blog/what-makes-seo-seem-so-damn-hard`). In it, I talked about the massive number of things that affect SEO, and that number has only grown. Today, a responsible SEO needs to be thinking about these things, to name a few:

- The business' overall product, marketing and sales strategy, and how SEO fits into that
- Keyword research and targeting (a process that requires tools, patience, intuition, testing and experience)
- Funnel optimization (CRO has both direct and indirect SEO impact these days)
- Testing and optimizing content for users (time on site, bounce rate, engagement, etc. all matter directly and indirectly)
- Content strategy (which ties into overall business strategy at the highest levels)
- On-page optimization. (Black hats were actually some of the earliest to notice that Google had become much smarter about on-page analysis than just keyword usage and repetition, so I'm sure Kris knows how in-depth this process can be.)
- Making the site search-engine friendly. (This has become a complex project for many otherwise simple sites as there are now features like faceted navigation, AJAX crawling, JavaScript, Flash and many, many others to consider.)
- XML Sitemaps. We recently presented a 90-minute webinar (`www.moz.org/webinars/getting-value-from-xml-sitemaps`) on this topic that generated dozens of questions; it's not the fire-and-forget tactic that many think it is.
- Analytics. Visitor monitoring is just the start. There are webmaster tools, link monitoring, brand mentions and alerts, social media tracking and more to consider now.
- Vertical search listings (such as local/maps/places, video, images, news, blogs, and shopping). Optimizing for just one of these categories can be a full-time job.
- Usability and user experience issues (since these can significantly impact rankings)
- Reputation tracking and management
- Competitive research
- Social media marketing. No SEO can afford to ignore social today, and that's a massive strategic and tactical undertaking.
- Syndication, scraping, copyright, and duplicate content issues

If Kris thinks pounding links at a page until it ranks is the majority of his SEO responsibilities, I'm worried. (Note: I don't actually believe that's the case; I've met Kris and he's a very smart guy. Instead, I suspect significant hyperbole went into his writing.) If anyone out there tells you that this is how they're going to do SEO, you'd better make sure they're either a highly specialized contractor, or find another provider who can help you think holistically about all of these factors.

# WHY WE CAN'T IGNORE BLACK HAT ENTIRELY

When I was in Munich keynoting SMX in 2011, I spent some time with a retiring black hat, Bob Rains. Bob, who's moving to the white hat world and joining TandlerDoerje in Germany, participated with me in a panel discussion on black hat social media tactics. In particular, Bob mentioned a tactic wherein he'd build Twitter and Facebook profiles for racehorses that would garner thousands of followers by making the profiles seem "more real than real," even pretending to be "official" Twitter accounts for the horses on occasion. On game day, he could then tweet/share a link to his gambling site. Users visited the site to place bets on the horses, netting Bob big affiliate payouts.

To do this manipulative work, though, Bob had to work incredibly hard to have real conversations on these social sites, upload photos from events, tweet interesting stats and experiences that could be verified. In other words ... he was building great content!

My recommendation was simple: just call the account a "fan page" and you'll be 100 percent white hat. You're building a great social profile; why not make it something that Twitter/Facebook won't shut down if they get word of it from the real owners? Why not go one extra step? Remove the "official" title and BE white hat! Yes, you might have a slightly harder time building up the profiles, but they'll last forever! And you'll be able to sleep at night!

I highlight this story because it perfectly illustrates how close black and white hat marketing often are. It also shows why I love talking to black hats and learning from them. There's almost always a way to take the knowledge and experiences from black hats—the best of whom, like Bob, are often massively creative—and apply it in white hat ways.

Three weeks prior to that event, first in London and next in New Orleans, Distilled hosted a one-day intensive seminar on link building. One of the talks at each event was called "Lessons from the Dark Side: What White Hats Can Learn from Black Hat SEO." Two presenters, Martin Macdonald (in London) and Kris Roadruck (in NOLA), gave talks about their experiences with web spam's effectiveness, limitations, and takeaways. I thought both presentations were excellent. They clearly indicated the danger of black hat SEO. Kris' deck started with almost a dozen slides about how and why not to do what he showed. They didn't pull any punches in showing the ups and downs of a spammer's life.

SEOs have a responsibility to understand and appreciate how and why black hat SEO operates. It's certainly not the first or most important step in an SEO education, but it's part of being a true professional. No one who does IT consulting would neglect to become educated about hacking and malicious attacks. No one who does public relations avoids studying the manipulative tactics practiced in their field. Even in industries like construction and contracting, it pays to understand how, why, and when shoddy work and cut corners happen. So, too, must professional, white hat SEOs know the range of tactics at play in our field.

In early 2011, I answered a related question on Quora (`www.quora.com/SEO/What-techniques-do-websites-use-to-game-the-Google-search-engine`):

Knowing more about each of the practices listed in that post can make you a better SEO. I'm not someone who pretends to have great expertise in this field. Every time, though, that I hear a black hat share a successful tactic that isn't illegal or just drive-by spam, I learn something, and am often able to come up with a way to leverage the same effect in a white hat way.

## WHY WHITE HAT IS ALWAYS BETTER

There are very few things in the world that I perceive as wholly black and white. Spamming the search engines versus practicing authentic, organic marketing, however, is one of them.

It's my opinion that for real brands and real businesses, the choice of going 100 percent white hat will pay massive dividends every time. Here's why:

1. **There's always a better way to spend that time and money.** Spam isn't free or easy, despite the image some black hats portray. When I hear about the actual costs and time commitments black hats invest, I'm blown away. For not much more time—and often less money—those same businesses and sites could invest in long-term, high value white hat tactics. Many just lack the creativity and willingness to do the hard work, while others are seduced by the promise of a quick win or simply ignorant of other options.

2. **White hat builds exciting companies, spam doesn't.** With a very small number of exceptions, spam doesn't build exciting, scalable, long-term companies. It creates relatively small amounts of temporary wealth. If you're unwilling to trade short-term gains for long-term success, you're probably hurting the online ecosystem. None of us should endorse that behavior.

3. **White hat rankings can be shared.** That means never having to sweat hiding dirty secrets, protecting your tactics or link sources, jumping through hoops to keep your footprint

anonymous, or refraining from showing off your site. The benefits of transparency improve your ability to do PR, branding, and networking. All of those, in turn, help SEO.

4. **Spam always comes with high risks.** Whether it's tomorrow, next month, or three years from now before you get knocked out of the search engines, it will happen. You can invest in multiple sites and tactics, shore up defenses, and build anonymity to hide your online profile. Honestly, though, if you applied that creativity and effort to white hat ... Just saying.

5. **You're renting rankings rather than buying them.** Devaluation of spam tactics means you have to stay one step ahead of the engines, and can never spend a week free from sweating what will and won't be found. White hat may take longer. If done right, though, it can put you in an unassailable position of strength for the long term.

6. **Reliability in the spam world sucks.** The people who sell spammy links or offer spam services are nearly always fly-by-night operations, moving from one business model to the next. Spammers are almost never long-term operators.

7. **Any victory is a hollow one.** I don't just mean in a touchy-feely way, I mean that no matter how many times you rank well with spam or how much you make, it's just money (and often far too little to sustain you, meaning you've got to go create more spam tomorrow). You're not building something real, long-lasting and sustainable— and you're rarely fulfilling any of the other requirements for job satisfaction or happiness.

8. **The money's not that good.** Ask yourself who the most prolific, talented, high profile spammers are in the world. I can name a good dozen or so and none of them are retired, only a few are millionaires, and not a one (to my knowledge) has made eight figures, with the exception of a few truly dark hat individuals who've earned their money from porn empires or illegal activities.

9. **There is legal danger.** I hesitate to bring this up because some folks in the search sphere have overemphasized this danger. However, the FTC, the British government and the EU all have regulations about disclosure of interests, and a lot of link buying and link spamming behavior violates these rules. We've yet to see serious enforcement. Personally, though, I have no tolerance for risk of this kind, and I suspect many others don't either.

10. **Spam never builds value in multiple channels.** What I love about the inbound/organic marketing philosophy is how it builds a site that attracts authentic traffic from hundreds of sources, often without any additional work. Spamming your way to a #1 ranking might send search traffic, but if the web shifts to Facebook/Twitter or if email marketing becomes the biggest tactic in your niche, or if a competitor wins purely on branding and branded search, you're up a creek. You've built nothing of real value—nothing to make people come back and share and like, +1, tweet, link, email, stumble, vote for, or shout to the heavens about. Spam builds a shell of a marketing strategy. One crack, and it's all over.

These graphics were in a slide presentation I made, but they're worth repeating here.

Who ranks #1 for "online dating?" It's not a black hat, but a site that found a genius way to become a content and media hub, OkCupid. How about "buy shoes online," one of the top converting terms in the apparel industry. It's Zappos, a brand that's put customer service, great product and a unique business model into their SEO campaigns. Big props to Adam Audette, who made Zappos a shining star in the SEO ecommerce world. Or "real estate values," an incredibly competitive term that's only risen in popularity with the market crisis? It's Zillow. Or "travel blog site," where some brilliant viral marketing earned Travelpod the top position. Or "art prints," where Benchmark-backed Art.com outranks even the exact match domain.

I could go on and on and on. The sites that people WANT to click on in the results are white hat. The ones that make searchers, technologists, marketers, and search quality engineers happy are sites that deserve to rank. When you build a brand that does that, and then optimize in a way that no web spam engineer would ever want to discount, you've earned yourself a truly competitive advantage in SEO. Black hat is, much of the time, a sad excuse for a lack of creativity, discipline, and willingness to invest in the long term.

Here's hoping that the SEO industry continues to grow, flourish, and attract brilliant, creative minds. Over the past nine years of my career in this field, I've seen great progress, but not enough. I can promise that Moz and our partners are going to do everything in our power to bring greater legitimacy, value, and economic opportunity to the field of search and inbound marketing. It's a fight I look forward to every day.

P.S. I put out a call on Twitter for great white hat sites ranking for competitive phrases, and received some terrific responses:

- Online budget app, Budget Simple (`www.budgetsimple.com`) has a well-designed site and top three rankings for "online budget" and "free online budget," competing against the likes of Mint and Intuit.
- Mini Mave in Denmark (`www.min-mave.dk`) has legendary SEO Mikkel deMib as a partner and top rankings for competitive terms like "gravid" (Danish for "pregnant"). Last year, they recorded over a million keywords sending many millions of visits to the site.
- Science equipment supplier Edmunds (`www.scientificsonline.com`) has a great site with links that rock and a brand that's trusted throughout the community. Their rankings for hyper-competitive searches like "science equipment" and "scientific supplies" along with a massive long-tail presence show the power of white hat in ecommerce niches.
- Online appliance retailer 8Appliances (`www.8appliances.com.au`) just started their online marketing, but they've already had success, earning more than 50,000 search visits monthly from top 10 rankings for queries like "miele kitchen appliances" (in Google Australia).
- Mexican-focused travel site Journey Mexico (`www.journeymexico.com`) has been having a lots of success in niche search results like "cultural travel mexico" and with its awesome blog.

White hat can be done, even in boring industries or for competitive queries. Anyone who says otherwise isn't telling the truth.

# 2

# SCHEMA.ORG: WHY YOU'RE BEHIND IF YOU'RE NOT USING IT

*By Craig Bradford*

---

**Editor's Note:** *This post was originally published on November 13th, 2011, on the The Moz Blog. Schema.org, which is approximately two years old now, includes vocabulary for health and medicine, technical publishing, genealogy, news articles, product offers, and external lists (to name a few) in addition to the examples Craig discusses. The full list of schema types is available at* `http://schema.org/docs/full.html`.

---

IF SOMEONE TOLD you that there was a quick and easy way to improve the click-through rate of your search results with minimal effort, you'd stop in your tracks and give them your full attention. Yet, `Schema.org` and rich snippets are still horribly underutilized.

Since Google, Yahoo, and Bing officially introduced Schema.org in June (`http://google webmastercentral.blogspot.com/2011/06/introducing-schemaorg-search-engines.html`), it's fair to say that the motivation to implement it has been mixed. However, it has already evolved a lot (Yandex, for example, has joined the initiative), and has added new stuff that people aren't paying attention to.

Here is the part where I try to persuade you that while there are a few downsides to using Schema.org, the upsides make it worth it.

# MYTH: SCHEMA.ORG MARKUP DOESN'T GET RICH SNIPPETS!

A common objection I hear from people who are not using schema is that there's no point because Google don't use it for rich snippets. WRONG!

At one point, Google did not use schema for rich snippets. However, this is no longer true. Lots of websites in different markets are seeing the benefits of taking a leap of faith in the form of rich snippets.

The following are all examples of websites that currently use the Schema.org vocabulary:

## Ecommerce (eBay)

**Logitech Revue** Google TV Dish Network Customers Only | **eBay**
rover.ebay.com › ... › Internet & Media Streamers
★★★★★ Rating: 4 - 105 votes
**Logitech Revue** Google TV - DISH Network customers ONLY in Consumer Electronics, TV, Video & Home Audio, Internet & Media Streamers | **eBay**.

## TV Series (IMDb)

The Wire (TV Series 2002–2008) - **IMDb**
www.imdb.com/title/tt0306414/  [+1]
★★★★★ Rating: 9.6/10 - 44,375 votes
Baltimore drug scene, seen through the eyes of drug dealers, and law enforcement. Starring Dominic West, John Doman, Deirdre Lovejoy.

## Movies (Rotten Tomatoes)

**The Adventures of Tintin - Rotten Tomatoes**
www.rottentomatoes.com/m/the_adventures_of_tintin/  [+1]
★★★★★ Rating: 85% - 41 reviews
Paramount Pictures and Columbia Pictures Present a 3D Motion Capture Film The Adventures of Tintin directed by Steven Spielberg from a screenplay by Steven Moffat and Edgar Wright & Joe Cornish....
Directed by Steven Spielberg. Starring Jamie Bell, Andy Serkis, Daniel Craig.

## Events (Ticketmaster)

**Washington Huskies Mens Basketball tickets**, and ... - **Ticketmaster**
www.ticketmaster.ca/Washington-Huskies-Mens-Basketball-tickets/art...  [+1]
Results 1 - 10 of 19 – Find and buy **Washington Huskies Mens Basketball** ...
Sat 12 Nov    Washington Huskies Mens ... - Alaska Airlines Arena at ...
Sun 13 Nov    Washington Huskies Mens ... - Alaska Airlines Arena at ...
Mon 14 Nov    Washington Huskies Mens ... - Alaska Airlines Arena at ...

### Recipes (iSaveurs)

As you can see, Schema.org markup is definitely being used by Google.

# SCHEMA.ORG IS NOT A LANGUAGE

Schema.org is a vocabulary, not a language in and of itself. Let me explain the difference, as there is still a lot of confusion in the SEO community.

There are various languages that do the job we're discussing:

- Microformats
- Microdata
- RDFa

When marking up any content on a page for rich snippets or similar (machine readable) reasons, both a language and a vocabulary are always used. See the following graphic, which shows an example of microdata being used with the Schema.org vocabulary.

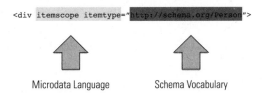

When it comes to using languages and vocabulary to mark up content, it's the vocabulary part that the major search engines have agreed to standardize with Schema.org.

When Google originally announced that they were going to support the Schema.org vocabulary, they also dropped the bombshell that they supported only microdata language.

**2) Schema.org uses microdata.**
Historically, we've supported three different standards for structured data markup: microdata, microformats, and RDFa. We've decided to focus on just one format for schema.org to create a simpler story for webmasters and to improve consistency across search engines relying on the data. There are arguments to be made for preferring any of the existing standards, but we've found that microdata strikes a balance between the extensibility of RDFa and the simplicity of microformats, so this is the format that we've gone with.

They also said that although they would continue to support the existing rich snippets markup, you should avoid mixing the formats together as doing so could confuse their parsers.

> **3) We'll continue to support our existing rich snippets markup formats.**
> If you've already done markup on your pages using microformats or RDFa, we'll continue to support it. One caveat to watch out for: while it's OK to use the new schema.org markup or continue to use existing microformats or RDFa markup, you should avoid mixing the formats together on the same web page, as this can confuse our parsers.

The fact that you couldn't mix Schema.org markup with microformats or RDFa annoyed a lot of people. Kavi Goel from Google later said this was a mistake and they would fix it (http://mz.cm/ZybF76.)

**BREAKING NEWS**—Two days ago, a pretty big announcement was made on the Schema.org blog (http://blog.schema.org/2011/11/using-rdfa-11-lite-with-schemaorg.html). There are plans in the pipeline for the Schema.org vocabulary to be compatible with the RDFa language, with support for using other vocabularies on the same page.

> *Editor's Note: Schema.org started officially supporting RDFa and RDa Lite 1.1, with support for using other vocabularies on the same page, in 2012. Although Google now states that they support microformats, RDFa, and microdata, microdata is their preferred format, and does not guarantee that it will show rich snippets in search results.*

## FIVE UNDERUSED SCHEMA.ORG APPLICATIONS

I personally believe Schema.org is the future, and if you've not already done so, you should implement it right now. Regardless of the type of website you have, there are ways you can use Schema.org markup, even if it's simply to define an article and the date it was published.

That said, there are cases where I think you can gain even more advantage by implementing it. Here are examples of the top five ways I think Schema.org should be used.

### #1 EVENTS

The Event schema lets you get really specific about what type of event you are describing. Right now, you can specify an event as any of the items shown in the following list.

- BusinessEvent
- ChildrensEvent

- ComedyEvent
- DanceEvent
- EducationEvent
- Festival
- FoodEvent
- LiteraryEvent
- MusicEvent
- SaleEvent
- SocialEvent
- SportsEvent
- TheaterEvent
- UserInteraction
- VisualArtsEvent

With the recent QDF update (Query Deserves Freshness algorithm—see `http://www.copyblogger.com/query-deserves-freshness`), it's important that you give Google as much information as possible. Events, by their very nature, are time sensitive, so using Schema.org to enforce event details is a good idea.

The Events schema is a pretty comprehensive vocabulary. You are able to mark up things like attendees, duration, performers, location, and start and end dates (see `http://schema.org/Event`).

## #2 JOBS

I don't think I can describe how amazing the Job markup is, which was announced just last week on the Schema.org blog. Even more amazing is what was announced on the Google blog today (`http://blog.schema.org/2011/11/schemaorg-support-for-job-postings.html`). Google just launched a custom search engine that specifically looks for Schema.org Job markup, and is used to find veteran-committed job openings (`http://googleblog.blogspot.com/2011/11/bringing-very-best-of-what-we-do-to.html`). I would love to see search-related queries return results like this example.

**SomeJobsite.com | Engineering Jobs**
www.somejobsite.com/EngineeringJobs...
Results 1 - 10 of 19 – Search and find engineering jobs...

| | |
|---|---|
| 10th November London | Product Engineer ... - $50,000... |
| 5th November Seattle | Mechanical Engineer... - $80,000... |
| 10th October New York | Washington Huskies Mens ... - $40,000 ... |

## #3 REPUTATION MANAGEMENT

This isn't groundbreaking news, so I'll make it quick. Use the Person schema (`http://schema.org/Person`) to make the best page online about the person in question. Not only can you mark up the basic facts about the person like their name and age, but you can mark up the tiny details such as what university they went to (`alumniOf`), what awards they have won (`awards`), where they work (`worksFor`), who their colleagues are (`colleagues`), and even the names of their family members (`parents`, `siblings`, `spouse`, `relatedTo`). This is an easy way to make a super-targeted page about a person that can be tested with Google's rich snippets tool. Look how much information Google is able to extract from my test page:

```
Item
    Type: http://schema.org/person
    image = http://craigbradford.co.uk/wp-content/uploads/2011/08/
    name = Craig Bradford
    homelocation = London
    birthdate = May 7th 1987
    alumniof = Strathclyde University
    awards = BEng (Hons) 2:1
    image = http://www.craigbradford.co.uk/wp-content/uploads/201
    performerin = football
    performerin = basketball
    performerin = martial arts
    performerin = Tae Kwon Do
    performerin = kickboxing
    awards = Super Middle Weight World Champion
    spouse = Lyndsay
    image = http://www.craigbradford.co.uk/wp-content/uploads/201
    worklocation = London
    jobtitle = SEO Analyst
    worksfor = Distilled
    affiliation
        text = SEOmoz Q+A
        href = http://www.seomoz.org/users/profile/296192
```

That is an amazing amount of information. Here is a preview of how the listing would look in the SERPs.

### Craig Bradford's Blog | About Craig Bradford
www.craigbradford.co.uk/about-craig/ - Cached
The excerpt from the page will show up here. The reason we can't show text from your webpage is because the text depends on the query the user types.

Craig Bradford

## #4 NEWS SITES

The recent QDF update reinforces how committed Google is to displaying fresh content. Schema.org has extended its vocabulary to include a section specifically for the news industry (`http://schema.org/NewsArticle`). This markup allows you to reference a particular page or column in the paper edition of a news public when appropriate to do so. The following image shows the recently added schema.

| Properties from NewsArticle | | |
|---|---|---|
| dateline | Text | The location where the NewsArticle was produced. |
| printColumn | Text | The number of the column in which the NewsArticle appears in the print edition. |
| printEdition | Text | The edition of the print product in which the NewsArticle appears. |
| printPage | Text | If this NewsArticle appears in print, this field indicates the name of the page on which the article is found. Please note that this field is intended for the exact page name (e.g. A5, B18). |
| printSection | Text | If this NewsArticle appears in print, this field indicates the print section in which the article appeared. |

News sites should be using this to markup to tell the search engines what their content is about and when it was published.

## #5 ECOMMERCE

I can't believe how many ecommerce websites I see without any markup at all. People spend so much time trying to rank higher that they forget to get the low hanging fruit in the SERPs. Rich snippets are an amazing way to increase click-through rates by drawing attention to your product listings. The following example shows how review stars make a search result for an eBay product stand out.

**Logitech Revue 097855070906 | eBay**
www.ebay.com/ctg/Logitech-Revue-/97019743 +?
★★★★★ from 51 users - $99.99 to $190.00
**eBay**: The **Logitech Revue** is a media streamer with Google TV, which serves as a complete entertainment system. With its Ethernet Interface, this **Logitech** ...

# WRAP-UP

I hope I've managed to convince you that Schema.org is worth implementing *right now*.

There are already the benefits of rich snippets to be had, but this isn't just about rich snippets. It's about creating content that machines can understand and reference. There are already services that try to make use of this kind of information such as Silk (`http://www.silkapp.com/?ref=DAipyl`) and Apple's Siri (`http://www.apple.com/ios/siri`). Ensuring that you are ahead of your competitors can only be a good thing.

# 3

# PERFECTING KEYWORD TARGETING AND ON-PAGE OPTIMIZATION

*By Rand Fishkin*

---

**Editor's Note:** *Although SEO has changed a lot since this post was originally published August 17, 2009 on* The Moz Blog, *it's still important to cover the basics of on-page optimization. Critical, in fact, which is why we have updated this post for 2013.*

---

"HOW DO I build the perfectly optimized page?" If you're in SEO, you probably hear this question a lot. Sadly, there's no cut and dried answer, but there are sets of best practices we can draw from and sharpen to help get close. In this chapter, I share our top recommendations for achieving on-page, keyword-targeting "perfection"—or, at least, close to it. Some of these recommendations are backed by data points, correlation studies and extensive testing, while others are simply gut feelings based on experience. As with all things SEO, we recommend constant testing and refinement, though this knowledge can help you kick-start the process.

# The "Perfectly" Optimized Page

### (for the example keyword phrase "chocolate donuts")

**Page Title: Chocolate Donuts | Mary's Bakery**

**Meta Description:** Mary's Bakery offers 9 varieties of the most delicious chocolate donuts you will ever taste. Voted Best Chocolate Donuts by Gourmet Donut 5 times!

## H1 Headline:

## Chocolate Donuts from Mary's Bakery

image filename:

**marys-chocolate-donuts.jpg**

photo of donuts
(with alt-img
attribute):
**Dozen Donuts,
Chocolate**

Body Text:_____

_____chocolate donuts____

_____

__Mary's Bakery_____

_____

_____

donut holes_____

_____

_____baked goods__

_____

_____

chocolate_____pastries_____

_____

_____

___breakfast pastry___

Try Our Donuts – Free!

Enter your email address

# BEST PRACTICES FOR OPTIMIZING PAGES

The following sections list our best practices for optimizing the following on-page SEO elements: head tags, URLs, body tags, internal links, and page architecture.

## HTML HEAD TAGS

Here are our suggestions for using HTML head tags to help optimize your pages.

- **Title**—The most important of on-page keyword elements, the page title should employ the keyword term/phrase as the first word(s). In our correlation data studies, the following graph emerged:

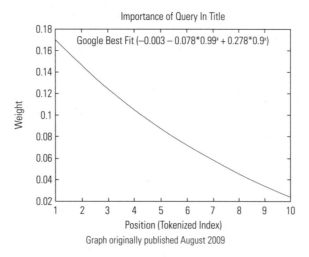

Importance of Query In Title

Graph originally published August 2009

Clearly, using the keyword term/phrase as the very first word(s) in the page title has the highest correlation with high rankings, and subsequent positions correlate nearly flawlessly to lower rankings. Title tags should sound like a human being wrote them without the express intent to rank for phrase after phrase, and they should be clickable since they show up in the SERPs.

- **Meta Description**—Although not used for rankings by any of the major engines, the meta description is an important place to use the target term/phrase due to the bolding that occurs in the visual snippet of the search results. It's also important for boosting click-through rate, thus increasing the traffic derived from any ranking position. What's the point of showing up in the top of the SERPs if no one clicks on your listing, after all?

- **Meta Keywords**—For quite a while, Yahoo! was unique among the search engines in recording and utilizing the meta keyword tag for discovery, though not technically for rankings. However, Microsoft's Bing now powers Yahoo! search results, and when Bing recognizes a meta keyword tag, it can trigger a spam flag. That, combined with the danger of others using keywords there for competitive research means that at Moz, we never recommend employing the traditional meta keywords tag. (The news_keywords tag, however, should be used by Google News publishers.)

- **Meta Robots**—This optional tag should not contain any directives that could inadvertently disallow access to search engines.

- **Rel="Canonical"**—The larger and more complex a site (and the larger/more complex the organization working on it), the more we advise employing the canonical URL tag to prevent any potential duplicates or unintentional, appended URL strings from creating a problem for the engines and splitting up potential link juice. See `http://mz.cm/15oH3Hb` for more details.

- **Rich Snippets and Structured Data Markup**—Embedding rich snippets into your pages and taking advantage of structured data markup can tell the search engines what they are about, as well as make them stand out in the SERPs. Examples of data that may benefit from structured data markup include author profiles, product ratings, and business reviews. Schema.org, a joint alliance of the major search engines, provides an exhaustive list of data that may benefit from structured markup.

- **Other Meta Tags**—Meta tags like those offered by the DCMI (`http://dublincore.org`) or FGDC (`www.fgdc.gov/metadata`) seem compelling, but currently provide no benefit for SEO with the major search engines and thus add unnecessary complexity and download time.

## URLS

Keep the following recommendations in mind for optimizing your use of URLs.

- **Length**—Shorter URLs appear to perform better in the search results and are more likely to be copied/pasted by other sites, shared and linked to.

- **Keyword Location**—The closer the targeted keyword(s) are to the domain name, the better. Thus, *site.com/keyword* outperforms *site.com/folder/subfolder/keyword* and is the recommended method of optimization (though this is certainly not a massive rankings benefit). An exception to this recommended structure is product pages on ecommerce sites. In most cases, *site.com/keyword-product-name* is best.

- **Subdomains versus Pages**—Despite the slight URL benefit that subdomains keyword usage has over subfolders or pages, the engines' link popularity assignment algorithms tilt the balance in favor of subfolders/pages rather than subdomains. The exceptions are certain franchise situations and content that is exceptionally different than the rest of the site. See `http://www.moz.org/blog/subdomains-subfolders-and-toplevel-domains` for more info.

- **Word Separators**—Hyphens are still the king of keyword separators in URLs, and despite promises that underscores will be given equal credit, the inconsistency with other methods make the hyphen a clear choice. NOTE: This should not apply to root domain names, where separating words with hyphens is almost never recommended (for example, *pinkgrapefruit.com* is a far better choice than *pink-grapefruit.com*).

## BODY TAGS

How should you use body tags to optimize your page? Here are our best strategies.

- **Number of Keyword Repetitions**—It's impossible to pinpoint the exact, optimal number of times to employ a keyword term/phrase on the page, but a general guideline is to use the exact match keyword a few times in the body of the copy. The same goes for partial match keywords. The most important thing, folks, is to write for the reader. If you do that, keyword repetition will come naturally. Panda has taught us that it is unwise to ever be aggressive with this metric.

- **Keyword Density**—While it's true that more usage of a keyword term/phrase can potentially improve targeting/ranking, it's also true that over-usage of a keyword/phrase can potentially incur an over-optimization penalty. So what's an SEO to do? Write good, relevant content about a subject that includes your keyword/phrase—content that will actually help someone and help your conversion rates. We've all seen those spammy blocks of text that look like they were written with the sole intent to get keyword rankings. Don't go there.

- **Keyword Usage Variations**—It's long been suspected that keyword usage variation can influence search engine rankings, though this has never been studied in a depth of detail that's convincing to me. The theory that varied keyword usage throughout a page can help with content optimization and optimization nevertheless is worth consideration. We recommend employing at least one or two variations of a term and potentially splitting up keyword phrases, and using them in body copy as well or instead. Don't be spammy, though. *Write for people, not rankings.* I keep saying this because it matters.

- **H1 Headline**—The H1 tag has long been thought to have great importance in on-page optimization. Recent correlation data from our studies, however, has shown that it has a very low correlation with high rankings (close to zero, in fact). While this is compelling evidence, correlation is not causation and for semantic and SEO reasons, we still advise proper use of the H1 tag as the headline of the page and, preferably, employment of the targeted keyword term/phrase.

- **H2/H3/H4/Hx**—Subheading tags appear to carry little to no SEO value in terms of keyword rankings, but are useful for telling search bots how pages are structured. With increased usage of responsive design and HTML5, this has become more important. Screen readers also rely on header tags and other HTML markup attributes to help visually impaired users navigate the Internet.

- **Alt Attribute**—Surprisingly, the alt attribute, long thought to carry little SEO weight, was shown to have quite a robust correlation with high rankings in our studies as long as you don't overdo it. Thus, we strongly advise the use of a graphic image/photo/illustration on important keyword-targeted pages with the term/phrase employed in the alt attribute of the img tag where it makes sense. Surrounding the image with relative, descriptive keywords can also improve rankings in image search

- **Image Filename**—Because image traffic can be a substantive source of visits, and image filenames appear to be valuable for this as well as natural web search, we suggest using the keyword term/phrase as the name of the image file employed on the page.

- **Internal Link Anchor Text**—Anchor text signals search engines what a page is about, which is useful for rankings, but if we use the same exact keyword match text over and over to link to the same page it makes our sites look really manipulative. A significant portion of the Penguin update deals with over-optimized anchor text. Don't get penalized, folks. Instead, go with logical, useful anchor text, and change it up when you're linking to your pages.
- **HTML Comments**—Apply the nofollow attribute to comments.

## INTERNAL LINKS AND LOCATION IN SITE ARCHITECTURE

Here are a few recommendations for handling internal links to optimize your page.

- **Click-Depth**—Our general recommendation is that the more competitive and challenging a keyword term/phrase is to rank for, the higher it should be in a site's internal architecture (and thus, the fewer clicks from the home page it should take to reach that URL).
- **Number/Percentage of Internal Links**—More linked-to pages tend to result in higher rankings and thus, for competitive terms, it may help to link to these pages from a greater number/percentage of pages on a site. Linking repeatedly to the same page with the same anchor text, though, is not helpful for SEO, and makes your sites look really spammy. So vary your anchor text, folks.
- **Links in Content versus Permanent Navigation**—It appears that Google and other search engines recognize location on the page as an element of link consideration. Thus, placing links to pages in the body content Wikipedia-style, rather than in permanent navigation, may potentially provide some benefit (if you do this in a way that is naturally useful to the reader). Don't forget, however, that Google only counts the first anchor text link to a page that they see in the HTML. Read `http://mz.cm/15oHaCB` for details.
- **Link Location in Sidebars and Footers**—Patent applications, search papers, and experience from inside Moz and many practitioners externally suggests that Google may be strongly discounting links placed in the footer, and, to a lesser degree, in the sidebar(s) of pages. Thus, if you're employing a link in permanent navigation, it may pay to use the top navigation (above the content) for SEO purposes. Use the footer and sidebar to link to things that people expect to find there, not to get exact-match, site-wide anchor text.

## PAGE ARCHITECTURE

Which page architecture factors are likely to influence rankings?

- **Keyword Location**—We advise that important keywords should be featured in the first paragraph of a page's text content. The engines do appear to have some preference for pages that employ keywords sooner, rather than later, in the text.

- **Content Structure**—Some practitioners swear by the use of particular content formats (introduction, body, examples, conclusion OR the journalistic style of narrative, data, conclusion, parable) for SEO, but we haven't seen any formal data suggesting these are valuable for higher rankings and thus feel that whatever works best for the content and the visitors is likely ideal.

## WHY DON'T WE ALWAYS OBEY THESE RULES?

The answer to this question is relatively easy. The truth is that in the process of producing great web content, we sometimes forget, sometimes ignore, and sometimes intentionally disobey the best practices laid out earlier. On-page optimization, while certainly important, is only one piece of a larger rankings puzzle, as illustrated in the following chart.

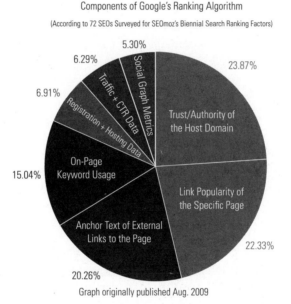

Components of Google's Ranking Algorithm

(According to 72 SEOs Surveyed for SEOmoz's Biennial Search Ranking Factors)

Graph originally published Aug. 2009

It most certainly pays to get the on-page, keyword-targeting pieces right, but on-page SEO, in my opinion, follows the 80/20 rule very closely. If you get the top 20 percent of the most important pieces (titles, URLs, internal links) from the list above right, you'll get 80 percent (maybe more) of the value possible in the on-page equation.

## BEST PRACTICES FOR RANKING #1

Curiously, though perhaps not entirely surprisingly to experienced SEOs, the truth is that on-page optimization doesn't necessarily rank first in the quest for top rankings. In fact, a list that walks through the process of actually getting that first position would look something more like:

- **Accessibility**—What content engines can't see or access cannot even be indexed; thus crawl-ability is foremost on this list.

- **Page Load Time**—This is part of Google's ranking algorithm, so write clean code that loads fast and isn't loaded down with lots of slow-loading images and scripts. More importantly, perhaps, users expect pages to load fast. If they have to wait more than a couple of seconds for your page to load, you've already lost them.

- **Content**—You need to have compelling, high-quality material that not only attracts interest, but compels visitors to share the information. Virality of content is possibly the most important/valuable factor in the ranking equation because it will produce the highest link conversion rate (the ratio of those who visit to those who link after viewing).

- **Social Sharing**—Social signals are important to ranking well in all of the major search engines. So create great content that people want to share, and make it easy to share. Social sharing will also naturally build great inbound links for you.

- **Basic On-Page Elements**—Getting the keyword targeting right in the most important elements (titles, URLs, internal links) provides a big boost in the potential ability of a page to perform well.

- **User Experience**—The usability, user interface, and overall experience provided by a website strongly influences the links and citations it earns as well as the conversion rate and browse rate of the traffic that visits. Make it easy for users to find what they want when they visit your site, and tell them what you want to do by using clear calls-to-action.

- **Marketing**—I like to say that "great content is no substitute for great marketing." A terrific marketing machine or powerful campaign has the power to attract far more links than content may "deserve," and though this might seem unfair, it's a principle on which all of capitalism has functioned for the last few hundred years. Spreading the word is often just as important (or more so) than being right, being honest, or being valuable (just look at the political spectrum).

- **Advanced/Thorough On-Page Optimization**—Applying all of the practices listed in the chapter with careful attention to detail certainly isn't useless, but it is, for better or worse, at the bottom of this list for a reason; in our experience, it doesn't add as much value as the other techniques described.

# 4

# DUPLICATE CONTENT IN A POST-PANDA WORLD

*By Dr. Peter Meyers*

**Editor's Note:** *In a post-Panda world, ignoring duplicate content is not an option. The potential damage is too great to risk. In this post, which was originally published on* The Moz Blog *on Nov. 16, 2011, "Dr. Pete" explains what duplicate content is, why it's such a big deal, and how inbound marketers can diagnose and fix duplicate content issues.*

IN EARLY 2011, Google launched the first phase of the "Panda" update, which would prove to be a wake-up call for SEO issues webmasters had been ignoring for too long. One of those issues was duplicate content. While duplicate content as an SEO problem has been around for years, the way Google handles it has evolved dramatically and seems to only get more complicated with every update. Panda upped the ante even more.

This chapter is an attempt to cover the topic of duplicate content, as it stands today, in depth. This is designed to be a comprehensive resource—a complete discussion of what duplicate content is, how it happens, how to diagnose it, and how to fix it. Maybe we'll even round up a few rogue pandas along the way.

# WHAT IS DUPLICATE CONTENT?

Let's start with the basics. Duplicate content exists when any two (or more) pages share the same content. If you're a visual learner, here's an illustration for you:

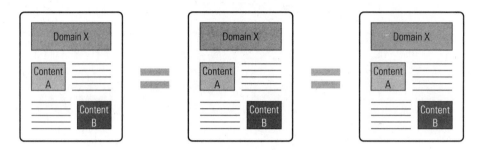

Easy enough, right? So, why does such a simple concept cause so much difficulty? One problem is that people often make the mistake of thinking that a "page" is a file or document sitting on their web server. To a crawler (like Googlebot), a page is any unique URL it happens to find, usually through internal or external links. Especially on large, dynamic sites, creating two URLs that land on the same content is surprisingly easy (and often unintentional).

# WHY DO DUPLICATES MATTER?

Duplicate content as an SEO issue was around long before the Panda update, and has taken many forms as the algorithm has changed. Here's a brief look at some major issues with duplicate content over the years.

## THE SUPPLEMENTAL INDEX

In the early days of Google, just indexing the web was a massive computational challenge. To deal with this challenge, some pages that were seen as duplicates or very low quality were stored in a secondary index called the *supplemental index*. These pages automatically became second-class citizens, from an SEO perspective, and lost any competitive ranking ability.

Around late 2006, Google integrated supplemental results back into the main index, but those results were still often filtered out. You know you've hit filtered results anytime you see this warning at the bottom of a Google SERP (search engine results page):

> *In order to show you the most relevant results, we have omitted some entries very similar to the 228 already displayed.*
> *If you like, you can repeat the search with the omitted results included.*

Even though the index was unified, results were still omitted, with obvious consequences for SEO. Of course, in many cases, these pages really were duplicates or had very little search value, and the practical SEO impact was negligible, but not always.

## THE CRAWL BUDGET

It's always tough to talk limits when it comes to Google, because people want to hear an absolute number. There is no absolute crawl budget or fixed number of pages that Google will crawl on a site. There is, however, a point at which Google may give up crawling your site for a while, especially if you keep sending spiders down winding paths.

Although the crawl budget isn't absolute, even for a given site, you can get a sense of Google's crawl allocation for your site in Google Webmaster Tools (under Diagnostics, select Crawl Stats).

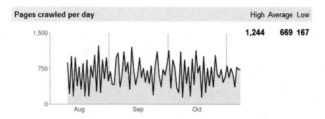

So, what happens when Google hits so many duplicate paths and pages that it gives up for the day? Practically speaking, the pages you want indexed may not get crawled. At best, they probably won't be crawled as often.

## THE INDEXATION CAP

Similarly, there's no set cap to how many pages of a site Google will index. There does seem to be a dynamic limit, though, and that limit is relative to the authority of the site. If you fill up your index with useless, duplicate pages, you may push out more important, deeper pages. For example, if you load up on thousands of internal search results, Google may not index all of your product pages. Many people make the mistake of thinking that more indexed pages is better. I've seen too many situations where the opposite was true. All else being equal, bloated indexes dilute your ranking ability.

## THE PENALTY DEBATE

Long before Panda, a debate would erupt every few months over whether or not there was a duplicate content penalty. While these debates raised valid points, they often focused on semantics—whether or not duplicate content caused a Capital-P Penalty. While I think the conceptual difference between penalties and filters is important, the upshot for a site owner is often the same. If a page isn't ranking (or even indexed) because of duplicate content, then you've got a problem, no matter what you call it.

## THE PANDA UPDATE

Since Panda (starting in February 2011), the impact of duplicate content has become much more severe in some cases. It used to be that duplicate content could only harm that content itself. If you had a duplicate, it might go supplemental or get filtered out. Usually, that was okay. In extreme cases, a large number of duplicates could bloat your index or cause crawl problems and start impacting other pages.

Panda made duplicate content part of a broader quality equation—now, a duplicate content problem can impact your entire site. If you're hit by Panda, non-duplicate pages may lose ranking power, stop ranking altogether, or even fall out of the index. Duplicate content is no longer an isolated problem.

# THREE KINDS OF DUPLICATES

Before we dive into examples of duplicate content and the tools for dealing with them, I'd like to cover three broad categories of duplicates: true duplicates, near duplicates, and cross-domain duplicates. I'll be referencing these three main types in the examples later in the chapter.

## TRUE DUPLICATES

A *true duplicate* is any page that is 100 percent identical (in content) to another page. These pages only differ by the URL.

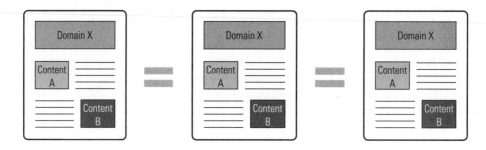

## NEAR DUPLICATES

A *near duplicate* differs from another page (or pages) by a very small amount—it could be a block of text, an image, or even the order of the content.

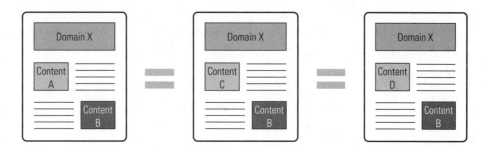

An exact definition of "near" is tough to pin down, but I'll discuss some examples in detail later.

## CROSS-DOMAIN DUPLICATES

*Cross-domain duplicates* occur when two or more websites share the same piece of content.

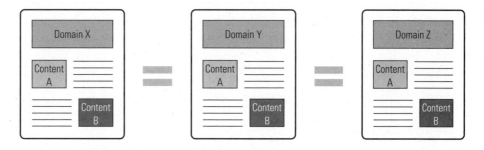

These duplicates could be either true or near duplicates. Contrary to what some people believe, cross-domain duplicates can be a problem even for legitimate, syndicated content.

# TOOLS FOR FIXING DUPLICATES

This may seem out of order, but I want to discuss the tools for dealing with duplicates before I dive into specific examples. That way, I can recommend the appropriate tools to fix each example without confusing anyone.

## 404 (NOT FOUND)

Of course, the simplest way to deal with duplicate content is to just remove it and return a 404 error. If the content really has no value to visitors or search, and if it has no significant inbound links or traffic, then total removal is a perfectly valid option.

## 301-REDIRECT

Another way to remove a page is via a 301-redirect. Unlike a 404, the 301 tells visitors (humans and bots) that the page has permanently moved to another location. Human visitors seamlessly arrive at the new page. From an SEO perspective, most of the inbound link equity is also passed to the new page. If your duplicate content has a clear canonical URL, and the duplicate has traffic or inbound links, then a 301-redirect may be a good option.

## ROBOTS.TXT

Another option is to leave the duplicate content available for human visitors, but block it for search crawlers. The oldest and probably still easiest way to do this is with a robots.txt file (generally located in your root directory). It looks something like this:

```
User-agent: *
Disallow: /dupe-page.htm
Disallow: /dupe-folder/
```

One advantage of robots.txt is that it's relatively easy to block entire folders or even URL parameters. The disadvantage is that it's an extreme and sometimes unreliable solution. While robots.txt is effective for blocking uncrawled content, it's not great for removing content already in the index. The major search engines also seem to frown on its overuse, and don't generally recommend robots.txt for duplicate content.

## META ROBOTS

You can also control the behavior of search bots at the page level, with a header-level directive known as the *Meta Robots tag* (or sometimes *Meta Noindex*). In its simplest form, the tag looks something like this:

```
<head>
  <meta name="ROBOTS" content="NOINDEX, NOFOLLOW" />
</head>
```

This page-level directive tells search bots not to index this particular page or follow links on it. Anecdotally, I find it a bit more SEO-friendly than robots.txt, and because the tag can be created dynamically with code, it can often be more flexible.

The other common variant for Meta Robots is the content value `"NOINDEX, FOLLOW"`, which allows bots to crawl the paths on the page without adding the page to the search index. This can be useful for pages like internal search results, where you may want to block certain variations (I'll discuss this more later) but still follow the paths to product pages.

> *One quick note: There is no need to ever add a Meta Robots tag with* `"INDEX, FOLLOW"` *to a page. All pages are indexed and followed by default (unless blocked by other means).*

News publishers who syndicate their content may ensure that only the original versions of their articles appear in Google News. They can do this by directing their syndication partners to use a Meta Robots tag that disallows Google News from indexing the syndicated version of the article. The tag looks like this:

```
<head>
  <meta name="GOOGLEBOT-NEWS" content="NOINDEX" />
</head>
```

Using this tag alone will prevent syndicated content from appearing in Google News search results, but still allow the content to be indexed by other by other crawlers. If a publisher would like to restrict syndicated content from appearing in *any* type of search results, they should have their syndication partners use the universal Meta Noindex tag instead.

News publishers can also point Google News towards the original version of the articles by using the `Rel=Canonical` directive, just as they would to specify a canonical version of any other type of page. For details on how to the `Rel=Canonical` directive, see the following section.

> **Editor's Note:** *In November of 2010, Google introduced a set of "experimental" tags for publishers of syndicated content to indicate the original source of a republished article. The Meta Syndication-Source directive, shown following, was deprecated in 2012.*

```
<head>
  <meta name="syndication-source" content="http://example.
com/news" />
</head>
```

## REL=CANONICAL

In 2009, the search engines banded together to create the `Rel=Canonical` directive, sometimes called just *Rel-canonical* or the *Canonical Tag*. This allows webmasters to specify a canonical version for any page. The tag goes in the page header (like Meta Robots), and a simple example looks like this:

```
<head>
  <link rel="canonical" href="http://www.example.com" />
</head>
```

When search engines arrive on a page with a canonical tag, they attribute the page to the canonical URL, regardless of the URL they used to reach the page. So, for example, if a bot reached the above page using the URL `www.example.com/index.html`, the search engine would **not** index the additional, non-canonical URL. Typically, it seems that inbound link equity is also passed through the canonical tag.

It's important to note that you need to clearly understand what the proper canonical page is for any given website template. Canonicalizing your entire site to just one page, or the wrong pages, can be very dangerous.

## GOOGLE URL REMOVAL

In Google Webmaster Tools (GWT), you can request that an individual page (or directory) be manually removed from the index. Click Optimization in the lefthand nav, and then choose Remove URLs from the dropdown list and you'll see a button called "Create a new removal request" in the main content area. Click that button and you'll see something like this:

Since this tool only removes one URL or path at a time, completely at Google's discretion, it's usually a last-ditch approach to fixing duplicate content. If you want to remove a page permanently, then you need to 404, robots.txt block or Meta Noindex the page before requesting removal. At Google's discretion, pages removed via GWT that are not blocked by other methods can reappear in the index after 90 days.

## GOOGLE PARAMETER BLOCKING

You can also use GWT to specify URL parameters that you want Google to ignore (which essentially blocks indexation of pages with those parameters). If you click Site Configuration, followed by URL parameters, you'll get a list that looks something like this:

| Parameter | URLs monitored | What Googlebot should crawl | |
|---|---|---|---|
| utm_source | 12 | Let Googlebot decide *(default)* | Edit / Reset |
| utm_medium | 11 | Let Googlebot decide *(default)* | Edit / Reset |
| utm_campaign | 7 | Let Googlebot decide *(default)* | Edit / Reset |
| id | 5 | Let Googlebot decide *(default)* | Edit / Reset |
| text | 5 | Let Googlebot decide *(default)* | Edit / Reset |

This list shows URL parameters that Google has detected, as well as the settings for how those parameters should be crawled. Keep in mind that the "Let Googlebot decide" setting doesn't reflect other blocking tactics, like robots.txt or Meta Robots. If you click Edit, you'll see the following options:

Personally, I find the wording a bit confusing. "Yes" means the parameter is important and should be indexed, while "No" means the parameter indicates a duplicate. The GWT tool seems to be effective (and can be fast), but I don't usually recommend it as a first line of defense. It won't impact other search engines, and it can't be read by SEO tools and monitoring software. It could also be modified by Google at any time.

## BING URL REMOVAL

Bing Webmaster Center (BWC) has tools very similar to GWT's options. In fairness to Bing, I think their parameter blocking tool came before Google's version. To request a URL removal in Bing, select the Index tab, followed by Block URLs and Block URL and Cache. You'll get a pop-up that looks like this:

BWC actually gives you a wider range of options, including blocking a directory and your entire site. Obviously, that last one usually isn't a good idea.

## BING PARAMETER BLOCKING

In the same section of BWC (Index) is an option called URL Normalization. The name implies that Bing treats this more like canonicalization, but there's only one option, ignore. Like Google, you get a list of auto-detected parameters that you can add or modify.

| Add Parameter | Enable | Disable | Remove Parameter |
| --- | --- | --- | --- |

| Parameter △ | Status | Source | Date |
| --- | --- | --- | --- |
| ft | Disabled | Bing | 11/7/2011 |
| id | Disabled | Bing | 11/7/2011 |
| max | Disabled | Bing | 11/7/2011 |
| msg | Disabled | Bing | 11/7/2011 |

As with the GWT tools, I'd consider the Bing versions to be a last resort. Generally, I'd only use these tools if other methods have failed, and one search engine is just giving you grief.

## REL=PREV AND REL=NEXT

In September of 2011, Google gave us a new tool for fighting a particular form of near-duplicate content known as *paginated search results*. I describe the problem in more detail in the next section. Essentially, though, paginated results are any content or searches where the results are broken up into chunks, with each chunk (say, ten results) having its own page/URL.

You can now tell Google how paginated content connects by using a pair of tags much like Rel=canonical. They're called Rel-Prev and Rel-Next. Implementation is a bit tricky, but here's a simple example.

```
<head>
  <link rel="prev" href="http://www.example.com/search/2" />
  <link rel="next" href="http://www.example.com/search/4" />
</head>
```

In this example, the search bot has landed on page 3 of search results, so you need two tags: a Rel-Prev pointing to page 2, and a Rel-Next pointing to page 4. Where it gets tricky is that you're almost always going to have to generate these tags dynamically, as your search results are probably driven by one template.

Google has pushed this approach harder over time, although the data on its effectiveness seems mixed. Bing didn't originally honor Rel=Prev/Next, but announced limited support for the tags in April of 2012. I'll briefly discuss other methods for dealing with paginated content in the next section.

## INTERNAL LINKING

It's important to remember that your best tool for dealing with duplicate content is to not create it in the first place. Granted, that's not always possible, but if you find yourself having to patch dozens of problems, you may need to re-examine your internal linking structure and site architecture.

When you do correct a duplication problem, such as with a 301-redirect or the canonical tag, it's also important to make your other site cues reflect that change. It's amazing how often I see someone set a 301 or canonical to one version of a page, while they continue to link internally to the non-canonical version and fill their XML sitemap with non-canonical URLs. Internal links are strong signals, and sending mixed signals will only cause you problems.

## DON'T DO ANYTHING

Finally, you can let the search engines sort it out. This is what Google recommended you do for years, actually. Unfortunately, in my experience, especially for large sites, this is almost always a bad idea. It's important to note, though, that not all duplicate content is a disaster, and Google certainly can filter some of it out without huge consequences. If you only have a few isolated duplicates floating around, leaving them alone is a perfectly valid option.

## REL="ALTERNATE" HREFLANG="X"

In 2012, Google introduced a new way of dealing with translated content and same-language content with regional variations (such as US English versus UK English). Implementation of these tags is complex and very situational, but here's a simple example of a site that has both an English and Spanish version (under a sub-domain):

```
<head>
  <link rel="alternate" hreflang="en" href="http://www.
example.com/" />
  <link rel="alternate" hreflang="es" href="http://es.
example.com/" />
</head>
```

These tags would tell Google where to find both the English and Spanish-language versions of the content. Like canonical tags, they are page-level and need to be placed on all relevant pages (pointing to the alternate language version of each specific page).

# EXAMPLES OF DUPLICATE CONTENT

So, now that we've worked backwards and sorted out the tools for fixing duplicate content, what does duplicate content actually look like in the wild? I'm going to cover a wide range of examples that represent the issues you can expect to encounter on a real website.

## WWW VERSUS NON-WWW

For site-wide duplicate content, this is probably the biggest culprit. Whether you've got bad internal paths or have attracted links and social mentions to the wrong URL, you've got both the www version and non-www (root domain) version of your URLs indexed:

```
www.example.com

example.com
```

Most of the time, a 301-redirect is your best choice here. This is a common problem, and Google is good about honoring redirects for cases like these.

You may also want to set your preferred address in Google Webmaster Tools. Under Configuration and Settings, you should see a section called Preferred domain that looks like this:

**Preferred domain**
- ○ Don't set a preferred domain
- ◉ Display URLs as **www.30go30.com**
- ○ Display URLs as **30go30.com**

There's a quirk in GWT where, to set a preferred domain, you may have to create GWT profiles for both your www and non-www versions of the site. While this is annoying, it won't cause any harm. If you're having major canonicalization issues, I'd recommend it. If you're not, then you can leave well enough alone and let Google determine the preferred domain.

## STAGING SERVERS

While much less common than the preceding issue, this problem is often also caused by subdomains. In a typical scenario, you're working on a new site design for a relaunch, your dev team sets up a subdomain with the new site, and they accidentally leave it open to crawlers. What you end up with is two sets of indexed URLs that look something like this:

```
www.example.com

staging.example.com
```

Your best bet is to prevent this problem before it happens by blocking the staging site with robots.txt . If you find your staging site indexed, though, you'll probably need to 301-redirect those pages or Meta Noindex them.

## TRAILING SLASHES ("/")

This is a problem people often have questions about, although it's less of an SEO issue than it once was. Technically, in the original HTTP protocol, a URL would be considered a completely different URL if you simply added a slash to the end of it. Here's a simple example:

```
www.example.com/products

www.example.com/products/
```

The first URL would represent a page, whereas the second URL would signal a folder. These days, almost all browsers automatically add the trailing slash behind the scenes and resolve both versions the same way. Google automatically canonicalizes these URLs in the majority of cases, but a 301-redirect is the preferred solution if you see duplicates in the index.

## SECURE (HTTPS) PAGES

If your site has secure pages (designated by the *https:* protocol), you may find that both secure and non-secure versions are getting indexed. This most frequently happens when navigation links from secure pages—like shopping cart pages—also end up secured. This is usually due to relative paths creating variants like this:

```
www.example.com

https://www.example.com
```

Ideally, these problems are solved by the site architecture itself. In many cases, it's best to Noindex secure pages—shopping cart and check-out pages have no place in the search index. After the fact, though, your best option is a 301-redirect. Be cautious with any site-wide solutions—if you 301-redirect all "https:" pages to their "http:" versions, you could end up removing security entirely. This is a tricky problem to solve, and it should be handled carefully.

## HOME PAGE DUPLICATES

While the three preceding issues can all create home page duplicates, the home page has a couple unique problems of its own. The most typical problem is that both the root domain and the actual home page document name get indexed. For example:

```
www.example.com

www.example.com/index.htm
```

Although this problem can be solved with a 301-redirect, it's often a good idea to add a canonical tag on your home page. Home pages are uniquely afflicted by duplicates, and a proactive canonical tag can prevent a lot of problems.

Of course, it's important to also be consistent with your internal paths. If you want the root version of the URL to be canonical, but then link to /index.htm in your navigation, you're sending mixed signals to Google every time the crawlers visit.

## SESSION IDS

Some websites (especially e-commerce platforms) tag each new visitor with a tracking parameter. On occasion, that parameter ends up in the URL and gets indexed, creating something like this:

```
www.example.com

www.example.com/?session=12345678
```

That image really doesn't do the problem justice, because in reality you can end up with a duplicate for every single session ID and page combination that gets indexed. Session IDs in the URL can easily add thousands of duplicate pages to your index.

The best option, if it is possible to implement on your particular site/platform, is to remove the session ID from the URL altogether and store it in a cookie. There are very few good reasons to create these URLs, and no reason to let bots crawl them. If that's not feasible, implementing the canonical tag site-wide is a good bet. If you really get stuck, you can block the parameter in Google Webmaster Tools and Bing Webmaster Central.

## AFFILIATE TRACKING

This problem looks a lot like session IDs and happens when sites provide a tracking variable to their affiliates. This variable is typically appended to landing page URLs, like so:

```
www.example.com

www.example.com/?affiliate=mozbot99
```

The damage is usually a bit less extreme than home page duplicates, but it can still cause large-scale duplication. The solutions are similar to session IDs. Ideally, you can capture the affiliate ID in a cookie and 301-redirect to the canonical version of the page. Otherwise, you'll probably either need to use canonical tags or block the affiliate URL parameter.

## DUPLICATE PATHS

Having duplicate paths to a page is perfectly fine, but when duplicate paths generate duplicate URLs, then you've got a problem. Let's say a product page can be reached one of three ways:

```
www.example.com/electronics/ipad2

www.example.com/apple/ipad2

www.example.com/tag/favorites/ipad2
```

Here, the iPad2 product page can be reached by two categories and a user-generated tag. User-generated tags are especially problematic, because they can theoretically spawn unlimited versions of a page.

Ideally, these path-based URLs shouldn't be created at all. However a page is navigated to, it should only have one URL for SEO purposes. Some will argue that including navigation paths in the URL is a positive cue for site visitors, but even as someone with a usability background, I think the cons almost always outweigh the pros here.

If you already have variations indexed, then a 301-redirect or canonical tag are probably your best options. In many cases, implementing the canonical tag will be easier, since there may be too many variations to easily redirect. Long-term, though, you'll need to re-evaluate your site architecture.

## FUNCTIONAL PARAMETERS

Functional parameters are URL parameters that change a page slightly, but have no value for search, and are essentially duplicates. For example, let's say that all of your product pages have a printable version, and that each version has its own URL.

```
www.example.com/product.php?id=1234

www.example.com/product. php?id=1234&print=1
```

Here, the `print=1` URL variable indicates a printable version, which normally would have the same content but a modified template. Your best bet is to not index these at all, with something like a Meta Noindex , but you could also use a canonical tag to consolidate these pages.

## INTERNATIONAL DUPLICATES

These duplicates occur when you have content for different countries which share the same language, all hosted on the same root domain (it could be subfolders or subdomains). For example, you may have an English version of your product pages for the US, UK, and Australia.

```
www.example.com/us/product/ipad2
www.example.com/uk/product/ipad2
www.example.com/au/product/ipad2
```

Unfortunately, this one's a bit tough—in some cases, Google will handle it perfectly well and rank the appropriate content in the appropriate countries. In other cases, even with proper geo-targeting, they won't. It's often better to target the language itself than the country, but there are legitimate reasons to split off country-specific content, such as pricing.

If your international content does get treated as duplicate content, you may want to try using the `hreflang` attribute (`http://mz.cm/YET7la`).

Even though Google seems to be taking it more seriously, this can be a complex situation to resolve, as Google uses many cues for internationalization.

## SEARCH SORTS

So far, all of the examples I've given have been true duplicates. I'd like to dive into a few examples of near duplicates, since that concept is a bit fuzzy. A few common examples pop up with internal search engines, which tend to spin off many variants—sortable results, filters, and paginated results being the most frequent problems.

Search sort duplicates pop up whenever a sort (ascending/descending) creates a separate URL. While the two sorted results are technically different pages, they add no additional value to the search index and contain the same content, just in a different order. URLs might look like this:

```
www.example.com/search.php?keyword=ipad
www.example.com/search.php?keyword=ipad&sort=desc
```

In most cases, it's best just to block the sortable versions completely, usually by adding a Meta Noindex selectively to pages called with that parameter. In a pinch, you could block the sort parameter in Google Webmaster Tools and Bing Webmaster Central.

## SEARCH FILTERS

Search filters are used to narrow an internal search—it could be price, color, features, etc. Filters are very common on e-commerce sites that sell a wide variety of products. Search filter URLs look a lot like search sorts, in many cases:

```
www.example.com/search.php?category=laptop

www.example.com/search.php?category=laptop?price=1000
```

The solution here is similar to the preceding one—don't index the filters. As long as Google has a clear path to products, indexing every variant usually causes more harm than good.

## SEARCH PAGINATION

Pagination is an easy problem to describe and an incredibly difficult one to solve. Any time you split internal search results into separate pages, you have paginated content. The URLs are easy enough to visualize:

```
www.example.com/search.php?category=laptop

www.example.com/search.php?category=laptop?page=2
```

Of course, over hundreds of results, one search can easily spin out dozens of near duplicates. While the results themselves differ, many important features of the pages (titles, meta descriptions, headers, copy, templates, etc.) are identical. Add to that the problem the fact that Google isn't a big fan of "search within search" (i.e., having their search pages land on yours).

In the past, Google has said to let it sort pagination out—problem is, Google hasn't done it very well. Recently, Google introduced Rel-Prev and Rel-Next, as described earlier. Google has championed this solution, but the effectiveness of it can be very situational.

You have three other, viable options (in my opinion), although how and when they're viable depends a lot on the situation:

1. You can Meta Noindex, Follow pages 2+ of search results. Let Google crawl the paginated content, but don't let it be indexed.
2. You can create a *View All* page that links to all search results at one URL, and let Google auto-detect it. This seems to be Google's other preferred option.
3. You can create a View All page and set the canonical tag of paginated results back to that page. This is unofficially endorsed, but the pages aren't really duplicates in the traditional sense, so some claim it violates the intent of Rel-canonical.

Pagination for SEO is a very difficult topic, and can be complicated by search sorts, filters, and other variables. Often, multiple solutions have to be brought into play.

## PRODUCT VARIATIONS

Product variant pages are pages that branch off from the main product page and only differ by one feature or option. For example, you might have a page for each color a product comes in:

```
www.example.com/product/ipod/nano

www.example.com/product/ipod/nano/blue

www.example.com/product/ipod/nano/red
```

It can be tempting to want to index every color variation, hoping it pops up in search results, but in most cases I think the cons outweigh the pros. If you have a handful of product variations and are talking about dozens of pages, fine. If product variations spin out into hundreds or thousands, though, it's best to consolidate. Although these pages aren't technically true duplicates, I think it's okay to Rel-canonical the options back up to the main product page.

> *I purposely used "static" URLs in this example to demonstrate a point. Just because a URL doesn't have parameters, that doesn't make it immune to duplication. Static URLs (i.e., parameter-free URLs) may look prettier, but they can be duplicates just as easily as dynamic URLs.*

## GEO-KEYWORD VARIATIONS

Once upon a time, *Local SEO* meant just copying all of your pages hundreds of times, adding a city name to the URL, and swapping out that city in the page copy. It created URLs like these:

```
www.example.com/product/ipad2/new-york

www.example.com/product/ipad2/chicago

www.example.com/product/ipad2/miami
```

These days, not only is Local SEO a lot more sophisticated, but these pages are almost always going to look like near duplicates. If you have any chance of ranking, you're going to need to invest in legitimate, unique content for every geographic region you spin out. If you aren't willing to make that investment, then don't create the pages. They'll probably backfire.

## OTHER "THIN" CONTENT

This isn't really an example, but I wanted to stop and explain a word we throw around a lot when it comes to content: *thin*. While thin content can mean a variety of things, I think many examples of thin content are near duplicates, like product variations. Whenever you have pages that vary by only a tiny percentage of content, you risk those pages looking low-value to Google. If those pages are heavy on ads (with more ads than unique content), you're at even more risk. When too much of your site is thin, it's time to revisit your content strategy.

## SYNDICATED CONTENT

These last three examples all relate to cross-domain content. Here, the URLs don't really matter—they could be wildly different. Syndicated content and scraped content (see the following section) differ only by intent. *Syndicated content* is any content you use with permission from another site. However you retrieve and integrate it, that content is available on another site (and, often, many sites).

While syndication is legitimate, it's still likely that one or more copies will get filtered out of search results. You could roll the dice and see what happens, but conventional SEO wisdom says that you should link back to the source and probably set up a cross-domain canonical tag. A cross-domain canonical looks just like a regular canonical, but with a reference to someone else's domain.

Of course, a cross-domain canonical tag means that, assuming Google honors the tag, your page won't get indexed or rank. In some cases, that's fine—you're using the content for its value to visitors. Practically, I think it depends on the scope. If you occasionally syndicate content to beef up your own offerings but also have plenty of unique material, then link back and leave it alone. If a larger part of your site is syndicated content, then you could find yourself running into trouble. Unfortunately, using the canonical tag means you'll lose the ranking ability of that content, but it could keep you from getting penalized or having Panda-related problems.

## SCRAPED CONTENT

*Scraped content* is just like syndicated content, except that you didn't ask permission (and might even be breaking the law). The best solution: QUIT BREAKING THE LAW!

Seriously, no de-duping solution is going to satisfy the scrapers among you, because most solutions will knock your content out of ranking contention. The best you can do is pad the scraped content with as much of your own, unique content as possible.

### CROSS-CCTLD DUPLICATES

Finally, it's possible to run into trouble when you copy same-language content across countries—see the functional parameters example—even with separate Top-Level Domains (TLDs). Fortunately, this problem is fairly rare, but we see it with English-language content and even with some content in European languages. For example, I frequently see questions about Dutch content on Dutch and Belgian domains ranking improperly.

Unfortunately, there's no easy answer here, and most of the solutions aren't traditional duplicate-content approaches. In most cases, you need to work on your targeting factors and clearly show Google that the domain is tied to the country in question.

## WHICH URL IS CANONICAL?

I'd like to take a quick detour to discuss an important question—whether you use a 301-redirect or a canonical tag, how do you know which URL is actually canonical? I often see people making a mistake like this:

```
<head>
  <link rel="canonical" href="http://www.example.com/prod-
  uct.php">
</head>
```

The problem is that `product.php` is just a template—you've now collapsed all of your products down to a single page (that probably doesn't even display a product). In this case, the canonical version probably includes a parameter, like `id=1234`.

The canonical page isn't always the simplest version of the URL—it's the simplest version of the URL that generates UNIQUE content. Let's say you have these three URLs that all generate the same product page:

```
www.example.com/product.php?id=1234

www.example.com/product.php?id=1234&print=1

www.example.com/product.php?id=1234&session=12345678
```

Two of these versions are essentially duplicates, and the `print` and `session` parameters represent variations on the main product page that should be de-duped. The `id` parameter is essential to the content, though—it determines which product is actually being displayed.

So, consider yourself warned. As much trouble as rampant duplicates can be, bad canonicalization can cause even more damage in some cases. Plan carefully, and make absolutely sure you select the correct canonical versions of your pages before consolidating them.

## TOOLS FOR DIAGNOSING DUPLICATES

So, now that you recognize what duplicate content looks like, how do you go about finding it on your own site? Here are a few tools to get you started—I won't claim it's a complete list, but it covers the bases.

### GOOGLE WEBMASTER TOOLS

In Google Webmaster Tools, you can pull up a list of duplicate title tags and meta descriptions that Google has crawled. While these don't tell the whole story, they're a good starting point. Many URL-based duplicates will naturally generate identical metadata. In your GWT account, navigate to Optimization, followed by HTML Improvements, and you'll see a table like this:

| Meta description | Pages |
| --- | --- |
| Duplicate meta descriptions | 149 |
| Long meta descriptions | 0 |
| Short meta descriptions | 0 |

| Title tag | Pages |
| --- | --- |
| Missing title tags | 0 |
| Duplicate title tags | 73 |
| Long title tags | 0 |

You can click on "Duplicate meta descriptions" and "Duplicate title tags" to pull up a list of the duplicates. This is a great first stop for finding your trouble spots.

## GOOGLE'S SITE: COMMAND

When you already have a sense of where you might be running into trouble and need to take a deeper dive, Google's `site:` command is a very powerful and flexible tool. What really makes `site:` powerful is that you can use it in conjunction with other search operators.

Let's say, for example, that you're worried about home page duplicates. To find out if Google has indexed any copies of your home page, you could use the `site:` command with the `intitle:` operator, like this:

Put the title in quotes to capture the full phrase, and always use the root domain (leave off www) when making a wide sweep for duplicate content. This will detect both www and non-www versions, as well as any other subdomains.

Another powerful combination is `site:` plus the `inurl:` operator. You could use this to detect parameters, such as the search-sort problem mentioned above.

The `inurl:` operator can also detect the protocol used, which is handy for finding out whether any secure (https:) copies of your pages have been indexed.

You can also combine the `site:` operator with regular search text, to find near duplicates (such as blocks of repeated content). To search for a block of content across your site, just include it in quotes.

I should also mention that searching for a unique block of content in quotes is a cheap and easy way to find out if people have been scraping your site. Just leave off the `site:` operator and search for a long or unique block entirely in quotes.

Of course, these are just a few examples, but if you really need to dig deep, these simple tools can be used in powerful ways. Ultimately, the best way to tell if you have a duplicate content problem is to see what Google sees.

## YOUR OWN BRAIN

Finally, it's important to remember to use your own brain. Finding duplicate content often requires some detective work, and relying too heavily on tools can leave some gaps in what you find. One critical step is to systematically navigate your site to find where duplicates are being created. For example, does your internal search have sorts and filters? Do those sorts and filters get translated into URL variables, and are they crawlable? If they are, you can use the `site:` command to dig deeper. Even finding a handful of trouble spots using your own sleuthing skills can end up revealing thousands of duplicate pages, in my experience.

## I HOPE THAT COVERS IT

If you've made it this far—congratulations—you're probably as exhausted as I am. I hope that covers everything you'd want to know about the current state of duplicate content. Some of these topics, like pagination, are extremely tricky in practice, and there's often not one "right" answer.

# 5

# FRESHNESS FACTOR: 10 ILLUSTRATIONS ON HOW FRESH CONTENT CAN INFLUENCE RANKINGS

*By Cyrus Shepard*

---

*Editor's Note:* This post was originally published on *The Moz Blog* on Dec. 12, 2011.

---

IN 2003, ENGINEERS at Google filed a patent application for a document-scoring program referred to as "Search Engine 125" that would rock the SEO world. Named "Document Scoring Based on Document Content Update," it not only offered insight into the mind of the world's largest search engine, but provided an accurate roadmap of the path Google would take for years to come.

In his series on the ten most important search patents of all time, Bill Slawski shows how this patent spawned many child patents (`www.seobythesea.com/2011/12/10-most-important-seo-patents-original-historical-data-patent-filing-children`). These are often near-duplicate patents with slightly modified passages, the latest discovered as recently as October 2011. Many of the algorithmic changes we see today are simply improvements of these original ideas conceived years ago by Google engineers.

One of these updates was Google's Freshness Update, which places greater emphasis on returning fresher web content for certain queries. Exactly how Google determines freshness was brilliantly explored by Justin Briggs in his analysis of original Google patents (`http://justinbriggs.org/methods-for-evaluating-freshness`). Justin deserves a lot of credit for bringing this analysis to light and inspiring this article.

Although the Freshness Update of 2011 received a lot of attention, in truth Google has scored content based on freshness for years.

### Reference

U.S. Patent Application "Document Scoring Based on Document Content Update" (`http://mz.cm/XsdNvm`)

## HOW GOOGLE SCORES FRESH CONTENT

In a blog post for *Inside Search,* Google's official search blog, Google Fellow Amit Singhal explains, "Different searches have different freshness needs." (`http://insidesearch.blogspot.com/2011/11/giving-you-fresher-more-recent-search.html`). The implication is that Google measures all of your documents for freshness, and then scores each page according to the type of search query. While some queries need fresh content, Google still uses old content for other queries (more on this later).

Singhal describes the types of keyword searches most likely to require fresh content:

- Recent events or hot topics: "occupy oakland protest" "nba lockout"
- Regularly recurring events: "NFL scores" "dancing with the stars" "exxon earnings"
- Frequent updates: "best slr cameras" "subaru impreza reviews"

Google's patents offer incredible insight as to how web content can be evaluated using freshness signals, and rankings of that content adjusted accordingly.

Understand that these are not hard and fast rules, but rather theories consistent with patent filings, experiences of other SEOs, and experiments performed over the years. Nothing substitutes for direct experience, so use your best judgment and feel free to perform your own experiments based on the following information.

## 1. FRESHNESS BY INCEPTION DATE

A web page is given a "freshness" score based on its inception date, which decays over time. This freshness score can boost a piece of content for certain search queries, but degrades as the content becomes older.

The inception date is often when Google first becomes aware of the document, such as when Googlebot first indexes a document or discovers a link to it.

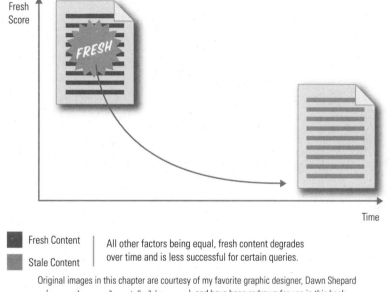

All other factors being equal, fresh content degrades over time and is less successful for certain queries.

- Fresh Content
- Stale Content

Original images in this chapter are courtesy of my favorite graphic designer, Dawn Shepard (www.shepardportfolio.com), and have been redrawn for use in this book.

*"For some queries, older documents may be more favorable than newer ones. As a result, it may be beneficial to adjust the score of a document based on the difference (in age) from the average age of the result set."*

All quotes in this chapter are from US Patent Application "Document Scoring Based on Document Content Update."

## 2. HOW MUCH A DOCUMENT CHANGES INFLUENCES FRESHNESS

The age of a web page or domain isn't the only freshness factor. Search engines can score regularly updated content for freshness differently from content that doesn't change. In this case, the amount of change on your web page plays a role.

For example, the change of a single sentence won't have as big of a freshness impact as a large change to the main body text.

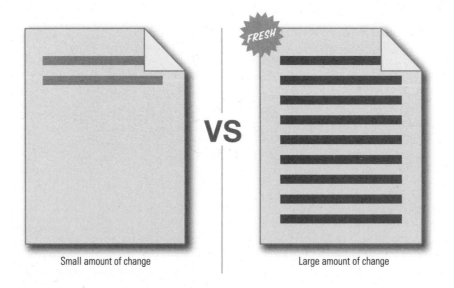

Small amount of change | Large amount of change

*"Also, a document having a relatively large amount of its content updated over time might be scored differently than a document having a relatively small amount of its content updated over time."*

## 3. THE RATE OF DOCUMENT CHANGE (HOW OFTEN) IMPACTS FRESHNESS

Content that changes more often is scored differently than content that only changes every few years. For example, consider the home page of *The New York Times*, which updates every day and has a high degree of change.

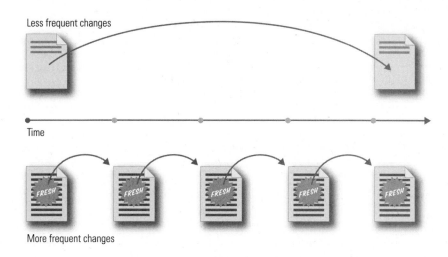

"*For example, a document whose content is edited often may be scored differently than a document whose content remains static over time.*"

## 4. FRESHNESS INFLUENCED BY NEW PAGE CREATION

Instead of revising individual pages, some websites add completely new pages over time. This is the case with most blogs. Websites that add new pages at a higher rate may earn a higher freshness score than sites that add content less frequently.

Some SEOs insist that 20 to 30 percent of the pages on your website should be new every year. This provides the opportunity to create fresh, relevant content, although you shouldn't neglect your old content if it needs attention.

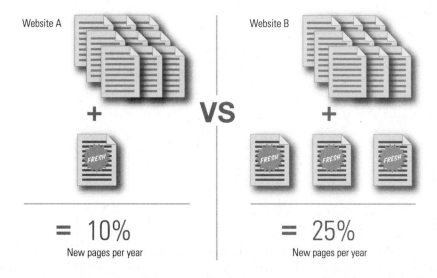

*"UA (the update amount score) may also be determined as a function of one or more factors, such as the number of "'new'" or unique pages associated with a document over a period of time. Another factor might include the ratio of the number of new or unique pages associated with a document over a period of time versus the total number of pages associated with that document."*

## 5. CHANGES TO IMPORTANT CONTENT MATTER MORE

Changes made in "important" areas of a document will signal freshness differently than changes made in less important content. Less important content includes navigation, advertisements, and content well below the fold. Important content is generally in the main body text above the fold.

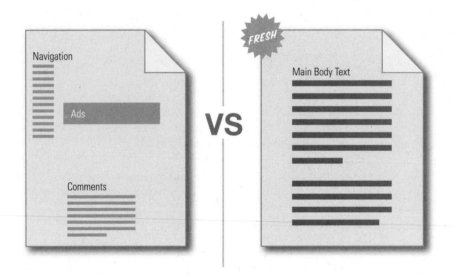

*". . . content deemed to be unimportant if updated/changed, such as JavaScript, comments, advertisements, navigational elements, boilerplate material, or date/time tags, may be given relatively little weight or even ignored altogether when determining the UA."*

## 6. RATE OF NEW LINK GROWTH SIGNALS FRESHNESS

If a web page sees an increase in its link growth rate, this could indicate a signal of relevance to search engines. For example, if folks start linking to your personal website because you are about to get married, your site could be deemed more relevant and fresh (as far as this current event goes).

That said, an unusual increase in linking activity can also indicate spam or manipulative link-building techniques. Be careful, as engines are likely to devalue such behavior.

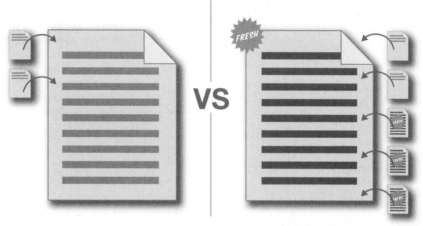

An increase in the rate of new links acquired can indicate relevance.

*". . . a downward trend in the number or rate of new links (e.g., based on a comparison of the number or rate of new links in a recent time period versus an older time period) over time could signal to search engine 125 that a document is stale, in which case search engine 125 may decrease the document's score."*

## 7. LINKS FROM FRESH SITES PASS FRESH VALUE

Links from sites that have a high freshness score can raise the freshness score of the sites they link to.

For example, if you obtain a link off an old, static site that hasn't been updated in years, this doesn't pass the same level of freshness value as a link from a fresh page—for example, the homepage of `Wired.com`. This is known as "FreshRank," a term coined by Justin Briggs (`http://justinbriggs.org/methods-for-evaluating-freshness.`)

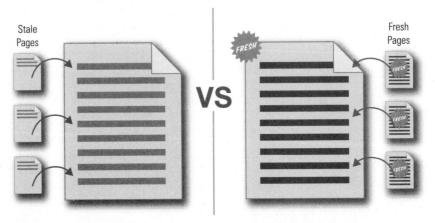

Links from fresh content, like *The New York Times* homepage, indicates freshness of the target page.

*"Document S may be considered fresh if n% of the links to S are fresh or if the documents containing forward links to S are considered fresh."*

## 8. CHANGES IN ANCHOR TEXT SIGNALS MAY DEVALUE LINKS

If a website changes dramatically over time, it makes sense that any new anchor text pointing to the page will change as well.

For example, if you buy a domain about automobiles and then change the format to content about baking, over time your new incoming anchor text will shift from cars to cookies.

In this instance, Google might determine that your site has changed so much that the old anchor text is no longer relevant, and devalue those older links entirely.

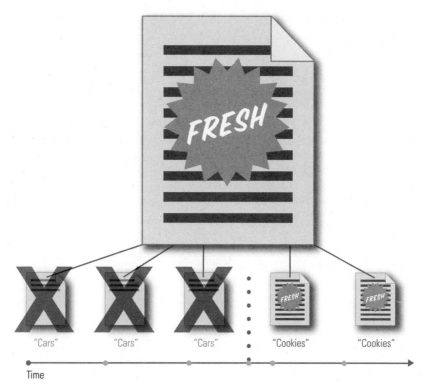

Over time, significant changes in anchor text can devalue links with older, less relevant anchor text.

*"The date of appearance/change of the document pointed to by the link may be a good indicator of the freshness of the anchor text based on the theory that good anchor text may go unchanged when a document gets updated if it is still relevant and good."*

## 9. USER BEHAVIOR INDICATES FRESHNESS

What happens when your once wonderful content becomes old and outdated? For example, your website hosts a local bus schedule... for 2009. As content becomes outdated, folks spend less time on your site. They press the back button to Google's results and choose another URL.

Google picks up on these user behavior metrics and scores your content accordingly.

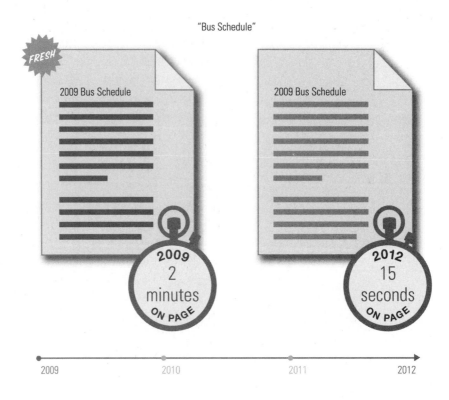

"If a document is returned for a certain query and over time, or within a given time window, users spend either more or less time on average on the document given the same or similar query, then this may be used as an indication that the document is fresh or stale, respectively."

## 10. OLDER DOCUMENTS STILL WIN CERTAIN QUERIES

Google understands the newest result isn't always the best. Consider a search query for "Magna Carta." An older, authoritative result is probably best here. In this case, having a well-aged document may actually help you.

Google's patent suggests they determine the freshness requirement for a query based on the average age of documents returned for the query.

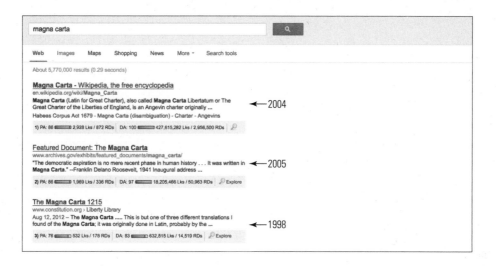

*"For some queries, documents with content that has not recently changed may be more favorable than documents with content that has recently changed. As a result, it may be beneficial to adjust the score of a document based on the difference from the average date-of-change of the result set."*

# CONCLUSION

The goal of a search engine is to return the most relevant results to users. For your part, this requires an honest assessment of your own content. What part of your site would benefit most from freshness?

Old content that exists simply to generate page views, but accomplishes little else, does more harm than good for the web. On the other hand, great content that continually answers a user's query may remain fresh forever.

Be fresh. Be relevant. Most importantly, be useful.

# 6

# ALL LINKS ARE NOT CREATED EQUAL: 10 ILLUSTRATIONS OF SEARCH ENGINES' VALUATION OF LINKS

*By Rand Fishkin*

---

*Editor's Note: It is surprising how little—and how much—has changed in how search engines evaluate and utilize links since this post was written three years ago. While links are no longer the only signals that search engines use to determine the importance and popularity of a web page, they are still the strongest ones.*

*For the most part, the principals of link valuation as explained here still hold water as well, especially if each one is updated within the current context of relevance and quality. As search engines have become more sophisticated, they have become increasingly adept at determining the relevance and quality of links, and they have adjusted the weight placed on those factors when valuing links accordingly.*

---

IN 1997, GOOGLE'S founders created an algorithmic method to determine importance and popularity based on several key principles:

- Links on the web can be interpreted as votes that are cast by the source for the target.
- All votes are, initially, considered equal.

- Over the course of executing the algorithm on a link graph, pages which receive more votes become more important.
- More important pages cast more important votes.
- The votes that a page can cast are a function of that page's importance, divided by the number of votes/links it casts.

That algorithm, of course, was named PageRank, and it changed the course of web search, providing tremendous value to Google's early efforts around quality and relevancy in search results. (Note: You can read the paper that Sergey Brin and Lawrence "Larry" Page presented to Standford on their prototype for a large-scale search engine at `http://infolab.stanford.edu/~backrub/google.html`.)

As knowledge of PageRank spread, those with a vested interest in influencing the search rankings (SEOs) found ways to leverage this information for the benefit of their web pages. But Google didn't rest on their laurels in the field of link analysis. They continuously improved the algorithm. Today, anchor text, trust, hubs and authorities, topic modeling, and even human activity are just a few of the signals Google takes into account when determining the weight a link carries. Yet, unfortunately, many in the SEO field are still unaware of these changes and how they impact external marketing and link acquisition best practices.

In this post, I walk through ten principles of link valuation that can be observed, tested, and (in some cases) patented. I'd like to extend special thanks to Bill Slawski from *SEO by the Sea* (`http://www.seobythesea.com`), whose recent posts on "Google's Reasonable Surfer Model" and "What Makes a Good Seed Site for Search Engine Web Crawls?" were catalysts (and sources) for this blog post.

> **Editor's Note:** *You can read these posts at* `www.seobythesea.com/2010/05/googles-reasonable-surfer` *and* `www.seobythesea.com/?p=3790`, *respectively.*

As you read through the following ten principles of link valuation, please note that these are not hard and fast rules. Based on our experience, testing, and observations, though, they are accurate from our perspective. As with all things in SEO, we strongly encourage our readers to test these principles for themselves. Nothing is better for learning SEO than going out and experimenting in the wild.

# PRINCIPLE #1: LINKS HIGHER UP IN HTML CODE CAST MORE POWERFUL VOTES

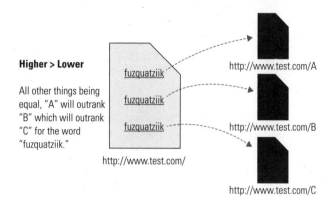

Whenever we test page features in what we hope are controlled environments on the web, we find that links higher up in the HTML code of a page seem to pass more ranking value than those lower down do. Many other SEOs we've talked to also find the same thing. This principle, that Links Higher Up in HTML Code Cast More Powerful Votes, certainly fits with the recently granted Google patent application "Ranking Documents Based on User Behavior and/or Feature Data" (www.google.com/patents/US7716225), which suggests a number of items that may be considered in the way that link metrics are passed.

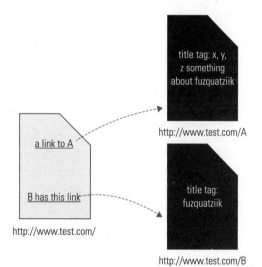

**Higher Up Links Can Overwhelm On-Page Factors**

Many other tests, as well as correlation and ranking models data, have shown that having the keyword at the front of the title element produces higher rankings. Thus, "B" should outrank "A." However, due to the power of the "higher link passes more weight" principle, the less optimal "A" still wins over "B" in test scenarios like the above.

In testing environments, SEOs often grapple with the power of the "higher link wins" phenomenon, and it can take a surprising amount of on-page optimization to overcome the power that the higher link carries.

## PRINCIPLE #2: EXTERNAL LINKS ARE MORE INFLUENTIAL THAN INTERNAL LINKS

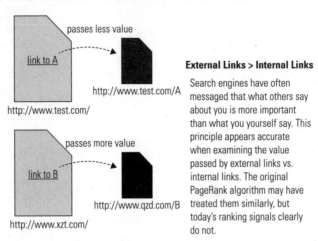

**External Links > Internal Links**

Search engines have often messaged that what others say about you is more important than what you yourself say. This principle appears accurate when examining the value passed by external links vs. internal links. The original PageRank algorithm may have treated them similarly, but today's ranking signals clearly do not.

There's little surprise here. If you recall, the original PageRank concept makes no mention of external versus internal links counting differently. It's quite likely that other, more recently created metrics (post-1997) do reward external links over internal links. You can see this in the correlation data from our post a few weeks back (see `www.moz.org/blog/the-science-of-ranking-correlations`). The external mozRank (i.e., the "PageRank" sent from external pages) had a much higher correlation with rankings than standard mozRank (PageRank).

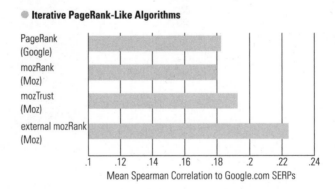

I don't think it's a stretch to imagine that Google calculates external PageRank and internal PageRank separately, and uses them in different ways for page valuation.

## PRINCIPLE #3: LINKS FROM UNIQUE DOMAINS MATTER MORE THAN LINKS FROM PREVIOUSLY LINKING SITES

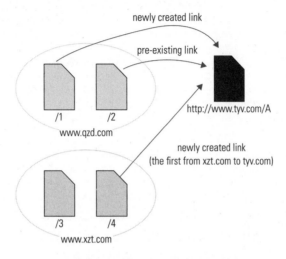

**Greater Domain Diversity of Links = Positive**
Search engines appear to highly value the domain diversity of external links in their ranking algorithms. Thus, in the scenario above (assuming all other things are equal), the newly created link from "1" to "A" will not be as valuable as the link from "4" to "A."

Speaking of correlation data, no single metric is more closely correlated with how Google determines search result rankings than the number of unique domains containing an external link to a given page. This strongly suggests that a diversity component is at play in the ranking system, and that it's better to have 50 links from 50 different domains than to have 500 more links from a site that already links to you. Curiously, the original PageRank algorithm makes no provision for this. This could be one reason that site-wide links from domains with many high-PageRank pages worked so well in Google's early years.

# PRINCIPLE #4: LINKS FROM SITES CLOSER TO A TRUSTED SEED SET PASS MORE VALUE

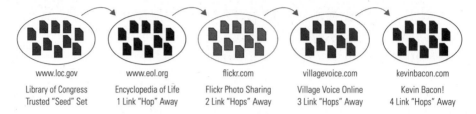

| www.loc.gov | www.eol.org | flickr.com | villagevoice.com | kevinbacon.com |
|---|---|---|---|---|
| Library of Congress Trusted "Seed" Set | Encyclopedia of Life 1 Link "Hop" Away | Flickr Photo Sharing 2 Link "Hops" Away | Village Voice Online 3 Link "Hops" Away | Kevin Bacon! 4 Link "Hops" Away |

**Link from Trusted Sites > Links from Untrusted/Unconnected Sites**

Numerous patent applications and IR papers from prominent search engineers have noted that by applying algorithms that bias towards links from trusted seed sites, webspam can be reduced significantly. It thus follows that legitimate sites will benefit if links originate from highly trusted domains.

We've talked about TrustRank on Moz (`www.moz.org/blog/whiteboard-friday-domain-trust-authority`), and Yahoo! has published a research paper on it, "Combating Webspam with TrustRank" (`http://www.vldb.org/conf/2004/RS15P3.PDF`). However, Google's certainly done plenty on this front as well. Bill Slawski speaks about this on his blog, *SEO by the Sea*, in the post "Google Trust Rank Patent Granted" (`www.seobythesea.com/2009/10/google-trust-rank-patent-granted`).

The abstract for Google's application to patent a search engine algorithm that selects trusted seed sites explains how the search engine determines its own trust metric:

> *A host-based seed selection process considers factors such as quality, importance and potential yield of hosts in a decision to use a document of a host as a seed. A subset of a plurality of hosts is determined, including some but not all of the plurality of the hosts, according to an indication of importance of the hosts, according to an expected yield of new documents for the hosts, and according to preferences for the markets the hosts belong to. At least one seed is generated for each host of the determined subset of hosts, wherein each generated at least one seed includes an indication of a document in the linked database of documents. The generated seeds are provided to be accessible by a database crawler.*

Linkscape's own mozTrust score functions in precisely this way, using a PageRank-like algorithm that's biased to only flow link juice from trusted seed sites rather than equally from across the web.

> **Editor's Note:** *The full text of Google's application Host-Based Seed Selection Algorithm for Web Crawlers can be read at* `http://mz.cm/15GWlsO`.

## PRINCIPLE #5: LINKS FROM "INSIDE" UNIQUE CONTENT PASS MORE VALUE THAN THOSE FROM HEADER/FOOTER/SIDEBAR NAVIGATION DO

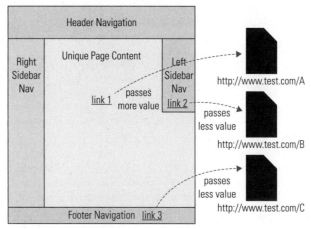

**Links in Content > Links Outside Content**
Search engines have been working on block analysis, vision-based page segmentation, and other forms of dissecting pages for many years. Today, it's quite likely that links inside relevant content blocks may pass more value than those from less contextually useful areas of a page.

Papers like Microsoft's "Vision Based Page Segmentation" (VIPS) and Google's "Document Ranking Based on Semantic Distance," as well as Google's recent patent on the Reasonable Surfer Model all suggest that valuing links from content more highly than those in sidebars or footers can have positive impacts on avoiding spam and manipulation. As webmasters and SEOs, we can certainly attest to the fact that a lot of paid links exist in these sections of sites and that getting non-natural links from inside content is much more difficult.

### References

"Microsoft's Vision Based Segmentation" (`http://mz.cm/16kR6Ai`)

Google's "Document Ranking Based on Semantic Distances" (`http://mz.cm/16kRFu2`)

Google's "Patent on the Reasonable Surfer Model" (`http://www.seobythesea.com/?p=3806`)

# PRINCIPLE #6: KEYWORDS IN HTML TEXT PASS MORE VALUE THAN THOSE IN ALT ATTRIBUTES OF LINKED IMAGES

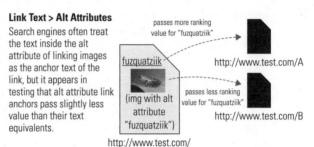

**Link Text > Alt Attributes**
Search engines often treat the text inside the alt attribute of linking images as the anchor text of the link, but it appears in testing that alt attribute link anchors pass slightly less value than their text equivalents.

While this principle isn't covered in any papers or patents (to my knowledge), our testing has shown that anchor text carried through HTML is somehow more potent than that from alt attributes in image links. That's not to say that we should run out and ditch image links, badges or the alt attributes they carry. It's just good to be aware that Google seems to have this bias. (Perhaps it will be temporary.)

# PRINCIPLE #7: LINKS FROM MORE IMPORTANT, POPULAR, TRUSTED SITES PASS MORE VALUE

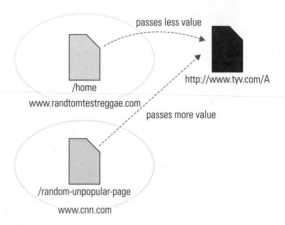

**More Valuable Domains = Higher Value Links**
Due to issues around trust, difficulty of acquisition, and the metrics passed from popular valuable domains in a link, it's often the case that pages/sites may benefit more from a link on an unpopular, unimportant page on a trusted, valuable site than the reverse (as illustrated above).

We've likely all experienced the sinking feeling of seeing a competitor outrank us with just a handful of links that appear to be from less powerful pages. When this happens, powerful domains may be passing value through links whose value is not fully reflected in page-level metrics. One reason search engines may do this is to combat spam and provide more trusted search results in general. Giving significantly more power to sites that rarely link to junk to pass value through links (even on less important pages) than they give to sites whose linking practices are questionable is one way for search engines to exercise quality control.

# PRINCIPLE #8: LINKS CONTAINED WITHIN NOSCRIPT TAGS PASS LOW, IF ANY, VALUE

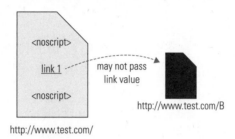

**Links in NoScript Tags May Not Pass Much (If Any) Value**
Because the links aren't visible on the page to visitors (and because they've had a history of manipulation for link value), links inside noscript tags appear to frequently pass minimal or no rank boosting ability.

While our testing certainly suggests that noscript links pass no value, we cannot say that this is true in all cases beyond the scope of our investigations. Over the years, this phenomenon has been reported and contradicted numerous times in the search community. Keeping this in mind, we included noscript links in Linkscape, but added the option for users to filter them out. All that said, the quantity of links that are inside this tag is quite small in comparison to the quantity of all links distributed across the web.

# PRINCIPLE #9: A BURST OF NEW LINKS MAY ENABLE A DOCUMENT TO OUTRANK "STRONGER" COMPETITION

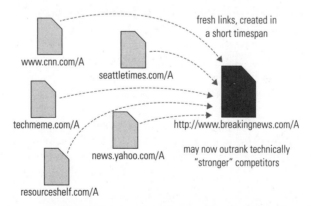

**A Fresh Burst of Links May Provide Exceptional Value**
When a page earns a relatively sizable volume of links in a short timespan, search algorithms may interpret this as a signal that the referenced page is a new and highly useful/interesting/timely resource. These temporally trending links may even provide a boost that places the page above competing documents with technically "better" ranking metrics.

Apart from Google's Query Deserves Freshness (QDF) algorithm (see `http://www.moz.org/blog/whiteboard-friday-query-deserves-freshness`), which may value more recently created and linked-to content in certain "trending" searches, it appears that the search engine also uses temporal signals around linking to both identify spam/manipulation and reward pages that earn a large number of references in a short period of time. While Google's patent on Information Retrieval Based on Historical Data first suggested the use of temporal data in 2005, the model has likely been revised and refined since then.

## PRINCIPLE #10: LEGITIMATE LINKS ON PAGES THAT ALSO LINK TO WEB SPAM MAY BE DEVALUED

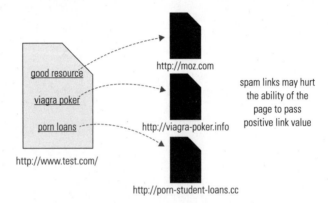

**Spam in Content or Links May Lead to Ranking Issues**

Links to known spam (even with the rel=nofollow applied) and high volumes of poison keywords or overly commercial anchor text in aggressive verticals may lower both a page's ability to perform well in the rankings and the link value passed through even legitimate internal/external links.

I was fascinated to see Richard Baxter's own experiments on this in his post "Google Page Level Penalty for Comment Spam" (`http://seogadget.co.uk/google-page-penalty-for-comment-spam-rankings-and-traffic-drop`). When his blog's comment spam filter failed, both traffic and rankings for the affected pages immediately dropped. When Baxter removed the spammy comment links, rankings and traffic returned to previous levels almost immediately.

Since then, I've been keeping an eye on some popular, valuable blog posts that have received similarly overwhelming amounts of spam. Lo and behold, the pattern seems verifiable. Webmasters would be wise to keep up to date on their spam removal to avoid arousing potential ranking penalties from Google (and the possible loss of link value).

## CONCLUSION

But what about classic PageRank, the score of which we get a tiny inkling of from the Google toolbar's green pixels? I'd actually surmise that while many (possibly all) of the features about links discussed here make their way into the ranking process, the classic concept of PR remains relatively untouched since its creation. My reasoning? Moz's own mozRank correlates remarkably well with the Google toolbar PR, and mozRank is calculated with very similar intuition to that of the original PageRank paper. (Moz's mozRank differs from the Google toolbar PR on average by 0.42, with 0.25 being "perfect" due to the two extra significant digits mozRank displays.) If I had to guess (and I really am guessing), I'd say that Google has maintained the classic PR because it finds it heuristically useful for performing some tasks such as determining crawling/indexation priority.

# 7

# THE RESPONSIBILITIES OF SEO HAVE BEEN UPGRADED

*By Rand Fishkin*

---

**Editor's Note:** *Since this post was originally published (on* The Moz Blog *in July of 2011), the responsibilities of an SEO have increased, and they vary from job to job and project to project more than ever. As Rand has since stated, the job of the SEO is to figure out how to drive traffic to a website that will achieve the marketing goals. It is not based on what anyone thinks the job of an SEO is. Period. One might say that is true of the SEO's job title, as well.*

---

WHEN I STARTED out as an SEO (circa 2003), the job responsibilities weren't easy, but the list was relatively short. Over the next five years, those responsibilities increased, primarily in tactical and knowledge areas. A 2003 versus 2008 rundown might look like this:

# SEO Responsibilities

| | Emerging 1999-2003 | Added in 2004-2008 |
|---|---|---|
| **Accessibility** | Crawlability of Site | XML Sitemaps |
| | Spider-Readable Content | Controlling for "Thin Content" |
| | Search-Friendly Architecture | Rel=Canonical |
| | Limiting Duplicate Content | Nofollow "Evaporation" Issues |
| | HTML Sitemaps | |
| **Keywords** | Basic Keyword Research | Keyword Difficulty Analysis |
| | On-Page Keyword Targeting | Keyword Usage in Images |
| | On-Site Anchor Text | Controlling for Keyword Manipulation (footers in particular) |
| **Link Building** | Site Owner Outreach | Social Media Outreaches |
| | Directories | Press/PR Tactics |
| | Blogs & Personal Sites | Content Syndication |
| | Guestbook/Signature Links | Badges + Widgets |
| | | Embeddable Content |
| | | Guest Blogging |
| | | Article Marketing |
| | | Many, Many More... |
| **Search Verticals** | Images | Maps/Local |
| | | Video |
| | | Shopping |
| | | News |

The last two and a half years, however, have brought about substantive changes in our field. We're facing large-scale, industry-shifting trends that have upset the classic model for search engine optimization, including the following:

- **Search engines favoring brands over smaller, lesser-known sites.** This is the result of Google's Vince update and similar search algorithm updates.
- **The release of Panda.** Panda has changed what it means to do SEO, just as the Florida update did at the end of 2003.

- **The shift in web user behavior toward social media.** More than 20 percent of the time we spend online is spent on social networking sites.

- **Fragmentation of the social media market.** LinkedIn just passed MySpace to become the #2 social network in the U.S., and Twitter, Facebook, Tumblr, Reddit, and Stumble-Upon each have 10 million+ active users. FourSquare also just passed that mark (and Google+ will, too, IMO).

- **The powerful increase in content creation as a marketing tool.** Fifty-seven percent of companies in HubSpot's recent survey have an active blog!

- **An overwhelming increase in mobile and local search.** As a result, portals like Google Maps, Bing Maps, Yelp, Citysearch, UrbanSpoon, and FourSquare have massive potential value to local businesses and service providers.

- **Lack of human resources.** The recession in 2008 caused a massive change in how businesses think about employment. Human resources are nearly the last thing companies will add to their costs these days. While that's generating amazing profits, it's having a rough impact on employment. As a part of this trend, SEOs have been asked to shoulder many new burdens.

Thus, the picture of an SEO's responsibilities today looks more like this:

## SEO Responsibilities in 2011

**Site Acessibility**
Creating a site engines can easily crawl & index

**Keyword Research/Targeting**
Choosing the right keywords and employing them effectively

**Content Strategy**
Set a plan of how to leverage the organization's resources to produce valuable, useful, relevant, share-worthy material

**Content Creation**
Execute on creation of blog posts, evergreen content, infographics, interactive works, apps, tools, etc.

**Link Building**
Investigating, tracking and acquiring link opportunities

**New Search Protocols**
Schema.org, Rel=Author, Video XML Sitemaps, etc.

**Search Verticals**
Images, local, video, news, blogs, social, mobile, product, etc.

**Community Management**
Creating & participating in conversations around your brand/sector in positive ways to drive awareness + adoption

**Social Media Promotion**
Employing Twitter, Facebook, LinkedIn, Google+, StumbleUpon, Reddit, Quora, et al. to improve your reach

**Social Network Reach**
Improving the size, depth and breadth of your social neworks to reach more potential customers and connectors

**Reputation Tracking**
Watching your brand's search results, social media remarks and web content to track success and monitor for danger

**Local / Maps Optimization**
Optimizing for placement in local search and portals, both web and social, plus monitoring local activity

**The job of "SEO" has been upgraded to "organic web strategist."**

> ***Author's Note:*** *While some of the new responsibilities listed here have been added due to changes in the SEO field, others reflect the fact that many companies have expanded the job duties of employees who perform SEO in lieu of replacing/ expanding staff.*

If you're in the SEO field, this shift is both a positive and a negative. If you can keep up with the workload, manage all the metrics, reporting, data, and platforms, AND perform effectively in all of these spheres, you're likely able to charge outsized fees (or earn a much higher salary). If you remain tactical and niche, you're either going to be undervalued, or you'll need to find ways to make that specialization and the ROI you can deliver visible to your clients/ managers.

The job of an "SEO" is so much more than what we think of when we talk about the basics of classic Search Engine Optimization. It almost feels as though we deserve a new title ... and probably a raise.

### References

"Google's Vince Update Produces Big Brand Rankings; Google Calls It A Trust 'Change'" *Search Engine Land*, March 5, 2009
`http://searchengineland.com/google-searchs-vince-change-google-says-not-brand-push-16803`

"How Google's Panda Update Changed SEO Best Practices Forever" *Moz Whiteboard Friday*, June 23, 2011
`www.moz.org/blog/how-googles-panda-update-changed-seo-best-practices-forever-whiteboard-friday`

"Google's Florida Update, A Fresh Look – WebmasterWorld.com" *Google News Archive Forum*, Dec. 12, 2003
`www.webmasterworld.com/forum3/20566.htm`

"HubSpot 2011 State of Inbound Marketing: Long Live Blogs!" by Tony Faustino, *Social Media Reinvention Blog*, June 27, 2011
`www.socialmediareinvention.com/2011/06/hubspot-2011-state-inbound-marketing-blogs.html`

"Study: Americans Use Mobile Apps More than Full Web Now" *TIME*, June 23, 2011
`www.techland.time.com/2011/06/23/study-americans-use-mobile-apps-more-than-full-web-now`

"Despite Poor Growth, Corporate Profits Soar" *The Globe and Mail*, July 10, 2011
`www.theglobeandmail.com/report-on-business/economy/despite-poor-growth-corporate-profits-soar/article599240`

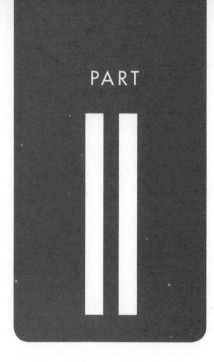

PART

# CONTENT

*By John Doherty*

ONLINE MARKETING, AND specifically SEO, are nothing without good content. Whether we are talking about on-page content, content meant to be shared via social media, or viral content such as videos, content is the backbone upon which we build rankings and businesses.

## HISTORY OF CONTENT WITHIN SEO

When people hear the term "SEO," they often think first of links. "I just want more links" is what we have been routinely been told by bosses and clients alike. In the early days of SEO, once the Link Graph began to take shape, the more links approach was useful. With some links and a URL, you could rank any page for pretty much any term.

All of this mostly came to an end with the Florida update in November 2003. It was arguably the biggest change to Google's algorithm up to that point. This update marked the beginning of the end for many SEO practices from the nineties, like keyword stuffing, invisible text, and hidden links.

Over the years, the SEO industry has experienced more updates, including Cassandra (hidden text and hidden links were the target), Austin (hidden text again), Mayday (the first thin content update), Panda (the next thin content algorithm, and its 20+ iterations as of

September 2012), and Penguin (targeting overly aggressive link building). Through all of this, content on the Internet has continued to improve, especially as richer media has become more indexable and supported by the search engines.

One potentially fundamental change happened in 2011 when Google launched Google+, an online social network, where Google is able to match up your identity to the content you consume and create on the Internet. While this feature allows Google to serve more relevant ads to searchers, it also provides the ability for Google to "learn" who the trusted authors are, and potentially rank their content higher due to higher source credibility.

## TYPES OF CONTENT

Before we jump into talking about opportunities and challenges with online content, we must first outline the types of content that web marketers should be leveraging. We can categorize content by its form as well as its purpose.

- **Text content** is still the easiest content available for the search engines to index, process, interpret, and use to rank web pages. Often the questions asked by online marketers are "how much content do I need?" and "how many words should I write?" when the real questions we should be asking ourselves are "who is my audience and what do they want to read?" This content (not to be confused with low-quality filler content) moves the reader towards conversion and helps with search engine rankings.

- **Images** are another kind of popular online content. Obviously, images work very well in certain verticals such as ecommerce, art, photography, and travel. In travel and photography verticals, images are used to elicit a "wow" reaction from users, which then drives them towards a conversion or sharing on a social network (also known as a micro-conversion). Images can also be used in ecommerce to show a product, and high-quality images have been known to increase conversions.

- **Video** is an underutilized type of content in most verticals. Some sites such as Zappos, Backcountry.com, and REI leverage video content to convert users, add richness to their site's pages, and enhance the visibility of their listings in search results. Videos can be used for social activity and brand building (e.g., YouTube and Vimeo), or for promotional and informational material.

- **Graphics** and visualizations have become very popular in the past few years as a way to showcase complex ideas in simple ways, and doing so in a visually appealing way can also attract links and build your brand. Low-quality visualizations and graphics do not net the same return as their high-quality, professionally designed and produced equivalents.

- **Presentations** can attract the attention of a new audience and set you apart as a thought leader in your space. By leveraging presentation display platforms like SlideShare, you are able to put your content in front of others—and even rank those pages for terms that would not make sense on your own site from a conversion perspective.

- **Apps** are another type of "content", but not one we often think of as content. A good product will attract users, which attracts links, which leads to rankings, which leads to more visitors and users. This is the ultimate type of product—product as content.

Content can also be broken down into two categories based on its purpose:

- **Informational content** shares knowledge or teaches a skill. This content is often delivered in the form of blog posts, instructional videos, and product images. When users visit your site looking for informational content, they are less likely to convert directly, but they do enter the marketing funnel. We must also note that while this content is at the top of the funnel, the ultimate goal is to meet your business customer's needs and drive them towards a conversion in the long term.
- **Transactional content** is content aimed at directly converting a user. This is on-page content, such as promotional copy about a specific hotel, or a call-to-action video encouraging a user to "Buy Now!"

As you can see, all of the content types listed above (with the possible exception of graphics), can fit into either one of these two categories. Websites need both types to truly win at marketing.

## TURNING CHALLENGES INTO OPPORTUNITIES

As search engines get smarter, content can and must become better. Smart marketers are realizing that they need content that speaks to a user's needs and enriches the online experience. This type of content leads to more customers, more links, and a better business. Creating this content is not without its challenges, however, so marketers must learn to overcome these difficulties.

Opportunities currently exist around imagery and video content. Very few websites are currently leveraging the power of these two, as they are hard to do well and can be expensive to produce, which is why stock photo sites charge a lot of money for their images.

### VIDEO CONTENT

Zappos has over 342,000 videos indexed in Google, and Backcountry.com has over 38,000 indexed. In many niches though, product videos do not exist, and there is an opportunity to become the leader in the space.

### HIGH-QUALITY CONTENT

The type of content we are talking about in not only in this section, Part II, but in the book overall, is high-quality content. This is the content that attracts links, shares, and readers. In the past, online writers (especially part-time bloggers) stuck to a "400-500 unique words, 2-3 optimized h1 tags, and a stock photo" equation for blogging. However, numerous studies have shown that this is not the most effective approach to producing excellent content, be it for readers or for marketing, links, and social activity.

## PRODUCING CONTENT ON BUDGET

One common issue with content is how to produce it on a budget. As with anything in business, the quality of content is directly correlated to how much you pay. There are many freelance writing sites available, such as:

- `oDesk.com`
- `FreelanceWriting.com`
- `BloggingPro.com`
- `BloggerJobs.biz`

Before you hire a writer to create content for your site, or produce any sort of content (such as video or images), always ask for samples of their work.

Video content can be produced cheaply with a $300 video camera, a tripod, and some free video editing software. If you realize that you would like to produce a lot of professional-level video content later on, the costs can skyrocket, but there is no need to pay an astronomical amount of money from the beginning.

## CONTENT AT SCALE

Content at scale is the most difficult challenge facing marketers. All websites can benefit from fresher, better content. What do you do, though, when you need a lot of it, such as unique product descriptions?

In the past, it was possible to procure good search rankings and traffic with templated content, but this is no longer the case. Websites have also discovered that templated content does not convert well. The problem of producing of content at scale has not yet been solved, but the beginning of solving this issue is doing a content audit to find out how much content you actually need. Often, this will be less than you think.

The next step is to create an editorial and content production calendar. Website owners must determine how much content they need to produce in what time period in order to reach their goals. We recommend writing original content moving forward, and working through the backlog of pages as quickly as possible. Prioritize based on high-margin products or pages that have the potential to convert well and drive large amounts of traffic.

For more ideas on creating content at scale, read Chapter 9, "Scaling White Hat Link Building—Scaling Content."

# THE FUTURE OF CONTENT

As content continues to become an even more integral part of online marketing, the need for new and innovative types of content will continue to grow, and the need for higher-quality versions of what already exists on the Internet will persist. One example is video infographics, which integrate well-designed graphics and pages into videos that explain an idea or how to accomplish a certain task. Other examples are described in Chapter 8, "Beyond Blog Posts: A Guide to Innovative Content Types."

The search engines are also trying to understand who the author of a piece of content is, as this is one way that they can learn which pieces of content are more likely to be of high quality. This especially applies to blog content, and is one way to deal with spam on the Internet. Potentially, the search engines will value and rank the content from reputable sources higher than content from anonymous sources to help reduce the amount of noise on the Internet.

We recommend that authors seeking to improve their reputation start by improving the quality of their work. If this applies to you, reading Chapter 10, "10 Super Easy SEO Copywriting Tips for Improved Link Building," may benefit you. We hope this chapter, and the others in this section, inspire you to create a unique strategy for producing high-quality, future-proof content in a way that works for your business.

# 8

# BEYOND BLOG POSTS: A GUIDE TO INNOVATIVE CONTENT TYPES

*By Tom Critchlow*

---

**Editor's Note:** *When we think about content production, it is often the end product that comes to mind. And when we do explore the process and the publishing platform, we often turn our attention to blogging. In fact, one of today's most popular blog categories is "blogging." In this post (originally published on The Moz Blog on May 11, 2011), Tom Critchlow introduces us to several alternative content platforms—from Q&A sites to product marketplaces—and challenges us to think about what makes each one successful.*

---

PRODUCING GREAT CONTENT is a high ROI activity. Too often, however, I see people focused on producing individual pieces of content aiming to get links and attention. Putting together a content strategy requires much more than creating a single piece of content. It requires creating a vision and strategy for how you're going to publish your content, what type of content you will be publishing, and how your audience will engage with it.

I like to think that instead of focusing on *pieces of content*, you should focus on the *content platform*. This shift requires lateral thinking, research, and creativity. In this post I break down some alternative content types that I've been consuming recently. Even though I've provided examples, try and look beyond the individual posts and *focus on the underlying platform. Think about what makes it successful.*

## Q&A CONTENT

The growth of Q&A content has exploded recently, primarily due to Silicon Valley's love affair with Quora. This platform is quite undervalued for generating marketing buzz, but there can be gold in Q&A sites. Here are some examples of powerful Q&A content.

- Here's a sliver of a Quora thread (`www.quora.com/Google-Wave/Why-did-Google-feel-that-Google-Wave-was-a-good-product`) that is answered by a Google employee with amazing details on why Wave failed, and how it was developed in the first place:

Google Wave   Software Quality Assurance   Google Inc. (company)   ⊘ Edit

★ **Why did Google feel that Google Wave was a good product?** ⊘ Edit
**Interested primarily in hearing from someone who worked on it.**

There must have been lots of internal testing and usage done on it prior to release, and they must have found it useful. Yet normal users (even "normal" early-adopter tech users) found it incomprehensible and ultimately useless. What usage patterns or experiences within Google prompted them to think that it was a really worthwhile product in that way that they thought Google Maps or GMail was? ⊘ Edit

- Here's one from the ever excellent Stack Overflow, with so many awesome questions it's difficult to pick one. From recent times I love this Q&A (`http://mz.cm/XPx791`) on how Stack Overflow optimized their load speed:

We looked closely at performance over the last few weeks, particularly in the last 4 or 5 business days

**52**

- we reduced the total number of queries happening on a lot of pages (question show, question lis user page, etc.)

- we deployed a page that shows us our worst query offenders in CPU time, total duration, reads, writes, etc. and optimized the stuff at the top of the lists

- we improved the way we call LINQ to SQL and moved to pre-compiled LINQ queries in certain hot code paths. This seems to have gotten much faster in .NET 4.0, we saw 8x gains over plain vanill LINQ and 2x over SQL-queries-as-LINQ-returns.

- we reduced the number of columns we return in some hot code paths, where we had effectively `select *` from users and posts.

- we were getting sloppy about the way we handled search engines, which was causing a lot of und load -- **Google's crawler is now indexing us at, and I am not making this up, 10 requests per second** which is the maximum. This is confirmed in Google Webmaster Tools. Google doesn

- Of course, we practice what we preach at Moz, and we are pumping out some awesome Q&A content. I love this thread on SEO secrets (`www.moz.org/q/what-s-your-best-hidden-seo-secret`):

We're seeing a lot of growth in our Q&A forum at the moment, so if you're not hanging out in there asking and answering questions, you're missing out!

- The Reddit AMA sub-reddit is my favorite daily read and has some super awesome threads. As I write this post, this AMA from John Resig, creator of jQuery is happening (`http://mz.cm/164K6Y4`):

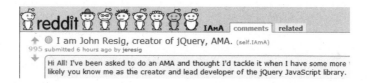

# PRESENTATIONS

I know what you're thinking: what place do stale PowerPoint presentations have in blog posts? Well, quite a lot, it turns out. Rand Fishkin of Moz regularly embeds his presentations in articles that often make for popular posts. In particular, I love his recent article, "4 Presentations with Tips, Graphics + Data You Can Use" (`www.moz.org/blog/4-seo-presentations-w-tips-graphics-data-you-can-use`).

So presentations work well online. I'm a big fan of how *Business Insider* is innovating in this space; they have full screen presentations you can flip through. (Enabling the use of arrow keys to scroll through them and # URLs is very slick, too.) Here's a screenshot of a presentation based on a recent survey of iPad users (`www.businessinsider.com/ipad-survey-two-thirds-of-ipad-owners-use-their-ipads-1-5-hours-a-day-1`):

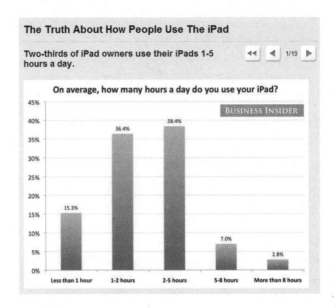

## CURATED CONTENT

I'm a big fan of online content curation. I think it's a largely untapped niche that has been steadily growing and will explode sometime soon. In the meantime, some pioneers are paving the way forward.

- *The Atlantic Wire* (www.theatlanticwire.com) is a phenomenal aggregation of hot news and information. It's a combination of reporting, journalism, investigation, and curation. They publish all kinds of different media depending on what's relevant to the story. They transparently cite sources and aren't afraid to post short-form content where it adds to the conversation. For example, this post about Obama having an iPad is just a link to the Whitehouse flickr stream and a paragraph of text (www.theatlanticwire.com/technology/2011/04/obama-has-his-very-own-ipad/37155):

■ I'm a big fan of personal storytelling. *Storify* is an awesome app that lets anyone quickly and easily create a story by curating content that appears elsewhere. A perfect example of how *Storify* can effectively be used is Danny Sullivan's awesome recap of the guy who live tweeted the Osama news (`http://storify.com/dannysullivan/the-death-of-osama-bin-laden-live-tweeted`):

### The Death Of Osama Bin Laden, Live Tweeted

By Danny ~~~~~~~, May 2, 2011 at 0:48

🔲 ✉ 👍 Like · 211                    Embed story ‹›

*Sohaib Athar (@ReallyVirtual) ended up live tweeting the raid that killed Osama bin Laden without realizing it. Here are the relevant tweets, as the raid unfolded (along with some of his retweets that lend to the story). You'll find his account here http://twitter.com/reallyvirtual*

## MAGAZINE AND LONG-FORM CONTENT

Let's jump from short-form content to long-form content. I'm a huge fan of the more editorial and in-depth content pieces. Although these are more effort, they can produce excellent rewards.

- *A List Apart* is an online magazine that's been running for years and has a wide audience. They produce phenomenal long pieces that are very well written and thoughtful. Of course, magazine and long-form content has been around for a long time, but it still delivers for you and I think it's relevant to highlight people still doing this well online. For example, see the excellent piece about orbital content that they recently published at `www.alistapart.com/articles/orbital-content`.
- the99percent.com is another awesome online content platform that publishes very strong editorial pieces, such as this one on Francis Ford Coppola: `http://99u.com/articles/6973/Francis-Ford-Coppola-On-Risk-Money-Craft-Collaboration`.

> **Editor's Note:** *the99percent.com is now 99U (*`http://99u.com`*), the educational division of Behance (*`http://behance.net`*), an online platform for showcasing and discovering creative work.*

- *Longform* (`http://longform.org`) and *Longreads* (`http://longreads.com`) are two excellent curators who showcase in-depth articles on a wide range of topics. This culture of long-form curation, however, has spawned some very innovative startups such as *Byliner* (`http://byliner.com`), which aims to publish very long-form content about current events.

**Introducing Byliner Originals.** Great writers. Great stories. Readable in a single sitting.

© 2012 BYLINER INC.

## IMAGERY AND PHOTOJOURNALISM

Say what? Your list of innovative content includes images? Aren't they a little dated? Not at all. We're only just scratching the tip of the iceberg when it comes to images.

■ *The Atlantic's* "In Focus" and *The Boston Globe's* "Big Picture" are leading the charge for high-quality online imagery and photo journalism. Who would have guessed that amazing, high-quality photos could be so appealing? For example, you can see a series of photos from the 1913 Women's Suffrage Parade at `www.theatlantic.com/infocus/2013/03/100-years-ago-the-1913-womens-suffrage-parade/100465/`.

Source: Library of Congress

■ Cinemagraphs—unless you live in a hole underground, or don't follow me on Twitter, you will have seen me raving about these awesome classy animated GIFs. Yes, you read that right; I'm including animated GIFs in my list of innovative content types. Just take a look at the cinemagraph online at `http://mz.cm/V2r2qg`, created by the stunningly talented duo Kevin Burg (`http://kevin.tumblr.com`) and Jamie Beck (`http://fromme-toyou.tumblr.com`). (Watch closely.)

# VIDEO

There are more innovations in video than I can cover in this blog post, so I'll stick to a few of the more attainable ones.

■ Interviews, *Mixergy* style. The video interviews from *Mixergy* are very low-budget and simple, but also very effective. The key here is in understanding your target audience and really getting the interviews your audience is hungry for. For example, check out the great interview with Paul Graham at `http://mixergy.com/y-combinator-paul-graham`.

*The Startup Foundry* (`http://thestartupfoundry.com`) also runs interviews using a split-screen style and it works very well. For example, check out their interview with Alexis Ohanian, the co-founder of Reddit, online at `http://mz.cm/YT59r6`.

- *Live Video! 2011* is going to be a big year for live video events. There are a lot of big players all pushing for live coverage and streaming media, which I think will shake up the way we consume content online. *YouTube* is obviously making a push for live streaming with *YouTube Live* (`www.youtube.com/live`). As you read this, *Google I/O* (`www.google.com/events/io/2011`) is likely streaming right now!

  But live streaming of events isn't just for conferences. As ever, entertainment is pushing the boundaries for what's possible. I really enjoyed the idea behind the recent live music video from Death Cab For Cutie (`www.youareatourist.com`).

- Of course, it's hardly innovative, but we're practicing what we preach at Moz by producing our Whiteboard Fridays and webinars (`www.moz.org/blog/category/whiteboard-friday` and `http://www.moz.org/webinars`), and they attract a lot of attention. Crucially, they also seem to have their own audience independent of the blog.

## INTERACTIVE INFOGRAPHICS

Are infographics dead? Hardly. At our #LinkLove conference in NOLA, Chris Bennett (`@chrisbennett`) said that infographics are alive and well, it's infocrapics that are dying out. It's so true, and it applies to any content form—if the substance is sub-par then you're not going to have success. That said, there are some very exciting interactive infographics coming out at the moment. My current favorite is *Where Did My Tax Dollars Go?* (`www.wheredidmytaxdollarsgo.com`). You input your salary, and the site creates a pie chart that reflects how much of your U.S. federal income tax was spent on Social Security, National Defense, Healthcare, etc.

© 2010 ANIL KANDANGATH

This is an excellent example of how you can turn complex and large data sets into something that is not only interactive, but personally engaging. I encourage you to go and lose 30 minutes of your life browsing the data. I'll wait.

## PRODUCT MARKETPLACES

Using products as marketing is nothing new, but there are a few really awesome examples of this.

- **Moleskine** (`www.moleskine.com`). Everyone at Distilled is a huge fan of the Moleskine brand and they're doing some innovative online marketing at the moment; for example, they launched the online Moleskine Artist Marketplace (`http://artistmarketplace.moleskine.com/en`), an online space where users can buy and sell Moleskin notebooks customized by artists.

  I really, really love this concept for inbound marketing! It has all sorts of benefits from gaining links, growing a user base of brand evangelists, generating social media buzz and also appealing to the hacker/Etsy crowd. (By the way, if anyone from the Moleskine marketplace is reading this and wants to create some Distilled branded moleskines for me that would be super awesome.)

■ **Threadless** (www.threadless.com). An oldie but a goodie and worth including since they're pretty much the perfect example of building a marketing plan into their product.

"I AM OLDER THAN THE INTERNET" Design by Peter Cardwell-Gardner
(www.threadless.com/profile/626592/Fluffy_Cheese)

# FACEBOOK NOTES

This really caught me unprepared but it's such a genius marketing tactic. *The New Yorker* published a story from author Jonathan Franzen on a Facebook page, which you can only access if you like the *The New Yorker's* Facebook page. There's a fascinating write up on *Business Insider,* but suffice to say, they gained over 17,000 Facebook likes and links from all over the place, including *Mashable, Forbes,* and *The Atlantic.*

## WHY EVERYONE NEEDS A MARKETING ORACLE FOR THEIR CONTENT PLATFORM

Everyone needs a Marketing Oracle. What's that, you ask? Simply put, it's someone who helps steer your brand's content vision. Taking lessons from a lot of the above content types, there is a strong editorial leaning, and I think people from the world of journalism often fill this role nicely. Think about this question: *"How would you innovate your brand's content model?"* If you're excited about tackling that question, you are passionate about creating content, have a strong editorial vision for your brand, and possess a deep understanding of social media, then you might make an excellent Marketing Oracle—if you're not already one.

I'll say it one more time: Everyone needs a Marketing Oracle. If you're producing content to aid your inbound marketing, you should think long and hard about what your content strategy looks like. There's value in building a content platform, defining your target audience, and building something that's going to provide long-term value for you. Think about becoming more like a media hub than a blog. Think about becoming a Marketing Oracle.

# 9

# SCALING WHITE HAT LINK BUILDING— SCALING CONTENT

*By Will Critchlow*

---

***Editor's Note:*** *This post, which focuses on scaling high-quality content as part of a successful link building strategy, is even more relevant than when it was originally published on <u>The Moz Blog</u> more than two years ago (March 13, 2011). Since then, Google has rolled out more than a dozen updates to its Panda algorithm, which rewards websites that have informative, unique content. Google has also introduced Penguin, an algorithm that favors quality over quantity when it comes to backlinks, and penalizes overoptimized sites that employ spammy link building techniques.*

*The introduction of the* `rel="author"` *attribute added yet another incentive for publishers to step up their game. Verifying Google Authorship adds an important level of trust to search results, and increases click-through rates for publishers who implement it in conjunction with a quality content creation strategy—not to mention that it humanizes authors and thought leaders, and rewards them individually with more exposure in the SERPs.*

---

ALTHOUGH SEO IS one of the "free" organic marketing channels, there is no doubt that competing with the biggest brands and most aggressive web marketers is not going to be free. In fact, it could be very expensive. I won't be sharing ways to compete with the link buyers for free with no effort, but I will be sharing real strategies that brands can use when they need to step it up a notch. In this chapter, I focus on one particular type of strategy—namely, *creating scalable content.*

## SCALABLE CONTENT

If you haven't already read the article in *Wired Magazine* about how Demand Media operates (`www.wired.com/magazine/2009/10/ff_demandmedia`), I can't recommend it highly enough. Even (or perhaps especially) in light of the Panda/Farmer update, I think it is important to think about how you would operate if you had to do what Demand Media does at this scale. Even more importantly, we should all look for the lessons we can learn that will make us better at what we do.

> *Editor's Note: Demand Media is a content and social media solutions company that commissions freelancers to produce content on subjects that it has identified as having a high ROI using its proprietary algorithm. Content usually provides advice of a "how-to" nature, and is posted on a number of highly visible sites, including eHow (www. ehow. com), YouTube (www. youtube. com), Trails. com, and Cracked. com. For information about Demand Media's other products and services visit their website at http://demandmedia.com.*

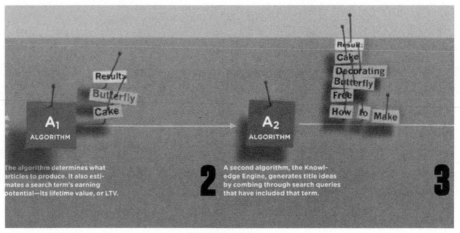

© 2012 Condé Nast

It strikes me that there are three particularly notable aspects to the Demand process: cost, scale, and quality.

## COST

> *"(I)t's fast, cheap, and good enough."*

The *Wired* piece was written before the recent Google update, and this sentiment is, in any case, debatable. Nonetheless, it's clear that there are major cost-saving efficiencies to be gained versus the process many of us use to create content.

## SCALE

> *"Demand will be publishing 1 million items a month, the equivalent of four English-language Wikipedias a year."*

This fact is interesting regardless of what you think of the quality of Demand's content—it's an amazing feat and there *has* to be something we can learn from it.

## QUALITY

> *"… every algorithm-generated piece of content produced 4.9 times the revenue of the human-created ideas."*

There are clearly things computers are *better at* than humans. One of these is mining data for patterns to see what is successful.

One of my long-running wish list ideas is a database of great headlines—based largely on offline media—that is categorized by predicted effectiveness. Have you ever stopped to look at the headlines on consumer magazines and compared them month over month? I feel like I should give credit for that tip—but I can't remember where it came from—perhaps Todd Malicoat's suggestion of a headline "swipe file" (www.stuntdubl.com/2007/01/12/linkbaiting-hooks)? Anyway, in a similar fashion, to I'd love to be able to run something like the following code to generate a list of keyword-rich headlines on a particular topic.

```
select * from headlines where subject like "<topic>" and
keyword like "<keyword>" and successful = 1
```

**Reference**

"Google's Farmer/Panda Update: Analysis of Winners vs. Losers," *The Moz Blog*, March 3, 2011 (www.moz.org/blog/googles-farmer-update-analysis-of-winners-vs-losers)

## WHAT'S THIS ALL HAVE TO DO WITH LINK BUILDING?

While "links" are pretty easy to understand, "link building" is a phrase that actually covers dozens of potential approaches and tactics. The consistent themes are:

- **[WHAT]**—a piece of content receives the link
- **[WHO]**—someone places the link
- **[WHERE]**—a piece of content contains the link

I would argue that there is not a single white hat link-building technique that would not benefit from better content either in the *what* or the *where*. And for every link that is not the result of a very close relationship or exceptional piece of evergreen content/functionality, scaling will come from either creating a greater volume of content for your own site, or creating greater volumes of content to appear elsewhere.

I will leave it as an exercise for the interested reader to think about the various forms of "good" links that you could get more of *if only you had a stream of great content.*

## GREAT CONTENT?

Well, while we are trying to learn from Demand Media, I'm not necessarily talking about *emulating* them. Especially if we are creating content for link building, the bar we're reaching for needs to be a little higher.

My research shows that on average, across my sample, *a piece of Demand Media content gathers links at less than 10 percent of the rate a piece of BBC or New York Times content does.* A December 2010 story on BBC regarding evidence that Neanderthals cooked and ate vegetables (`www.bbc.co.uk/news/science-environment-12071424`), for example, has links from almost 4,000 unique domains!

So, we know we need to raise the bar. The question is "how" do we do it?

I think the answer looks something like:

- Use only great writers.
- Apply quality control at multiple stages of the process.
- Automate what you can.
- Fill the content hopper intelligently, based on what the Linkerati really wants.
- Don't be afraid to scale.

Here's how I think this pans out in more detail.

## USE ONLY GREAT WRITERS

We have some great writers on our team (in my opinion), but when we start talking about increasing scale, it doesn't always come with full-time employees. My mantra for this is that we want to be a *model agency for writers* when we are doing this kind of work. Whereas many of the writing services I've come across seem to be more like marketplaces, we want to behave more like a model agency. Model agencies don't just take on anyone—they have a selection process to make sure candidates have the looks, attitude, and skills to succeed. We don't just want people who can string a sentence together; we want people who can make words sing.

This does affect the cost part of the equation. You simply can't achieve this at the rates Demand is paying. By paying many times as much (as much as freelance journalist rates in many cases), we can create the selective environment we are seeking.

## QUALITY CONTROL

A benefit of the "model agency" approach is that you can apply much of the quality control early in the process *to the writer instead of the writing*. Once you are confident in the skills of the writer, the quality control can become much more light-handed. As even high-profile journalists have proven, however, you can never give up quality control entirely. We think about three kinds of quality control:

- Automated (see the following section)
- "Second opinion" from another writer
- Editorial review from a dedicated editor or consultant (or, occasionally, a client)

## AUTOMATION

Much of the automation we have layered onto this process is driven from third-party APIs that make it easy to do relatively complex things. We already have a workflow, plagiarism checking, the ability of qualified writers to select the jobs they want, and automated Google Doc sharing based off the workflow/approval process.

Future automation might also include these features:

- Additional quality checks (spelling, reading level, etc.)
- Headline suggestion/refinement tools for consultants
- Resource suggestion for writers (useful links, a la Zemanta (`www.zemanta.com`), images, videos, etc.)
- Better notification and alerting around the process and deadlines
- Additional services such as transcription

## FILLING THE HOPPER WITH GOOD CONTENT

At the moment, generating good content is probably the least-thought-out part of our system. In contrast to the apparently almost-fully-automated Demand system, we are still at the stage of having our consultants (in conjunction with clients and writers) suggest and decide upon the specific content to be written.

In contrast to Demand, whose model targets keyword volume, I think our hopper should be filled with link-worthy content ideas. Perhaps this starts to look like a traditional newsroom.

## SCALING

As I started thinking about how to scale content, one of my first thoughts was to emulate the industries that have been scaling content for decades. News organizations have been refining the systems and processes needed to address several tasks:

- Gather ideas from a diverse set of sources.
- Write copy using both staff writers and freelancers.
- Apply quality control.
- Write compelling headlines.

I think we can learn several lessons from examining the work of masters. My wife is a journalist, and these are some of the things that have impressed me most about her team:

- It turns out that the people who are good at quality control are often good at writing headlines (they're called copy editors or sub-editors).
- A small core team can manage a large volume of *high quality* output using a team of trusted freelance writers.
- The person writing the copy isn't necessarily the same person that decides the topic *or* the same person who writes the headline.

However, I do think there are some things many journalists could learn from the geeks among us—mainly lessons about the utility of web apps:

- **Version control**—one of the first things I built into our spec was the ability to see who had made which change to a draft and when. I was amazed to learn that this simple feature (present in such ubiquitous software as Microsoft Word and Google Docs) is not standard on all news desks.

- **Project management apps**—for similar reasons, there is often no end-to-end system managing the process of where everything is in the system. One of the things I wanted our system to have was a simple way for all interested parties to see the status of everything. In my mind, this includes:
  - Editors/owners being able to see all outstanding jobs
  - Writers having their own dashboards to see what they are working on
  - Consultants having project dashboards
  - Finance having reports on spend (both across the board and on specific projects)

**Reference**

"CORRECTING THE RECORD: Times Reporter Who Resigned Leaves Long Trail of Deception," *The New York Times,* May 11, 2003 (`http://mz.cm/15NGTfy`)

## DO WE HAVE ALL THIS STUFF?

The short answer is "no." We have made big leaps forward in automation, but we still aren't hitting the lofty heights we'd love to achieve when it comes to quality, or scaling at the volume we know we need to be doing. As we put significant five-figure monthly spends through the system, however, we learn the patterns that will enable us to be more successful in the future.

# 10

# 10 SUPER EASY SEO COPYWRITING TIPS FOR IMPROVED LINK BUILDING

*By Cyrus Shepard*

---

**Editor's Note:** *Writing for the web is different than writing for print. Readers consume content differently online. Copywriters who can write for both types of audiences will have a definite advantage in today's world, where eBooks, blogs, iPads, and PDFs are as popular as their print counterparts. In this post, which was originally published on* The Moz Blog *on May 3, 2011, Cyrus Shepard shares simple tips copywriters can use to increase engagement with their online content and, in turn, increase shares and attract links.*

---

COMPARE THE TWO following posts, both written by the exact same SEO expert and each containing around the same number of words. Without knowing the subject, can you guess which post earned more links?

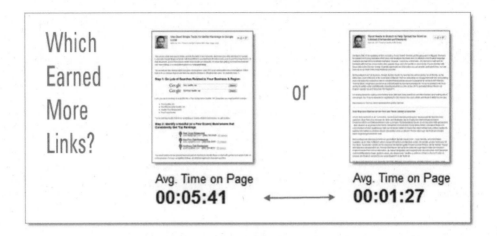

Try 378 to 6. In addition to its visual appeal, the left post was more timely, useful and informative—all hallmarks of copywriting grace.

The "secrets" of copywriting have existed since before the ancient Greeks. Generations of Don Drapers have perfected the craft. Today we use computer analysis and data mining to uncover the most effective SEO practices. The Moz biannual Ranking Factors (`www.moz.org/article/search-ranking-factors`) explores many common data points. My colleague Casey Henry conducted a study of link-worthy material that included elements such as title length and word frequency (`www.moz.org/blog/what-makes-a-link-worthy-post-part-1`). Fantastic stuff, and I hope he does another such study soon.

So why don't more authors take advantage of these lessons? Why all the cardboard-looking blog posts?

Here's the takeaway. To earn links, *use copywriting to organize your content.*

## 1. WRITE FOR POWER SKIMMERS

Steve Krug's words of wisdom for website usability in his book *Don't Make Me Think* ring true for all elements of SEO copywriting.

> *"We don't read pages. We scan them."*
> —*Steve Krug*

Krug advocates for a billboard style of design. This means using language, images, layout, and color to make your material stand out and shine. Think of motorcycle riders speeding past billboards. Which one will they remember?

To be fair, prettying up mediocre content won't make it any better. But does your best work look like it belongs in an encyclopedia?

*Unless you are Wikipedia, don't look like Wikipedia.*

## 2. WHY HEADLINE FORMULAS WORK

Headlines organize your content by *making a promise to the reader*. The body of your content delivers on that promise.

Consider the following headlines, all found on the cover of a single edition of *Wired Magazine*:

> **What** Japan Can Learn From Chernobyl
> **Why** Android Beat the iPhone
> **Why** America's Funniest Home Videos Won't Die
> **How** the Internet Saved Comedy

Using the "who-what-why" formula isn't the only way to format your headlines, but it works. Another technique I like is to ask a question, e.g., **"Have You Been Secretly Penalized by Google?"**

Don't be scared of headline formulas. Instead of "gimmicky," think of them as a framework for the promise you make. When I'm stuck for headline inspiration, I surf the fantastic resources over at *Copyblogger* (`www.copyblogger.com/magnetic-headlines`).

There are literally dozens of effective headline formulas out there, so you need never worry about repeating yourself.

## 3. GET 20% MORE WITH NUMBERS

I made that number up. Why?

Numbers grab our attention. Look at the titles to some of the most linked-to posts on Moz:

> **21 Tactics** to Increase Blog Traffic
> **8 Predictions** for SEO in 2010
> Launching a New Website: **18 Steps** to Successful Metrics & Marketing
> **17 Ways** Search Engines Judge the Value of a Link

It makes you want to click one of those links right now, doesn't it?

Whether in a headline or a list, numbers light up the ordered, mathematical part of your brain to make content more attractive. It also provides you with a way to structure your material in a way that makes sense.

## 4. FREE AND EASY POWER WORDS

My writing life changed when I read Robert W. Bly's seminal work, *The Copywriter's Handbook*. He introduced me to the power of choosing the right language for successful communication.

Although some of his "power" words belong in the back of a Sunday newspaper advertisement, their effectiveness can't be denied. These include words like **quick, easy, guarantee,** and **free.**

> "Free is the most powerful word in the copywriter's vocabulary. Everybody wants to get something for free."
> —Robert W. Bly

Words are magic. The opposite of power words includes language like **try, maybe, might, possibly**, and **perhaps**. These "halfway" words kill your writing.

The point is not to use a rote list of words like a checklist in your copy, but rather be conscious of the power (or lack of) your language. Don't hedge your bets with weak prose.

## 5. A PICTURE IS WORTH 1,000 CLICKS

Rethink your visuals. Visuals are essential to any story and include:

- Photographs
- Artwork
- Charts and graphs
- Slide decks
- Video
- Infographics

The wrong way to add images is to buy stock or steal them off of the web. Instead, make every effort to include original media in your content. A simple, 100 percent original hand drawn image attracts more interest any day of the week than using Parked Domain Girl.

Original Pineapple Artwork by Dawn Shepard Graphic Design http://www.shepardportfolio.com)

It doesn't matter what you use, just make it *original*.

## 6. USE SUB-HEADLINES OR DIE TRYING

This is a no-brainer. Imagine the front page of a newspaper with just one headline. All other text is equal. You wouldn't read it, or you would tire quickly if you did. Our brains don't work that way.

We want things broken up and organized.

If your text is longer than 250-400 words, you *must* use sub-headlines. No exceptions.

## 7. WHEN IN DOUBT, LIST IT OUT

This entire post is a list. Try these numbers on for size:

- **75 percent of the top 20 posts on Moz contain a bulleted list**
- **60 percent feature a numbered list**

Why do lists work so well? Why is David Letterman's Top Ten the most anticipated part of his show, even if it's not as funny as the rest of the show?

Lists are the building blocks of ideas. When we go to the grocery store, we don't write a story—that's ineffective. To communicate your thoughts quickly and effectively, nothing gets to the root of the matter like a list can.

Humans crave order. Use lists to create structure and build your content from the ground up.

## 8. QUOTES

My all-time favorite use of effective quoting comes from Michael Crichton's science fiction work *Timeline*. He juxtaposes two ideas against each other to explain a single concept about quantum theory.

> *"Anyone who is not shocked by quantum theory does not understand it."*
> —*Neils Bohr, 1927*

> *"Nobody understands quantum theory."*
> —*Richard Feynman, 1967*

Utilize quotes to set your ideas apart.

## 9. THE BOLD AND THE ITALIC

Along the same lines, use **bold** to emphasize important points. If you don't have important points, **you have bigger problems**.

*Italics* do the same job, but sound more European. Italics can provide a smoother look on the printed page than bold, so consider how your readers will consume your content.

## 10. BE HONEST

Effective SEO copywriting should never alter or misrepresent your work. Indeed, its purpose is to help you communicate your core ideas more clearly and effectively.

> *"All you have to do is write one true sentence. Write the truest sentence that you know."*
> — *Ernest Hemingway*

Writing from the heart is always the best copywriting technique.

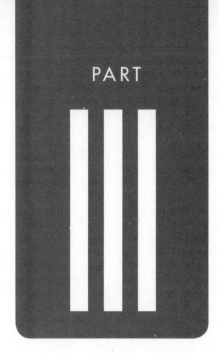

PART

III

# SOCIAL MEDIA

*By Jennifer Sable Lopez*

THERE WAS A time, not so long ago, when getting your blog post on the homepage of Digg meant receiving more traffic in one day than your blog had seen all year. Remember when Twitter was simply a "micro blogging" platform where you'd tweet about your trip to the zoo or what you had for dinner? (Okay, perhaps that hasn't changed so much.) What about before your mom got on Facebook? That was back in the day, right?

## SOCIAL MEDIA MARKETING: THE EARLY YEARS

It used to be enough for a company to simply update their Twitter and Facebook pages every now and then. Social sites were used as a way to push your message and increase your following. Think back—how often did you participate in contests asking you to retweet a tweet, or like a Facebook page, for the chance to win a brand new iPad (or whatever the gadget du jour was)?

Remember, this was not all that long ago. However, we could argue that social media has been around for many, many years; remember Yahoo! profiles and build-your-own avatars, Internet Relay Chat (IRC), and user groups? These were all early forms of social media, but it wasn't until sites like MySpace and Friendster came around that we really started to understand the power of connecting people online.

At some point along the way, marketers began to realize that social media was a great way to reach the masses. With more and more people flocking to Facebook, Twitter, LinkedIn, and countless other sites, marketers jumped in as well.

The biggest problem was that we (marketers) were focusing too much on the "us" and not enough on the "them." Social media seemed to be an easy way to get our message out to more people, so that's what we did. We shouted our messages from the social media rooftops—and sometimes, people listened. However, more often than not, they didn't.

## SOCIAL MEDIA AWAKENING: IT'S NOT JUST ABOUT ME, IT'S ABOUT YOU

Social media has become an integral part of everyday life. It is no longer something that just geeks or technology folks use. It's now part of mainstream communication. As a result, businesses and organizations have been forced to think about it much differently as well.

Companies are finding that social media is a great way to build and nurture a community online. What once was thought of as a way to push a message and agenda has now become an opportunity to have a conversation. Marketers are finding that when they become a part of the discussion and start focusing on the community, rather than themselves, they make more headway.

On that same note, it would be almost impossible to build a community without having some sort of help or support structure in place. Customer service now has a whole new life, and it comes in the form of social media. Some brands dedicate 100 percent of their social media accounts to helping customers, while others like to create separate accounts for support. This is simply another way to have a conversation and "engage" with the community. (I put that in quotes because it has become an annoying buzzword, and I want you to picture me saying it while I do air quotes and make a face "en-GA-ge.")

We've learned that social media is far more than simply a way to broadcast, but a way to be a part of something bigger. It also makes a brand or company feel more human and approachable. Take a look at a couple of examples.

### EXAMPLE 1

Twitter user @proby tweets that he likes his new Red Wing shoes, but links to a photo of his broken shoelaces. @RedWingShoes was closely monitoring its brand mentions, saw the tweet, and immediately let him know that he could replace the shoelaces for free. Being available to help the customer and promote a service is a great way to build positive brand awareness. How much do you want to bet that the customer will buy Red Wing shoes again?

## EXAMPLE 2

A mother has tried several times via phone and email support to make sure that she will be seated next to her children on an 18-hour flight from South Africa to the U.S. She finally gets frustrated and tweets to @DeltaAssist asking for help. Within an hour, Delta responds, asking the customer to send the flight information to them via a DM (direct message). The customer was able to get her issue resolved via Twitter faster and easier than she could using other avenues. This is a great example of why you should make sure your Social Media Manager has the power to make decisions quickly for the company (or has direct access to the decision maker).

# SOCIAL MEDIA MANAGEMENT: THE ONLINE COMMUNITY MANAGER IS BORN

Although it's taken some time for us to figure it out, social media has become an integral part of the greater Marketing team. It's no longer just a fun add-on that we ask the intern to manage without any pay.

With a greater focus on social media in companies and organizations, it's been imperative for a new breed of marketers to emerge. More recently, the role of Community Manager has begun to blossom. This role isn't always focused solely on social media, but that often is a huge portion of the job. Whatever their title, this person (or team!) is in charge of anything and everything from overall social strategy, to online customer service, to tracking social analytics—and usually does it all with a positive attitude.

# SOCIAL MEDIA STRATEGY: A PART OF THE TEAM

As a part of the greater marketing effort, the social media strategy is (or should be) aligned with the SEO strategy, the branding strategy, the blogging/content strategy, the advertising strategy, etc. If you're going to be a part of the future of social, you're going to need the full marketing team's support.

Right along with the other marketing team members, the social media strategist will also need to track specific key performance indicators (KPIs), set and accomplish goals, etc. While each organization may focus on different KPIs, some of the central metrics will include increases in social followings/fans/likes, brand mentions, response time (for more customer service focused accounts), and traffic coming from social sites.

The goals of the social marketer will also differ depending on the company, niche, size of community, and many other factors. It's often a good idea to start small and focus on one area, then expand from there. For example, at Moz, we started by focusing on Twitter with the goals of increasing followers, mentions, and replies. Once we met these goals, we increased them for Twitter, and then started building up Facebook. Since we only had one person focused on Community/Social Media at the time, it was necessary to prioritize. We simply couldn't afford to jump into every social channel imaginable.

As you build and grow the social portion of your marketing team, be sure to set goals that are realistic and make sense for your organization. It's okay to take things slow, and build up organically!

## SOCIAL MEDIA: WHAT DOES THE FUTURE HOLD?

As we move forward at Moz, the role of social media will continue to grow into a bigger portion of the overall marketing strategy. The focus will be on joining and becoming "one" with the community, and being human. As someone said (I seriously feel bad I can't remember who it was) at a conference I recently attended, "You're no longer competing against other companies; you're competing against the user's mom, sister, friends, and coworkers." It's time for you to participate in the conversation and talk about things your community wants to discuss, rather than just your own agenda.

# 11

# THE RICH GET RICHER: TRUE IN SEO, SOCIAL, AND ALL ORGANIC MARKETING

*By Rand Fishkin*

> **Editor's Note:** *Launching a new brand in a competitive online marketplace can be extremely challenging for inbound marketers. This is true today, and it was true in 2010, when this blog post was penned. While some of the tactics may have changed, the basic principles for successfully edging out competitors remain the same.*

MANY YEARS AGO, one of the search marketing industry's first thought leaders, Mike Grehan, wrote the seminal piece *Filthy Linking Rich* (www.e-marketing-news.co.uk/ Oct04/RichLinking.html). Mike's point was well encapsulated in a few sentences:

> *The Mathew effect, when applied to networks, basically equates to well connected nodes being more likely to attract new links, while poorly connected nodes are disproportionately likely to remain poor.*
>
> *In fact, it has been proposed that "the rich get richer" effect drives the evolution of real networks. If one node has twice as many links as another node, then it is precisely twice as likely to receive a new link.*

For those in the field of SEO, social media, and all forms of organic marketing (content development, blogging, email list building, etc.), it probably comes as no surprise that this same principle applies to each of these activities. The email marketer with a giant email list has much greater leverage to add 100 new subscriptions through the power of their existing influence than their new competitor does. The website ranking in position #1 for a high volume search query likely earns a few natural links each day, while a struggling competitor—even one who might have better prices, quality, value, or content—must struggle out of obscurity before any of those "links via discovery" come their way.

This principle applies cross-channel equally well.

High search rankings can earn you lots of visitors who might subscribe to an email list. Thousands of Twitter followers can mean direct SEO benefit and second-order effects such as more links and branding. A popular LinkedIn group can drive traffic that converts into more RSS subscribers, getting you noticed by industry lists, which gives you more media attention and links that deliver higher rankings. It's a virtuous circle—unless you're sitting on the sidelines.

Many of the marketers I talk to complain bitterly about this challenge, though not all of them necessarily comprehend why the difficulty is so great. Thankfully, there are ways you can give yourself a step up, even in those early stages:

1. **Build basic competency everywhere.** Because your email marketing efforts will boost your link building, and your social media traffic can convert into RSS subscriptions, make sure you have the basics of every channel covered. An accessible website is key to attaining any rankings—and basic keyword targeting is, too. Get a presence on the major social media networks with your brand name and include a basic email signup form on your site. Establish a blog, an RSS feed and a presence on some major industry sites (forums, Q+A sites, blog comments, etc.). These basics will serve you well no matter what shape your marketing takes.

2. **Focus on your strongest channels.** Which marketing channel should you choose? It depends. If earning links is hard for you, search is still low ROI, and email newsletters are a mystery, don't start with these. Go with what you know and build up your social media presence, your research-based white papers, or your subscription-worthy blog content. With cross-channel leverage, you can shore up those weaker sectors when you have the strength to take them on.

3. **No matter what, get analytics and conversion tracking right.** All your efforts, in any spectrum of organic marketing, will be for naught if you can't measure and improve. Analytics and conversion tracking can show you which channels work for you and where you efforts are best spent. These aren't the only consideration, as passion and aptitude should figure into the mix as well, but they're the critical baseline. Get tracking right or suffer the consequences.

Overtaking a competitor or earning your way into a crowded field with strong existing players is hard, and it's getting harder, at a faster pace, every day. I've shared this graphic before when writing about how SEO can be a competitive advantage (`www.moz.org/ blog/how-to-make-seo-an-unfair-competitive-advantage-for-your- business`), but it's worth showing again.

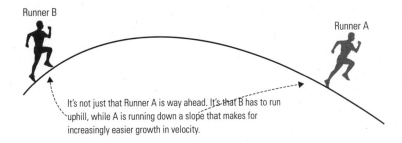

Runner B

Runner A

It's not just that Runner A is way ahead. It's that B has to run uphill, while A is running down a slope that makes for increasingly easier growth in velocity.

Don't be discouraged, but do be wary, and start investing in organic now. Like Manhattan real estate in the '80s, it might seem like there's a peak in how hard it is to enter the market, and it's only going to get worse if you delay your efforts.

# 12

# LIFE AFTER GOOGLE IS NOW: 9 PIECES OF ADVICE ON HOW A NEW SITE CAN SUCCEED WITHOUT SEARCH

*By Stephen Croome*

**Editor's Note:** *After producing print content for 170 years, <u>Illustrated London News</u> finally launched one of its print publications online—with Social, not Search. In this post, which was originally published on <u>The Moz Blog</u> on Nov. 8, 2011, Stephen Croome gives us the inside scoop on this groundbreaking strategy, which proved to be as successful as it was risky.*

*PODIUM* IS THE magazine with "an intelligent view of sport" (http://www.thepodium-magazine.com). Our major articles are in-depth interviews with sports stars, our commentary is from globally renowned pundits, and we often do our own photo shoots. Cover stars so far have been Usain Bolt and Frankie Dettorri. Other articles have focused on golf, F1, the All Blacks, horse racing and the 2012 Olympics.

On the face of it, that sounds like an SEO's dream—rich, unique content that search engines love. It's a pity that it did not help us one little bit.

Was I going to get search engine traffic for "Usain Bolt" on a brand new website? Enough to beat his own website, his sponsor, Puma, the *BBC,* or *The Guardian*? Not a chance.

*So I decided to abandon the un-loyal scraps of long-tail Search and design for Social instead.*

This is the tale of what I did to grow online traffic for *PODIUM Magazine* when SEO wasn't a viable option.

# WHAT DOES DESIGNING FOR SOCIAL MEAN?

*We had a clear strategy to leverage Social from Day One.*

## 1. ONLY THE BEST GOES ONLINE

I chose to put less content online. Only the best articles, and pieces that we thought would spark debate, made it online. This means that we didn't water down the user experience—readers only got the good stuff. Where Search would say, "Stick everything online and pray for long tail," I believe the mantra for Social is, "Don't bore me. Blow me away!"

## 2. TWITTER IS FOR THE INSIDER'S VIEW

Twitter was owned by the Print Editor, Andy Tongue (@andytongue). This meant we got a highly knowledgeable sportswriter who is able to engage online with the people we cover. When you cover Usain Bolt and your writers are guys like F1's David Croft, getting them to retweet your coverage of them IS your Twitter strategy.

This is a virtuous circle of promotion; everybody taking part wins. Build this into your products, and you will have a marketing beast.

## 3. FACEBOOK IS FOR DEBATE

For Facebook, we decided to pick the most contentious article in each edition and put it behind a "Like" wall on Facebook.

The article sits on the site's homepage, looking like an article; but when readers click on it, it takes them to the Facebook page. Our hope is that people will debate these articles on our Facebook page, thereby taking advantage of Facebook EdgeRank to make these articles pop up into everyone's feeds.

## 4. IT'S ALL ONE PRODUCT CONCEPT = BETTER USE OF TIME AND ENERGY

Using this strategy meant we could cut down our energy expenditure on trying to funnel people to each site. Instead of diluting our energy trying to get people to Facebook, Twitter, and the website, we focus on the website and allow the strategy and mechanisms built into our use of Twitter and Facebook to naturally gather users on those platforms.

# WHAT WE LEARNED

Here are the top lessons.

## 5. DO MORE OF WHAT IS SUCCESSFUL

By the time we got around to Version 2, we found that Twitter was a steady audience builder. We wanted to promote Twitter in the same way as Facebook. We didn't do that by slapping a Twitter button onto the webpage.

In the new design, we made Twitter and Facebook living parts of the website. Social is not an afterthought; the website is now a Social Content Delivery Mechanism.

## 6. NOT EVERYTHING SUCCEEDS

Facebook is hard for us, and we haven't cracked how to create the level of conversation we want there yet. This is partly due to the exciting rigors that come with turning print writers into digital writers. But each success that we do make, as measured by traffic spikes and new Twitter followers, builds a stronger internal business case to pursue this route with other titles.

## 7. JUMP ON EVERY OPPORTUNITY

This means *monitor your analytics daily*. You must turn every scrap of attention into engagement. To do this, you need to react quickly.

### The Debate Piece

Take a look at the following graph. The first spike was a forum that had picked up our F1 piece, which certainly provoked some controversy.

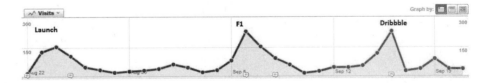

I read their discussion and realized that I could add something to it, so I joined the forum and posted. This engagement kept the debate going and drove more traffic to the site, which means we can go back and promote other F1 stories in the future.

> *Author's Note: I posted openly and clearly as Podium, clarifying a point without appearing spammy.*

### The Wow! Piece

I saw this traffic spike in the analytics and tracked it back to the artist's *Dribbble* page (`http://dribbble.com/WeaslyGrizzly`). He had created a Pixorama for us to illustrate a story, and linked to us from his *Dribbble* account to say it was going to be in the magazine shortly.

This was not originally going to appear online. When I saw it and the traffic it was generating to our site from *Dribbble*, though, I knew it had to go on the site. I'm sure it is going to turn out to be awesome link bait.

## 8. PARTNERSHIPS = WIN-WIN

The partnership value comes in two forms. First, making connections with brands builds new relationships. We always try to make our first interaction with a brand be one that is helpful to them (retweet, brand mention, etc.), with nothing expected in return.

Second, as we write our own, exclusive content with major stars, we can share some of it with another website. They will send traffic to our site and link to us to read the full article. Sharing your unique content is something that would be hard to do if you had your SEO hat on, but in the Social world, it's fine.

As long as you have mechanisms set up to capture traffic to Facebook and Twitter, you are building long-term marketing channels.

## 9. TOOLS HELP

We learned what generated buzz and discussion, and we keep that in mind as we plan for the future. F1 has a crazy community!

Using a tool like Moz's Followerwonk (`www.followerwonk.com`) would be heresy to traditional print journalists as a means for deciding who is newsworthy, but it can now become part of our process in choosing who to cover, and who to talk to about when writing specific sports articles.

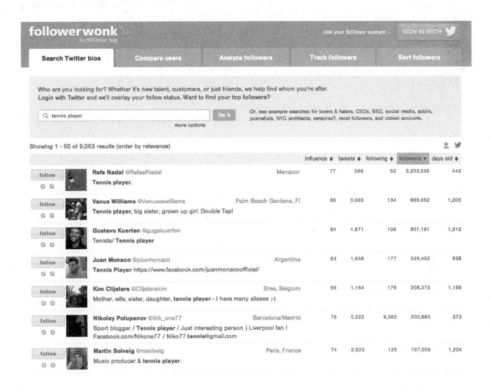

Followerwonk, by the way, allows you to see the most influential people in your Twitter network who have the keywords you specify in their bios.

## IN CONCLUSION

We still have a ton to do. But we have great, unique content at our disposal, and real subject matter experts to create our conversations.

Long term, I am sure (and relieved) that the traffic we have seen and the community we are building will be a much better investment for us than having devoted all our resources to pure SEO would have been.

# 13

# TRACKING THE KPIS OF SOCIAL MEDIA

*By Rand Fishkin*

---

**Editor's Note:** *This post was originally published on* <u>The Moz Blog</u> *in September of 2011. While marketers still struggle to measure the impact social marketing activities have on the bottom line, the gap between social and ROI is narrowing. This progress can be attributed in part to the increased sophistication of many of the social media management and analytics tools mentioned in this post—including Followerwonk, which was acquired by Moz last summer.*

---

SOCIAL MEDIA RECEIVES a massive amount of attention on the web and attracts a great deal of interest from marketers, too. The primary complaint of those who invest in it seems to be consistent: It's hard to measure the impact on the bottom line. On this point, I must concede. While social is an exciting new area for online marketers, its value isn't always commensurate with the effort required. Even when it is, it's tough to prove that point to clients or executives.

This chapter is here to help you improve your ability to track the impact of your social media actions. In it, I take a brief look at the topics surrounding this problem, and offer some solutions, tools, and methodologies to make things easier.

# WHY AND WHERE SOCIAL MATTERS

Social media has an analytics problem. Whereas many other sources—ads, organic search, referrals, bookmarks—drive traffic that directly converts into a desired action (such as a purchase or signup), social traffic is temporal. Visitors from Twitter, Facebook, LinkedIn, Google+, StumbleUpon, and the like are known to visit a page and quickly depart. This leaves marketers struggling to understand the value of these channels. High bounce rates, low browse rates, and awful conversion rates make social the black sheep of referral traffic sources.

I'll try to explain the analytics problem—and the reason why social still matters despite its poor KPIs—in visual form.

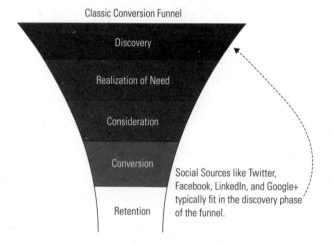

Web users rarely become buyers (or "conversion action" takers of any kind) on their first visit to a website. The web's a tool for discovery, research and investigation, and people use it that way. They browse around the web, find things that are interesting, discover potential needs or desires, further examine the options, and eventually make a purchase decision.

For most people, the web is less like the checkout aisle at the grocery store (stocked with tempting treats and not-so-tempting magazines, at least IMO), and more like the considered purchase of a grill, television set, or automobile. Social media isn't the deal closer—it's the channel that creates potential for a future conversion. Social media can create brand familiarity and drive visitors to content that further draws them in, but it rarely fills an expressly stated need.

The figure on the facing page shows the various roles of social for a visitor who took a free trial of Moz software in 2011 and was converted.

# Typical Lifecycle of Brand Impressions & Visits Prior to Conversion

### #1: Mention on Facebook

### #2: Visit from Tweeted Link

### #3: Video from a Search Query

### #4: Re-Targeting Ad

### #5: Brand Search Query

### #6: RSS Link

**Q:** Which of these channels/sources should get credit for the conversion?

**A:** Probably all of them, but that's not how most analytics tools measure.

CONVERSION!

Twitter and Facebook are involved early on in the buying cycle, likely before a customer has knowledge about the product or realizes their need for it. Social channels are likely to be partially responsible for thousands of free trials at Moz. Given the social analytics tools currently available, we have a very tough time quantifying just how much value social participation and presence bring to our company.

Another great illustration of this phenomenon is Eloqua's Content Grid, which explores how the types of content shared through various channels (including social media) impact the buying process (see `http://blog.eloqua.com/the-content-grid-v2`).

Social media does lots of good things for brands on the web:

- Drives traffic
- Builds brand familiarity
- Creates positive associations with the brand
- Delivers social proof (built when people share content and discuss the brand)
- Attracts brand followers, including brand evangelists, who help spread the word about products and services

*The Atlantic* published an insightful article about why good advertising works at `http://mz.cm/ZYsMiA`. Many of the same principles that apply to good advertising apply to social media. In my opinion, they are even more powerful because they're not interruption-based, but inbound and organic. If ten of the people I follow on Twitter or Google+ start sharing links to a new startup's website, I'm going to be far more engaged, impressed, and enticed to make a purchase than if that same startup puts banner ads on the websites I browse. Both channels create brand awareness, but social is more personal, more trustworthy, and more likely to capture my click.

We know that social is a softer, more-difficult-to-measure traffic source, but we're inbound marketers. That means we can't live without data, so let's explore some of the ways we can monitor this channel.

## WHICH SOCIAL METRICS TO TRACK

In the social media analytics world, there are several key types of metrics we're interested in tracking:

- **Traffic data**—How many visits and visitors did social drive to our sites?
- **Fan/follower data**—How many people are in our networks, and how are our networks growing?
- **Social interaction data**—How are people interacting with, sharing, and re-sharing our content on social networks?
- **Social content performance**—How is the content we're producing on social sites performing?

Getting the right metrics to answer these questions requires segmenting data by network.

## FACEBOOK

Facebook Insights, the social network's built-in analytics product for brand pages, offers a wealth of data for nearly all the metrics we care about (see `www.facebook.com/insights`).

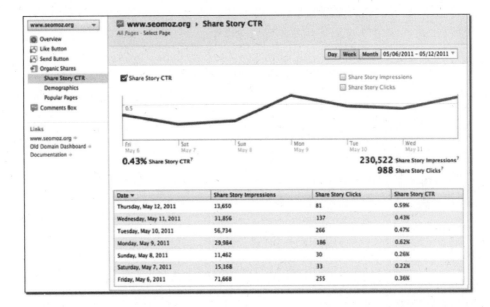

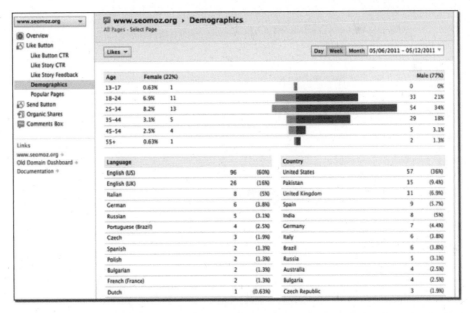

As these images show, you can track key metrics over time with Insights, including the size and demographics of your fan base, the reach and effectiveness of your content, and the quantity of likes and content shares.

Insights also offers a unique, powerful feature—integration with your website. Using a snippet of JavaScript code, you can embed the Facebook Insights functionality on your site. This gives you information about all the users who visit your pages while logged into Facebook. Since Facebook Insights is a topic that has been well-covered on Moz (and elsewhere on the web), I won't dwell too much on it other than to say it's the most robust built-in social analytics platform by far.

To learn more about Facebook Insights, check out these resources:

- Official Facebook Insights Page for Developers
  `https://developers.facebook.com/docs/insights`
- "4 Facebook Marketing Tactics You Might Not Know About," *Moz*
  `www.moz.org/blog/4-facebook-marketing-tactics-you-might-not-know-about`
- "6 Areas You Need to Monitor for Effective Messaging," *Search Engine Watch*
  `http://searchenginewatch.com/article/2097426/Facebook-Insights-6-Areas-You-Need-to-Monitor-for-Effective-Messaging`

## TWITTER

Twitter and Facebook likely refer more traffic to websites than other social networks do. (StumbleUpon purportedly sends more outbound traffic, but it is more of a discovery/browsing engine than a true social network.) Unlike Facebook, Twitter does not have a relatively sophisticated analytics product built into its platform. This means that you need third-party tools (or a lot of time to collect data manually) to track metrics for Twitter over time, as I discuss later in this chapter.

The metrics I care about tracking on Twitter are:

- Followers—The unique number of Twitter users who've "followed" my account.

- Active Followers—The number of followers who've logged into Twitter in the past 30 days. This data is challenging to get, and requires software that runs through your followers and determines which ones are actively using Twitter via the API. Some third-party tools (discussed later) show this information.

- @ Replies—The number of tweets sent that begin with my account name (Twitter handle), @randfish.

- @ Mentions—The number of tweets that include my Twitter handle inside the tweet. Anyone who follows me will see these tweets in their feed, regardless of whether they follow the people who tweet about me.

- Brand Mentions—The number of tweets that mention a brand but do not use the twitter handle preceded by the @ symbol.

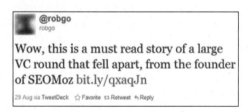

- Domain/URL Mentions—The number of tweets that include a link containing my domain name. These now include, by default, any shortened URL that contains domain name, as Twitter automatically parses the final destination URL for matches to the query.

- Direct Retweets—The quantity of my tweets that my followers share with their followers using Twitter's native retweet (RT) button. These tweets are unedited by those who share them.

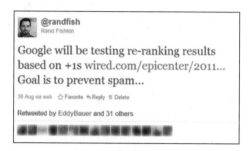

- Other RTs—The quantity of my tweets that my followers shared with their followers using a method other than Twitter's native retweet button. These tweets credit me by preceding my Twitter handle with the abbreviation "RT" or word "via." They are similar to direct retweets, but contain a modification of the original message. Because of this, they appear to come from a unique source, and aren't necessarily counted by Twitter's automatic RT system.

- Best Performing Content—The content I made available to Twitter that earned the most clicks, retweets, and shares. Twitter does not currently make this information directly available. However, it can be obtained through some third-party tools like Buffer (`http://bufferapp.com`), TweetReach (`http://tweetreach.com`), and Twenty Feet (`https://www.twentyfeet.com`).

- Direct Traffic and Non-Twitter.com Drivers—The sources that sent traffic to my site via Twitter's ecosystem, including desktop clients and other third-party applications. Thanks to a recent change made by Twitter, these sources now show up (for the most part) as coming from `http://t.co` (Twitter's native URL shortener).

| Source/Medium | None ≽ | Visits ↓ |
|---|---|---|
| 1. t.co / referral | | 23,990 ±3% |
| 2. facebook.com / referral | | 19,847 ±3% |
| 3. linkedin.com / referral | | 13,101 ±3% |
| 4. twitter.com / referral | Twitter-ecosystem | 9,520 ±4% |
| 5. stumbleupon.com / referral | | 4,761 ±5% |
| 6. twitterfeed / twitter | | 3,115 ±6% |
| 7. hootsuite.com / referral | | 2,369 ±8% |

In addition to these relatively standard metrics, I'd love to be able to see how my Twitter activities impact follower count, engagement, etc. For example, if one of my tweets earns me 100 new followers, it would be terrific to see that growth. However, it currently isn't possible to make these types of connections (to my knowledge).

All these metrics show the growth, reach, and traffic-level impact of my Twitter activities, but none of them fully integrate with the buying cycle mentioned earlier. In an ideal world, I'd want to see the bottom-line impact that all of my Twitter activities have, but this is very challenging to achieve.

It's often mentioned that in analytics, nothing is worth tracking unless it leads to actions that improve performance. For the metrics listed in this section, the primary actions you're tracking are your own. The key to improving performance is to compare successful interactions, tweets, and content against less successful ones. This will help you determine what actions grow your audience, bring visits to your site, and eventually, drive conversion actions.

*Author's Note: For more information about tracking Twitter metrics, see "Social Media Analytics: Twitter: Quantitative & Qualitative Metrics" by Avinash Kaushik, Google Analytics' evangelist (*www.kaushik.net/avinash/social-media-analytics-twitter-quantitative-qualitative-analysis*).*

## LINKEDIN

LinkedIn functions like a hybrid of Twitter and Facebook. Making a personal connection on LinkedIn require mutual acceptance from both parties. Public entities like company pages and groups, though, can be followed one-way. LinkedIn tends to be a great social network for those who are recruiting talent, or are involved in B2B sales and marketing. This particular social network is far less effective as a pure consumer/B2B channel.

Like Facebook, LinkedIn has some built-in analytics for businesses—and individuals, too. Some data points that are useful to track include:

- Company Page Views and Uniques—The number of times your company's LinkedIn profile has been viewed over time and the quantity of unique visitors to the page.

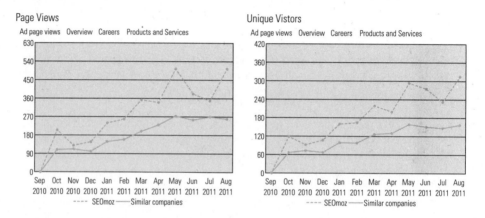

- Quantity of Followers—As with Twitter, individuals can "follow" a brand account on LinkedIn and receive status updates in their "updates" stream. The more followers you have, the greater your ability to reach people on LinkedIn with your content.

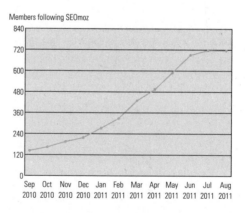

■ Connections—The number of unique connections an individual has on LinkedIn is a worthwhile metric to track. Unfortunately, though, I couldn't find built-in functionality for tracking that data, just the raw, current count (on the "Network Statistics Page") and some data about the geographic and industry reach of those connections.

### Your Network of Trusted Professionals

You are at the center of your network. Your connections can introduce you to 14,087,200+ professionals — here's how your network breaks down:

| | | |
|---|---|---|
| 1 | **Your Connections**<br>Your trusted friends and colleagues | **3,125** |
| 2 | **Two degrees away**<br>Friends of friends; each connected to one of your connections | **888,700+** |
| 3 | **Three degrees away**<br>Reach these users through a friend and one of their friends | **13,195,200+** |
| | Total users you can contact through an Introduction | **14,087,200+** |

**19,793 new people** in your network since September 5

■ Messages and Invitations—The number of invitations to connect and email messages sent to your account. (I clearly need to find a free hour or two and comb through mine—sorry if I haven't added you yet.) This data is also excluded from LinkedIn's built-in analytics.

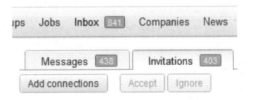

■ Profile Views—The number of people who have looked at your profile over time. Tracking some data about who they are might also be useful. (Note: If someone who views your profile is a first degree connection, LinkedIn will show their name; if not, they'll display the company name or industry associated with their profile.)

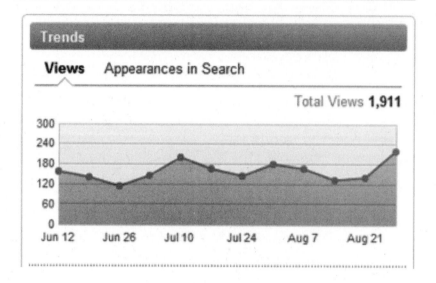

- Top Keywords—The top keywords LinkedIn users searched for prior to discovering your profile.

| Top Search Keywords | | |
|---|---|---|
| 1. | rand fishkin | 48% |
| 2. | seomoz | 36% |
| 3. | rand | 4% |
| 4. | seo | 2% |
| 5. | fishkin | 1% |
| 6. | social media | 1% |
| 7. | marketing | 1% |
| 8. | internet marketing classes | <1% |
| 9. | nfl | <1% |

- Content Shares—Tragically, I couldn't find a way to measure or record the number of status updates and shares to one's personal LinkedIn feed, nor the number of "likes" received for them. While LinkedIn has not added this functionality for engagement with personal profiles, they do offer limited analytics data for Company Pages that they can use to track engagement with their company status updates (i.e., content shared).

- Traffic—While LinkedIn isn't a huge driver of referral traffic for most users, it can be for certain B2B sites. For these sites, the quality of the traffic from LinkedIn is often higher than traffic from other social sources.

| Visits ? | Pages/Visit ? | Avg. Time on Site |
|---|---|---|
| **407,083** | **3.66** | **00:04:52** |
| % of Site Total: 31.33% | Site Avg: 3.53 (3.74%) | Site Avg: 00:04:32 (7.10%) |

| | Source ⌄ | None ⌄ | Visits ↓ |
|---|---|---|---|
| 1. | seomoz.org | | 69,503 |
| 2. | pro.seomoz.org | | 53,172 |
| 3. | t.co | | 24,940 |
| 4. | opensiteexplorer.org | | 24,035 |
| 5. | facebook.com | | 19,197 |
| 6. | linkedin.com | | 14,038 |

Over the past month, LinkedIn has been Moz's fourth largest source of referral traffic; not too shabby! (Note: Referrals from `moz.org` and `pro.moz.org` are technically internal referrers.)

Few third-party tools exist to help with measuring the success of LinkedIn activities. Over time, though, I hope to see more tools in the social media analytics field developed that successfully track actionable data for Twitter, Facebook, LinkedIn, and beyond.

## GOOGLE+

Google's social network is still relatively young. Given Google's intent to make it part of the signals that influence web search rankings, and the dramatic growth (25 million+ members) it achieved in its first two months, it's already worthy of marketers' attention.

Unfortunately, the network doesn't yet have any sophisticated metrics-tracking capabilities, very few third-party apps have integrated Google+, and robust API and oAuth functionality isn't currently available. There are plenty of interesting metrics worth tracking. It's just insanely frustrating that even raw counts are unavailable for many of these. Hopefully, Google will add some soon. (Heck, if you work on the Google+ team and are doing analytics for users/brands, please consider the following list.)

- **Number of Followers**—It is at least possible to manually track this. Technically, on Google+, people who subscribe to your updates aren't called "followers." They "have you in circles." You can see this metric on your profile page.

■ **+Name Mentions**—It's tough to even manually compile a list of name mentions. Unfortunately, I could not find a raw quantity of name mentions on Google+, either, making it nearly impossible (and certainly not pragmatic) to track the number of name mentions you receive on Google+ today.

■ **Brand Mentions**—I'm unaware of any way to find the number of brand mentions in Google+; another bummer. However, you can use Google's "site:plus.google.com" search modifier and query for your brand name with date restrictions to produce a list of brand mentions in the SERPs (see `http://mz.cm/ZEtBNq`).

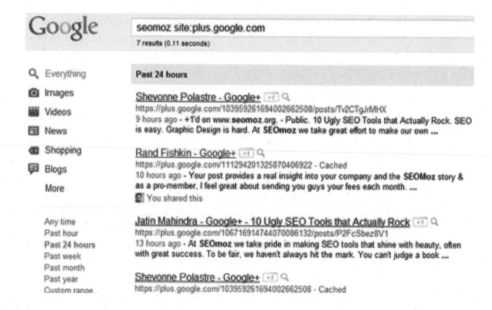

■ **Content Shares, Content +1s, Link Shares, & Link +1s**—These would all be excellent metrics to add to our list, but we currently have no way to extract this data from Google+ system (to my knowledge, anyway).

■ **+1s of Your Site's Content**—While this number is currently unavailable in Google+, it is possible to track it via Google's Webmaster Tools (`www.google.com/webmasters`). Webmaster Tools provides the quantity of +1s of your site's content, as well as where they came from and where they point to, allowing you to analyze their impact.

## Activity

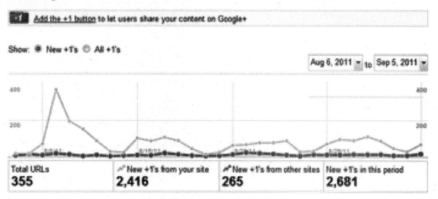

| Total URLs | New +1's from your site | New +1's from other sites | New +1's in this period |
|---|---|---|---|
| 355 | 2,416 | 265 | 2,681 |

- **Traffic**—Google+ is already a traffic powerhouse for many tech-forward brands and those that reach early adopters in general, especially considering their relatively small market share (one-eighth the size of Twitter based on total number of users, probably even smaller when comparing active number of users). For the record, Google+ has been the ninth-largest referrer of visits to Moz over the past 30 days.

## Referring Site:
plus.google.com

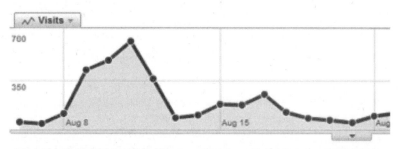

## This referring site sent 4,782 visits via 1 referral p

| Site Usage | Goal Set 1 | Goal Set 2 | Goal Set 3 | Goal Set 4 | Ecommerce |
|---|---|---|---|---|---|

| Visits ⑦ | Pages/Visit ⑦ | Avg. Time on Site |
|---|---|---|
| **4,782** | **1.90** | **00:02:19** |
| % of Site Total: 0.37% | Site Avg: 3.53 (-46.17%) | Site Avg: 00:04:32 (-48.83%) |

| | Referral Path ⌄ | None ⌄ | Visits ↓ |
|---|---|---|---|
| 1. | /url | | 4,782 |

Perhaps due to privacy issues, Google+ uses a single referring URL for all traffic. This helps consolidate traffic from Google+ in analytics reports, but makes it frustrating to determine the value of actions taken on the social network beyond driving traffic.

For more information about tracking Google+ metrics, see these articles:

- "Google Explores Re-Ranking Search Results Using +1 Button Data," *Wired.com* `www.wired.com/business/2011/08/google-studying-re-ranking-search-results-using-1-button-data-but-its-touchy`

- "Google+ Hits 25 Million Users, is the Fastest Growing Website Ever," *Business Insider* `www.businessinsider.com/google-plus-growth-25-million-users-2011-8`

## REDDIT, STUMBLEUPON, QUORA, YELP, FLICKR, AND YOUTUBE

Depending on the quantity and value of the traffic that other social networks send, there may indeed be additional metrics worth tracking. StumbleUpon, SlideShare, Reddit, and Quora are all in our top 50 referrers for Moz, and each sends 500+ visits per month. Investing more effort in analyzing data from these social networks is likely worth it, and if this yields large returns, additional investment is likely warranted.

## BLOGS AND FORUMS

The world of social started out as one where discussion sites (forums, Q&A, bulletin boards, and the like) and the blogosphere reigned supreme. Eventually, consolidation and massive adoption of the major networks took over the hearts and minds of the press. The social web, however, is still very much alive in the blogosphere and forum world.

Marketers have massive opportunities available to them in these spaces, too. At Moz, we have tens of thousands of visits each week from blogs and discussion sites of all sizes. Interaction with those sources often yields fantastic results in terms of referral traffic, mindshare, and links. Many brands use similar tactics, hiring community managers or evangelists to engage in industry topic discussions while building strong, recognizable profiles that increase brand awareness and produce traffic and links.

Thus, as responsible inbound marketers, it's our job to measure actions taken through these channels, and to quantify the impact each one has on our brand.

- **Site & Brand Mentions**—Monitoring mentions of a site or brand name (such as Moz or `www.moz.org`) in the blogosphere can lead you to content and conversations worthy of engagement, as well as allow you to track the quantities (and possibly sentiment) of those mentions over time. Google Alerts (`www.google.com/alerts`) is potentially worth looking at as a tool to help you monitor these mentions.

- **Links**—Direct links are nice because they appear either in link-tracking tools like Google Webmaster Tools (`www.google.com/webmasters`), Open Site Explorer (`www.opensiteexplorer.org`), or Majestic SEO (`www.majesticseo.com`), OR directly in your web analytics. Note new referral sources (quantity and location) and apply metrics. (I like Domain Authority personally, but am biased, of course.)
- **Traffic**—A must-have for any inbound channel, visit-tracking is the most simple metric I've mentioned here. (Honestly, though, I wish it could be tracked alongside the quantitative metrics for mentions/links and stats like `follow` versus `nofollow/ DA/ #` of linking root domains/etc. to help give a sense of the SEO value, too.)

For any inbound marketing channel (social or otherwise) that you're considering tracking, I really like this process:

Step #1: Discover
Find inbound marketing paths that look promising and make a list.

Step #2: Test
Invest a few days/hours building authentic value in that niche/sector.

Step #3: Measure
Use your web analytics to track primary + second-order impact.

Step #4: Repeat
Throw out low ROI projects; repeat high ROI ones.

Losing a few hours to channels that don't provide value is a minimal cost to pay for discovering and participating in those that do!

If you're curious about this process and want to dive deeper, you may be interested in viewing my SlideShare presentation, *The Power of Inbound Marketing* (`www.slideshare.net/randfish/the-power-of-inbound-marketing`).

## TOOLS FOR MEASURING SOCIAL MEDIA METRICS

The number of tools available to track social media has grown exponentially over the last three years. While I'm unable to list all of them here, this list will hopefully provide you with a good sample set:

- **bit.ly**—Excellent for tracking click-throughs on content from any source—on any device or medium. It's frustrating to have an extra layer of analytics required. Given the non-reporting of many desktop and mobile clients, though, bit.ly (`https://bitly.com`) has become a must for those seeking accurate analytics on the pages they share.
- **Social Mention**—The equivalent of "Google Alerts" for social media, Social Mention (`www.socialmention.com`) has real-time brand monitoring, search functionality, and several plugins.
- **Raven Tools**—A toolset that tracks basic metrics for both search and social, Raven (`http://raventools.com/tools`) pulls data from Twitter, Facebook, and YouTube, and will likely expand into other networks in the near future.

- **Converseon**—A very impressive social and web-monitoring tool out of NYC, Converseon (`http://converseon.com`), like Radian6, is geared toward enterprises, but offers human-reviewed sentiment classification and analysis. This is a very powerful tool for those seeking insight into brand perception on the social web.

- **PageLever**—Specifically focused on tracking interactions on Facebook pages, PageLever (`http://pagelever.com`) provide more depth and data than Insights does.

- **Twitter Counter**—A phenomenal tool for monitoring the growth of Twitter accounts over time, Twitter Counter (`http://twittercounter.com`) tracks data latently. This makes it possible for you to access historical data for many accounts, even if you haven't used Twitter Counter before. Upgrading to a "premium" account provides analytics on mentions and retweets as well.

- **Followerwonk**—Technically more of a social discovery tool, Followerwonk (`https://followerwonk.com`) helps you find profiles that meet your specific criteria. It also offers very cool analytics on follower overlap and opportunity, and is based on a paid credits model. (Note: Followerwonk was acquired by Moz in 2012, and is now available to PRO members with added functionality.)

- **Social Bakers**—While it provides basic stats for Twitter and Facebook, Social Bakers (`www.socialbakers.com`) also tracks metrics for several unique Facebook sources, including Places and Apps.

- **Crowdbooster**—More than a raw analytics tool, Crowdbooster (`http://crowdbooster.com`) provides tips for optimizing social media activities that will increase engagement and social reach. Examples including recommending times for posting content and suggesting users to connect with.

- **Awe.sm**—This product offers link and content tracking, along with traditional social analytics. Awe.sm (`http://totally.awe.sm`) also has a very pretty interface.

- **TwentyFeet**—Aggregates metrics from Facebook, Twitter, and YouTube in a single data stream (`www.twentyfeet.com`).

- **SimplyMeasured**—Reports on social media analytics are made available via Excel exports; includes some very cool streams of data (`http://simplymeasured.com`).

- **Most Shared Posts**—This plugin shows the posts that are most shared on Google +1, Twitter and Facebook on the Wordpress site it is installed on. Most Shared Posts (`http://www.tomanthony.co.uk/wordpress-plugins/most-shared-posts`) was developed by Tom Anthony.

> *Editor's Note: PostRank and BackType were originally included in this list. The services have since been shut down after being acquired by Google and Twitter, respectively.*

One member of our community, OnReact, mentioned that *SEOptimize* has a great post on tools designed specifically for Google+, some of which can be useful to gather the data mentioned earlier (see `www.seoptimise.com/blog/2011/08/more-than-30-google-tools-extensions-tutorials-and-other-resources.html`).

Other tools mentioned by our community include the following.

- **Klout**—Scored-based system that measures the social influence of brands and individuals across multiple networks. Scores are based on hundreds of factors, and users can earn "Klout Perks" based on their level of engagement with the Klout community (`http://klout.com/home`).

- **Viralheat**—This unified platform for social media management is unique in that it has publishing capabilities (`www.viralheat.com`).

- **HootSuite**—This web-based app allows users and teams to manage campaigns across multiple social media networks in a single dashboard. Provides analytics in custom-built reports. Other features provided based on membership level (`http://hootsuite.com`).

- **SharedCount**—Tracks URL shares, likes, and tweets via a simple interface (`http://sharedcount.com`).

- **PeerIndex**—Measures your interactions across the web to help you understand the impact of your social actions (`www.peerindex.com`).

Obviously, there are a ton of metrics and data worthy of attention, and no analytics product measures all of them in a single platform—at least, not yet. For now, marketers are stuck with measuring the value of social media by combining tools, manual collection, visit tracking via analytics, and plenty of questions about the value of social media. However, much like the SEO space, I expect that we'll see an increasing growth of metrics, tools, and sophistication from marketers, and value derived through participation and network growth. It's exciting to be an early adopter in this space.

# 14

# EVERYONE SHOULD HIRE "SOCIAL MEDIA EXPERTS"

*By Rand Fishkin*

> **Editor's Note:** *Some marketing professionals are still hesitant to trust anyone who calls themselves a "social media expert" these days, believing that the rules of the game—and its players—change too quickly for anyone to master the field. This contrasts sharply with the nature of the complaint about the social media expert that Rand disputes in this post (originally published on* The Moz Blog *in 2011), as it is based on the premise that social media skills are merely common sense.*

I CAUGHT A post from Peter Shankman entitled "I Will Never Hire a Social Media Expert and Neither Should You." It's not the first of its kind, nor was it the best argued, but it struck a nerve and has made a number of waves around the web. Needless to say, as someone who employs multiple team members with a great deal of social media expertise, I strongly disagree with the substance and sentiment of the piece.

Here's Mr. Shankman's argument in his own words:

> *No business in the world should want a "Social Media Expert" on their team. They shouldn't want a guru, rock-star, or savant, either. If you have a "Social Media Expert" on your payroll, you're wasting your money.*
>
> *Being an expert in Social Media is like being an expert at taking the bread out of the refrigerator. You might be the best bread-taker-outer in the world, but you know what? The goal is to make an amazing sandwich, and you can't do that if all you've done in your life is taken the bread out of the fridge.*

The full piece (see `http://shankman.com/i-will-never-hire-a-social-media-expert-and-neither-should-you`) makes a passionate case, but an entirely false one. There's no evidence, only opinion; no examples, just speculation; no data, but loads of stereotyping. Peter founded and sold HARO, the social media service that connects journalists to subject-matter experts. He is certainly one of the premier benefactors of social traffic and of a new, more socially connected web, yet Mr. Shankman somehow manages to ignore the benefits social media has brought him (and his company and its clients) to write a scathing post that dresses down anyone who dares claim expertise in this marketing discipline.

As with my arguments against Mr. Roadruck's sensationalist post "White Hat SEO is a Joke" (see Chapter 1), I'm worried that I'm falling for troll bait. Regardless, the people who do great social media marketing deserve a strong defense, and I believe the evidence is almost entirely in their favor. Besides that, as an SEO, I've long felt the brunt of baseless attacks by ignorant skeptics. I feel a kinship with those who've had their profession ridiculed, and have a duty to stand up for them.

Let's start by exploring the popularity of the social media expert in comparison to a more traditional marketing job role Mr. Shankman points out, media traffic planner:

> *Marketing involves knowing your audience, and tailoring your promotions in specific bursts to the correct segments. "Social media experts" don't know this. They'll build you a fan page, and when all that work doesn't convert into new sales, they'll simply say, "Well, we'll just post more." Don't be that guy. Real marketers know when to market using traditional methods, social media, or even word of mouth. Go ahead. Ask a "social media expert" what a traffic planner does at an agency, then laugh as they quickly ask Google for help finding the answer.*

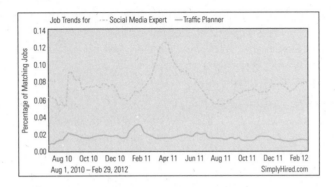

As you can see from the figure, there's a dramatic rise in interest and demand for social media folks over the last couple of years. I don't think this is because companies are "wasting their money." In the current economic climate, companies are watching the bottom line more closely than they have in the past 20 years when hiring. These businesses are investing in high ROI projects and people, and social media is part of that.

The primary point Mr. Shankman appears to make is that social media skills are merely "commonsense" abilities that every marketing professional has. Thus, there's no need for specialists or experts to assist marketing departments with understanding the nuances of the field.

I beg to differ.

Product, marketing, engineering, and customer service departments can all benefit from gaining more knowledge of how social media works, and very little of it is merely common sense. From knowing the difference between an original tweet and a retweet (on the basic end of the spectrum) to crafting lifecycle attribution by melding tools like bitly and Facebook Insights with Google Analytics (on the advanced end), leveraging social media expertise is often critical to improving overall performance.

Facebook has 600 million users; Twitter's at nearly 200 million; LinkedIn is over 100 million. Blogs have hundreds of millions of readers and tens of millions of publishers. The microblogging platform and social media network Tumblr alone has 250 million pageviews in a day. Disqus reaches 500 million visitors each month, and has become the community/commenting system of choice for webmasters and bloggers. Social's driving an increasing proportion of the web's traffic, conversions, and value. How can anyone logically proclaim that experts are worthless?

*Editor's Note: In October 2012, Facebook hit 1 billion monthly users. The following month, LinkedIn reported reaching the 200,000,000 member mark. Headed into 2013, Tumblr now has 91.1 million blogs, Twitter has 200,000,000 monthly users and Google+, which many predicted would fail as quickly as Google Wave did, has more than 500 million members with public profiles.*

*Business meetings are held in Google Hangouts. 72 hours of video are uploaded every minute to YouTube. 72 hours, every minute! With music services like Spotify, music "collections" are becoming a relic of the past for many. An undocumented number of weddings (both real and imagined) are currently being planned on Pinterest, which is now 10.4 million members strong. And 18,712 tweets per minute were sent as Barack Obama was sworn in for a second term as President of the United States of America.*

As a thought exercise, I created the following chart that highlights some of the critical knowledge areas in social media.

### Spheres of Social Media Expertise

| | Basic Knowledge | Intermediate Knowledge | Advanced Knowledge |
|---|---|---|---|
| **Platforms** — Options available, potential applications, focus, user profile, etc. | Twitter, Facebook, LinkedIn, Reddit, YouTube, TripAdvisor | Yelp, StumbleUpon, Wikipedia, Google Profiles | Quora, HARO, StackOverflow, Fark, Hacker News |
| **Tactical** — How to effectively build a presence, how to contribute, make connections, etc. | Comments that contain obvious SEO anchor text will be removed | Including links to images w/ [img] label increase CTR | Profiles w/ certain headshot angles increase engagement |
| **Psychology** — How do users behave, what do they respond well/poorly to, how can behaviors be encouraged/discouraged, etc. | Obvious promotional messaging rarely works (w/a few exceptions) | Shorter tweets = higher CTR on average | Female profiles receive lower engagement on women-centric networks like Etsy |
| **Creative** — What content, contests, messaging, branding, graphics, media, etc. will be well received? | Brand mascots may outperform brand logos in social profiles | Facebook contests w/low barrier to entry work well | Videos from YouTube can be embedded + use XML Sitemaps to get GG rich snippets |
| **Analytics** — How can social activity be tracked + measured; what metrics are right to work on vs. which should be ignored, how can data improve processes? | Track clicks with Bit.ly; track actions with Google Analytics | Use custom segments in GA to partition social visits | Use rel=canonical + landing page code to help track specific CTAs + campaigns |
| **Tools** — What tools are available to track important metrics, improve productivity, reduce unmeasured data, etc. | Tweetdeck, Google Analytics, Bit.ly PRO w/ custom domain name | Facebook Insights for Websites, Unbounce, Tatango | Statdash. Trunk.ly, Rowfeeder |

(Note: As I am not a social media expert, this chart is likely to be more illustrative than accurate.)

*Editor's Note: In 2013, you don't even need a "computer" to participate in social media networking. There are apps for that. Some social networks, such as Instagram, are only accessible with a mobile app. Despite last's year's privacy gaffe, the mobile app based, photo sharing community remains immensely popular. While it recently launched an online presence with limited features, users still upload all of their photos to the network through the Instagram app.*

*As social media networks and the services they offer become integrated into more aspects of users' personal and professional lives (often blending the two), many marketers are now faced with the enviable problem of having more data than they know what to do with. Marketers with social media expertise are in high demand.*

I don't see how Mr. Shankman can believe A) that these pieces of knowledge won't help organizations improve, and B) that such knowledge is innate, requiring no specialization, research, or study.

As further evidence, I'll call to the witness stand some exemplary individuals and companies that I've seen have a massive impact on improving KPIs, processes, and internal use of social media. While I'm a passionate supporter of social media marketing, these are the true experts:

- **Marty Weintraub** of AimClear is one of the industry's brightest stars. His work, research, and client list speak for themselves. Everyone who sees Marty speak about social media is in awe of the passion, dedication, and level of expertise he brings to the field (and stage). (`www.aimclearblog.com/author/aimclear`)

- **Dan Zarrella** of HubSpot has put together some of the most respectable and useful research in the field of social media, and helped to turn HubSpot into a shining beacon of knowledge dissemination across the web. His presentations, webinars, and research have made him the web's pre-eminent social media scientist, and his expertise is backed by more data than nearly anyone else in the marketing field. (`http://danzarrella.com`)

- **Ciarán Norris** of Mindshare Digital, whom I've known for years, has grown from being a talented search marketer into being an even more talented social and brand marketer. He now runs digital media marketing for Mindshare in Ireland, and has helped dozens of big brands build remarkable, revenue-generating social strategies. (`ie.linkedin.com/in/ciaranj`)

- **Jen Lopez** runs community management here at Moz. She has helped us scale our social presence and increase user engagement across multiple networks. Jen is directly responsible for a substantial portion of our efforts to increase traffic, conversions, retention, and brand value. Her knowledge of social media tools, management platforms, branding concepts, and program design is vast. Jen also has a creative, innovative mind, and she knows how to inspire people to do great things. For example, she recently turned the Mozcation program into an amazing outpouring of community effort and attention. (`www.moz.org/team/jen`)

- **Kristy Bolsinger** of Ant's Eye View has helped dozens of local and national firms create successful social media and web marketing programs. I've personally heard great feedback from folks who've worked with her, which is why I continue to refer those seeking a consultant her way. (`www.linkedin.com/in/kristybolsinger`)

There are remarkable people with social media expertise. Some of them even use the highly appropriate title "social media expert" or "social media specialist." They provide a ton of value to the organizations they work with. Neither Mr. Shankman, nor anyone else, should belittle their profession.

In fact, I recommend the opposite. Do as we've done, and hire folks with social media knowledge and expertise. You will be given opportunities that wouldn't be available to you otherwise. And if other processes around monetization and customer acquisition scale, social is a phenomenal complement to whatever channels you are currently pursuing.

# 15

# A PEEK UNDER THE HOOD: HOW WE MANAGE THE MOZ COMMUNITY

*By Jennifer Sable Lopez*

---

*Editor's Note: This post, which reveals the inner workings of the world's most vibrant—and possibly largest—inbound marketing community, was originally published January 18th, 2012, on The Moz Blog. It was completely updated for this book in March of 2013.*

---

HAVE YOU EVER been a part of a community and wondered, "How does all the magic happen?" Or maybe you've never quite understood what a community manager actually does. In the spirit of *TAGFEE*, I've decided to lift the Moz hood and show you how we manage our large, active community. In this chapter, you'll get a look at the who, what, when, and how of managing the Moz community. Hopefully, you'll gain some insights on how to grow your community, too.

> *Editor's Note: To be TAGFEE is to be as Transparent, Authentic, Generous, Fun, Empathetic, and Exceptional as possible. To learn more about Moz's core values, read, "What We Believe and Why: Moz's TAGFEE Tenets" (www.moz.org/blog/ what-we-believe-why-seomozs-tagfee-tenets).*

# WHO ARE WE?

Over the last couple of years, the community has grown rapidly. It quickly became imperative to build a team to help take care of different aspects of the community. I simply couldn't handle all the community tasks on my own anymore. So, before I jump too far into the what, when, and how of managing the Moz community, I'd like to introduce you to the "who."

## KERI MORGRET

Keri is well-known in the SEO industry as one of those amazing conference live-bloggers. She is also known for her ability to remember almost all our community members. Having managed many forums and community sites in the past, including being a moderator at Sphinn, she is perfectly positioned to be a part of the Moz community team as our On-Site Community Manager.

Having recently relocated to Seattle for the love of Moz, Keri also runs her business Strike Models with her husband. (Go check out the site, it's super cool—`www.strikemodels.com`.) She has quickly become an integral part of the team, as well as the community in general.

As the Mozzer who leads management of our user-generated content blog, *YouMoz*, and our Q&A forum, she interacts all day long with community members. You may not realize it, but Keri pretty much knows everything that's going on all the time in the community. You think I'm kidding … I'm not.

Not only does she spend her time managing some of the on-site areas, but Keri can jump in to help out on Twitter—or any other of our social media properties. If you're ever curious about what's going on right now within the Moz community, Keri is your woman. You can ping her `@KeriMorgret` on Twitter.

## ERICA MCGILLIVRAY

When we found out that Erica was a founder of GeekGirlCon (geekgirlcon.com), we just knew she'd fit right into our community. With a background in SEO, social, email marketing, and event planning (pretty much marketing awesomeness), she easily jumped into the role of Social Community Manager.

A ninja in her own right, Erica can essentially do anything and everything that has to do with managing the community. Right now, Erica focuses on the management and strategy behind our social media properties (Twitter, Facebook, LinkedIn, Pinterest, etc.); community voice documentation and evolution; running our weekly Mozinar series; and organizing our annual MozCon (including wrangling speakers).

Oh, and did I mention she's a badass SEO? I've always felt strongly that you can't manage a community unless you're a part of the community yourself. Well, Erica can talk the talk and walk the walk. If you want to keep up with all of Erica's geekery, follower her on Twitter @emcgillivray.

## MEGAN SINGLEY

From her initial stint on our Moz customer support team, we knew we wanted Megan's expertise and ability to wow our community. As a bonus, she knows our software inside and out. As an exceptionally TAGFEE person—especially the Generous, Fun, and Empathic parts—Megan focuses on keeping the community extra happy as our Community Coordinator.

Megan regularly tweets, Facebooks, G+s, and LinkedIns to keep our community growing strong. She also can jump in at any point to help out with Q&A, blog comment moderation, and running Mozinars. If you're racking up those MozPoints, Megan's the one who makes sure you get your t-shirt, Q&A access, and more.

Megan has an uncanny ability to find out what each person loves. From celebrating community accomplishments to sending out thank you cards to amusing community members with surprises, Megan is always sharing her joy with the Moz community, including our Seattle office. With Megan around, for instance, you may come back from vacation to find your desk filled with Grumpy Cat photos. Get to know more about Megan by following her on Twitter @megansingley.

## LINDSAY WASSELL

After her time as a Mozzer back in the day, we bribed Lindsay to return—at least for a couple hours a day—as an Associate on our community team. Lindsay is our East Coast voice. As our community grew, we realized that none of us are morning people, and we were still sleeping while many of you were tweeting from work—or, in the case of Europe, sitting down for dinner!

In stepped Lindsay to fill the gap. While we're dreaming, she's answering your questions, sharing today's content across our social networks, and taking care of any immediate needs like combating spam. Not to mention, Lindsay's often the first one to notice if anything on our site's gone down or customers aren't seeing what they expect.

When Lindsay's not moonlighting as Roger, she's running her own SEO auditing and consulting company, Keyphraseology (keyphraseology.com) and running after her young twins. All from sunny Florida. Follow our own canary in the community coalmine on Twitter @lindzie.

## CHRISTY CORRELL

As our customer base flourished and our community built up MozPoints, we soon found ourselves needing more help with our Q&A forum. Good thing we knew Christy. Both Lindsay and I worked with Christy back in the day—way back before I was an SEO!—and I knew she was top-notch.

Christy mostly focuses on wrangling our other Associates to answer Q&A questions. She makes sure you're getting answers to your questions—and are happy with your answers. Christy pokes Associates and Mozzers (in the most TAGFEE way) when questions go too long without replies or need follow-up. Or she can assign them to someone else if a Mozzer's on holiday, for instance.

When she's not in Q&A, Christy spends her Associate time working on special content projects for Moz—like editing this book! She also owns Honey Tree Media (`honeytreeme-dia.com`), an SEO and new media consultancy. Get to know more about Christy by following her on Twitter `@denverish`. Especially if you're in Denver, as she's a huge advocate for her local SEO community. Make sure you ask her about her dog.

## MELISSA FACH

As our community exploded, so did the submissions to *YouMoz*. We were getting roughly nine a day—or around 60 a week! Poor Keri needed more help, and that's when we found Melissa and got her on board as an Associate. Having worked as an editor at *Search Engine Journal*, among other jobs in the SEO industry, Melissa knows a ton about inbound marketing and the who's who of blogging.

If you submit a YouMoz, whether we decide to publish it or reject it, you'll probably hear from Melissa. She's making sure your info's ready to be published and your screen caps are sized correctly. Melissa has quickly become an essential member of our team and an advocate for helping our *YouMoz* writers become even more awesome.

When she's not editing *YouMoz*, Melissa runs her own consulting and business training company, SEO Aware (`seoaware.com`). If you want to make her day, tweet *Star Wars* photos at her. You can find her sharing promoted *YouMoz* posts and Mozzy love on Twitter `@SEOAware`.

## MIRIAM ELLIS

You know when you meet someone and you say to yourself, "Wow, they're incredibly TAGFEE, why don't they work at Moz?" Okay, maybe you don't say that, but we do. That's Miriam. As an Associate, she helps out on *YouMoz* and in Q&A.

While most of our Associates and Staff in Q&A know more than a little about SEO, we often find ourselves with specific Local SEO questions. They are usually along the lines of, "Why isn't my business address updated? I stood on my head and did the hokey pokey while mailing off my postcard to Google." While the rest of us scratch our heads,

Miriam jumps in and reminds you that you need to wear purple while doing it. Which is why she's also the owner of Solas Web Design, a firm that offers optimized website design, Local SEO/SEM and copywriting services (`solaswebdesign.net`).

Additionally, Miriam plays a woman behind the curtain in *YouMoz*. She reads just about every submission and gives us her opinion on the post's quality and if she thinks it's worthy of publication. Especially when we're swamped, we build our acceptance, rejection, and "needs more editing" emails on her thoughts. She's pretty magical.

## JEN LOPEZ

Oh, hi! Just a quick background: I have a degree in journalism with an emphasis on public relations, but spent ten years as a web developer before I turned into an SEO. Got hired as an SEO Consultant with Moz in early 2009, then in January 2010 we gave up consulting. Doh! Hello Community Management.

I started out by creating this new position and doing ALL the tasks myself. And as both the community and I have grown, I'm now Director of Community with both an in-house team and a gaggle of Associates reporting to me. Not to mention all you awesome community members that I love getting to know better!

So what will you find me doing on an average day? I manage my team, advocate for the community both inside and outside of Moz, help out where my team needs me, respond to help tickets as needed, comment on community posts outside of Moz, tweet from my personal account (`@jennita`), and handle any other random issues that comes up during the day.

The truth is, my job rocks. Sure I deal with trolls sometimes, but that's what makes the job interesting.

## COMMUNITY DOESN'T STOP THERE

Community and content go together like cheese and spiral macaroni, and at Moz, one would not exist without the other. Along with our internal community team, there are a few others who make a big impact on the community by serving up hot content for our readers. Let me introduce you to the "external" members of our community team!

## ASHLEY TATE

Ashley joined the Moz team in early 2012 after spending a few years in the startup trenches as a content manager. With a background in blogging, content strategy, and community management, she took on the role of Content Lead to help spread her obsession with actionable, delightful content to the far corners of the Interwebs.

You'll find Ashley managing the blog schedule and content, heading our overall content strategy, creating and editing content on the *Moz* and *YouMoz* blogs, and working with authors throughout the content curation process. You can also find her tweeting from her personal account, `@ashletate`, mostly about inbound marketing and her adorable dog, Darwin.

## PETER MEYERS (AKA DR. PETE)

Dr. Pete has been around the Moz community for about as long as Rand himself. He was an essential part of the community long before we even called it a community. Rand made the smart move long ago to bring Pete on board as an Associate, and now he's our full time Marketing Scientist.

Pete spends much of his time working on big content projects, writing on the blog, and answering questions in Q&A. (You'd be amazed at how much stuff this guy knows!) In fact, he's written some of the top content on the blog for the past three years (check out `www.moz.org/users/profile/22897`). He pretty much makes the rest of us look bad with our unworthy content.

When he's not helping manage the chaos of Q&A, writing on the blog, or being one of the funniest guys on Twitter (`@dr_pete`), he's busy being Dad to a toddler and new baby. Oh, and if you've ever wondered if he's a real doctor, he has created a web page just for you (see `www.areyouarealdoctor.com`.)

## MOZZERS

That's you, you, and YOU. Whether it's Gianluca responding to a Tweet about Moz from Italy while us West Coasters are sleeping (`www.moz.org/users/profile/108403`), or Ryan Kent answering a question in Q&A about a technical PRO issue (`www.moz.org/users/profile/312503`), you guys help us manage the community every day. This is a very important aspect of the community and one that makes people want to be a part of it. It's not just one person managing everyone else with an iron fist. It's all the Moz staff and community members helping each other out. Holy. Geeky. Happiness.

## WHAT DO WE DO?

Obviously, there's no way to really describe everything that we do in one blog post. When you work with a community, your day can change in an instant. Sometimes an issue comes up and you help manage it since you're the public "face" of the community on the social sites. Other times, you wake up and find out that a hashtag has been created about you, along with hundreds of posts.

Let me take a few moments to walk you through the major aspects of managing the Moz community. This really is only a high-level look at what we do each day. Here are the what, when, and how, of what it means to manage the Moz community.

## BLOG

When Rand started the *Moz* blog years ago, I'm sure he never quite imagined that it would be the base of such an expansive and amazing community. It really has become the center of everything Moz. Think about this: an average blog post gets around 60 thumbs up, 70 comments, and 900+ Tweets. That's a lot to keep up with each day! Here's a post from the blog in 2013, prior to the launch of Moz.

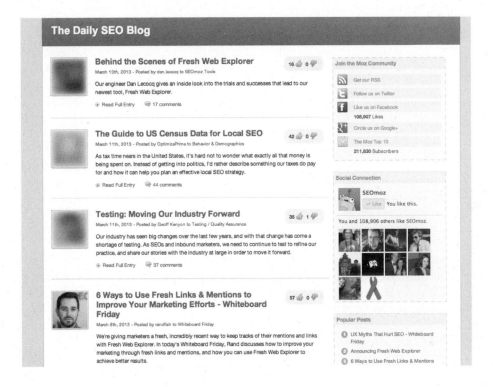

## What

You probably know that we post content not only about SEO, but about inbound marketing in general. We focus on creating actionable takeaways and look for authors who can bring something new to the community. We like to cover hot topics in the industry, but we don't necessarily cover them as "news." We also post major new updates, improvements, or issues related to our software products on the blog as well.

## When

We publish at least one new post per night, and sometimes publish a second a second one during the day (U.S. Pacific Time).

## How

We use a custom blog editor to create the posts. When it comes to managing comments, we have a system that helps us moderate those that meet certain criteria. If we suspect that a comment is spam, one of us has to manually approve it for it to be published. If it is spam, it doesn't get published.

When it comes to comments, we take the community very seriously and will ban users if they don't "play by the rules." Essentially, you're in our home and we request that you handle yourself as a professional.

## Who

Ashley manages the blog schedule and makes sure we have a post going up each night. The idea is to set the schedule at least a couple weeks out, with openings here and there for hot topics or new authors we want to introduce. All of us watch for spam comments throughout the day, and our wonderful Inbound Engineering Manager, Casey Henry (www.moz.org/team/casey), set up a way to moderate and kill spam before you guys ever even see it.

The entire team helps manage the comments, detect spam, and make sure things don't get out of hand anywhere. We also might alert other Mozzers when their expertise is needed to answer a question. Sometimes a comment might require the deep technical knowledge of one of our amazing engineers, for instance.

## YOUMOZ

Any member can create a blog post using our blog editor and submit it to be read by our editors. If it's approved, it gets published to the *YouMoz* blog, shown here in a screenshot from March, 2013. Writing a post for *YouMoz* is a great way to get your name out in the community. Plus, you get a nice link. *YouMoz* publishes posts by anyone in our community who has creative ideas or deep insights to share, whether you've been around the industry forever—or are just starting your career.

## What

Similar to posts on the main blog, the community loves to read actionable posts. However, in *YouMoz*, we do have a little more leeway than we do on the main blog. We'll publish posts on topics that we don't normally cover on the blog. The best part about that is if the post does really well in *YouMoz* and gets promoted to the main blog, we see more diversity in the subjects and voices.

## When

We try to post at least one *YouMoz* submission per day, and some days, we even have two. It used to take four to eight weeks to get through the queue, but now it's only two weeks—and we're always working towards making it even faster.

## How

As mentioned, any community member can create a blog post and submit it. We also provide a "Read Me First" page that has helped us to get higher quality posts submitted (see www. moz.org/posts/ugc_guidelines). It provides style guidelines, detailed information about what we're looking for, and practical tips like image width. If your post is approved, it gets published to the *YouMoz* blog. But more often than not, we tend to work with authors whose posts show promise, but may need more fine tuning—which is why that queue gets so long.

## Who

Keri and Melissa are the main points of contact when it comes to *YouMoz*. They both work hard on cleaning up the queue and making it easier and quicker for authors to get their posts published. Miriam also reviews posts and leaves us great thoughts what we should do with them. Whenever necessary, Erica, Megan, and I also jump in and help out by editing and approving content, declining posts, etc. We also may need to pull in an expert, like Pete, to check on the technical merits of a post.

When it comes to promoting *YouMoz* posts to the main blog, it's a team decision. Usually Ashley or Keri recommend the post and the rest of us chime in. There is no "golden rule" to follow in order get a *YouMoz* post promoted, and it sometimes depends on whether or not there's a spot open on the main blog. When it's good and the community likes it, though, it will get promoted.

## Q&A

As Moz moved away from the consulting business model, we realized that our community still had questions about inbound marketing. We also realized that our community, in addition to us Mozzers, wanted to help answer those questions. Thus, our Q&A forum was born. We were pleasantly surprised to see how much people love to both ask and answer questions, as you can see in this post from March, 2013.

## What

You'll find pretty much any and every kind of question related (sometimes barely related) to Internet marketing in Q&A. Since this feature is for subscribers only, and blatant spammers don't like to pay money, it's fairly easy to keep spam in check. So we spend most of our time here making sure questions get answered and people keep in line with our Community Guidelines and TAGFEE principles.

## When

Twenty-four hours a day, our community asks and answers questions. Thankfully, we're lucky enough to have many Associates helping out on the forum, including some who live in London and other cites "across the pond." This means we're able to have coverage all day long. Whee!

## How

This all happens through our own proprietary Q&A system. We get asked quite often if we built this ourselves or used an out-of-box solution. This is a 100% homegrown system, which does have its own set of bugs. In fact, we've completely rebuilt the backend twice to make it faster and easier for you to use.

## Who

Keri heads our Q&A efforts by monitoring activity and making sure things are up and running. If there is an issue, she works with our technical project manager Jamie Seefurth (`www.moz.org/team/jamies`) to get our engineers on the problem. On the public side, Keri and Christy try to make sure no question is left behind by assigning some to our team of Staff and Associate experts. Dr. Pete, Megan, Erica, and myself also hop in and help out when we can, which in Dr. Pete's case means he's answered over 1,000 questions! Many of our Associates play a role in Q&A, and you'll see a number of them answering questions and endorsing answers every day. Even Rand goes in quite often and replies to questions personally.

# SOCIAL COMMUNITY

With the help of social media sites, our community has grown by leaps and bounds the last couple of years. You may have noticed that we engage with users quite frequently on Twitter, Facebook, Google+, and LinkedIn, while slowly branching out into Pinterest and YouTube, and maintaining a Twitter account for Followerwonk. It's not that we've ignored other sites; we just tend to focus our energies on these first four as that's where the bulk of our community is.

Since many of our members follow us on these sites in addition to the blog, we had to figure out a way to be somewhat unique in all areas. Nothing worse than content overkill. Here's a quick walkthrough of how we manage the big four social media sites here at Moz.

# TWITTER

Twitter is a bit of a "catch-all" platform for us, and is the social media site where we have the most followers (well over 200k). As expected, we use this channel for many different activities, including providing customer service, offering SEO and online marketing advice, and promoting content.

## What

We tweet about Moz content and events, product upgrades and improvements, subscriber perks, site outages, tool issues, *YouMoz* posts, and anything else related to the Moz community. Additionally, you'll see a ton of replies to customer service type inquiries, issues, problems, questions, kudos, high-fives, and kitten photos.

We keep the tone of the tweets as Mozzy as possible, and speak on behalf of Roger. It makes my day when someone tweets, "Hey Roger, thanks for great app," or something along those lines. It's all about Roger!

## When

Our community is very international, so we can't just tweet from 9am to 5pm Pacific time. We need to be available as often as possible to respond to questions, requests, and such. While we do need to sleep at some point, you'll notice that we have people covering Twitter from about 4am until around 11pm Pacific.

Lindsay jumps on in the early morning, which isn't so early for our Florida office, a.k.a. her home. She usually spends an hour so responding to urgent issues, handing out some high fives, and making sure everything's starting out on the right foot. Then Erica and Megan jump on when they get into the office. They typically trade off days where one's in charge in the morning and the other in the afternoon. I help out if they need extra coverage.

We also schedule some of our tweets in advance. While we don't schedule tweets that specifically ask for user engagement, we do need to schedule them to promote our content during our international community's "on" hours. (On a side note, our most popular tweets are usually retweeted between 2am and 4am Pacific Time.)

### How

We use CoTweet to manage Twitter, which allows multiple users to manage multiple accounts. It makes it easy to assign tweets to others; plus, you can tag tweets and set up extensive searches. We also like CoTweet because it acts like an inbox, letting us reach the illustrious "inbox zero" multiple times a day, ensuring that don't miss any activity in our community.

> ***Editor's Note:*** *CoTweet is now SocialEngage, and is part of ExactTarget's suite of premium marketing products and services (see* `http://mz.cm/138Ftxx`*).*

### Who

While Erica's the main person managing the account, at any time throughout the day you may find Megan, Keri, Lindsay, or me tweeting as well.

I also encourage staff to reply to tweets if they see them and simply cc: @moz so we know it's been handled. For example, Rand will often do this. He'll see a tweet before we do and will respond. It's a great way to give people direct interaction with every Mozzer!

## FACEBOOK

As I mentioned before, we wanted to figure out a different approach to using Facebook. So we decided to make Facebook the "face" of Moz.

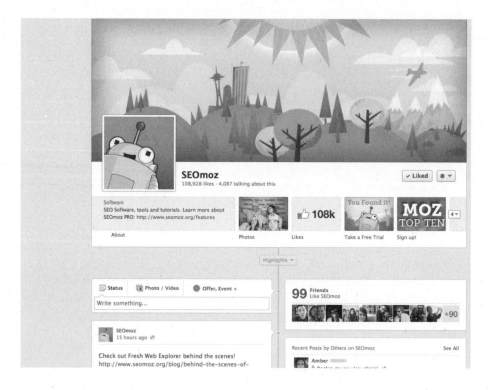

## What

Yes, we do post all of our content on Facebook, the same as we do on Twitter, but we also post fun facts about the company and event photos to Facebook. One thing I enjoy doing is posting photos from a Meetup or conference to Facebook. We find we get a boost in "likes" each time someone is tagged in our photos. Our community loves to see our Mozzy culture.

Additionally, I often ask the community questions here. People love to share their opinions, and Facebook is a simple and easy way to do it. With so many people logged in all day, it's very easy to get people's attention on Facebook.

We also love to change Roger's outfit and add some "life" to him.

We manage comments and wall posts on Facebook just as we would manage comments on our site. If it's spam, we remove it; if it's obscene or someone cusses, we remove it; and if you need help or have something cool to share, we'll respond. Essentially, as long as you're on-topic and not a jerk, we keep your posts.

## When

The timeframe for when we use Facebook is similar to the one for Twitter. However, we don't schedule Facebook posts in advance. We haven't quite nailed down when the best times for us to post are, but it's something we're slowly figuring out.

## How

Although I could use an outside app to manage Facebook, I choose not to. Posts made from outside apps don't seem to show up in people's feeds as often as posts made directly from

Facebook do. I want us to show up in those feeds as often as possible, so I don't use outside apps for Moz. Plus, I like knowing that what I'm seeing on our wall is what our fans are seeing on our wall.

## Who

Again, Erica and Megan are the main people managing our Facebook page. However, Lindsay, myself, and quite a few others who are not officially part of the Community team also have admin rights.

## GOOGLE+

As soon as Google+ brand pages came out, we jumped right on it. It took us a couple months to shake the bones out and figure out a strategy, but I think we're going on a nice track now.

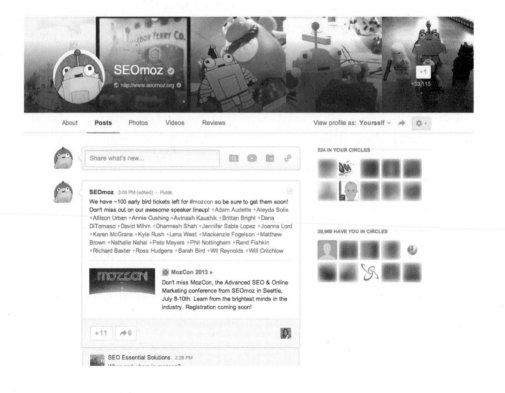

## What

In order to not seem like drones who publish the exact same content over and over, on our Google+ page we not only promote our own content, but other's as well. This is also a great place for us to introduce our readers to hot topics that we think they'd be interested in.

However, the hottest content on our Google+ page, we've found, is our very own White-board+ video series. Whiteboard+ video is essentially a Whiteboard Friday video, but it is only posted to Google+. We'll keep testing this and see what works best, so you might find some new content on there soon.

## When

Right now, we generally have at least one post in the early morning and then another post sometime during the day. But we're always testing and refining how we manage our Google+ account. One weekend, we posted a special Whiteboard+ video on Friday at 8 pm Pacific, and it went crazy! It had 353 pluses, 382 shares, and 101 comments. And most of this happened over the weekend! I think we may be onto something here.

## How

We prefer to stay logged into Google+ all day long and use its interface to manage our account. I'm very happy that it now shows alerts when we get a new follower, comment, plus, etc. This makes it easier to manage the page, as opposed to hitting refresh and scanning the page for updates like I did previously. (Although I wish it would turn off those community invites!) The Google+ search is also really helpful for finding people who aren't tagging us in their posts.

## Who

Erica and Megan do most of the daily management, with Lindsay jumping in early in the morning to post recent content. While G+ is pretty chill, either Keri or myself can hop in as needed.

# LINKEDIN

Ahh, LinkedIn, the stepchild of our social efforts for far too long! Luckily, we've made it part of our main strategy, because so many people from the community are there. We mostly focus on growing our Group, and use our Company Page for content updates and recruiting.

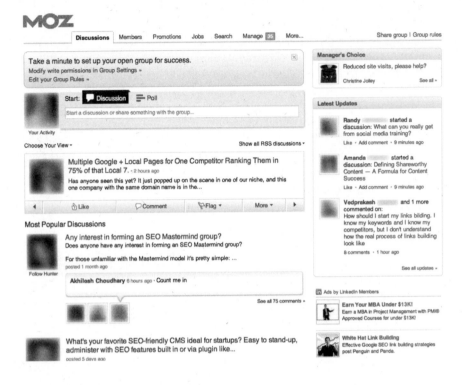

## What

Initially, we tried to set up RSS feeds of our content to go to our Group, and then manually posted updates to our Company Page. However, LinkedIn's feeds were a bit buggy, so we now manually post in the Group, too. We also make sure to promote updates to our tools, upcoming Mozinars, special events, and other information we think the Group may be interested in. LinkedIn is a great place to share content from others, too.

We also manage who joins the group. As with our other social media accounts, we manage comments and posts the same way we manage them on our own blog. We spend time trashing spam and sales pitches, too.

We're also trying new things on LinkedIn, like creating a book club.

## When

While we usually update LinkedIn during "regular business hours" on the West Coast, we do find ourselves peeking in on the weekend, too. Unlike other social networks, we find that our community is pretty active here on the weekends; that's probably when people are taking time to look for new jobs, update their personal portfolios, and do other professional leveling up.

## How

Unlike other social networks, LinkedIn posts made in our Group come directly from the individual community manager, not Roger. We always make sure we're maintaining our Mozziness, and if we need to put on a moderator hat, we make sure that we identify ourselves as such. Roger does update our Company Page, though, on LinkedIn.

Unfortunately, we've found that LinkedIn attracts a lot of spammers. This means that our team, mostly Megan and Erica, manually approve new members and reach out, in a Mozzy way, to double-check we're not dealing with spambots.

We also manage posts, the moderation queue (only approved members can post in the Group), and any other issues that come up. All this happens directly through LinkedIn's user interface.

## Who

Erica and Megan manage the LinkedIn Company Page and Group. Others on the team have admin access, though, and can jump in at any time. But honestly, they do such a great job, we haven't really had to!

## WHEW.

Whether you're a member of the Moz community or you manage a community of your own, I hope you've found this post insightful and that you now have a better understanding of our community management process. Honestly, this barely scratches the surface of what happens behind the scenes in the Moz community. There's a lot to learn and change happens all the time, but our community is amazing. We couldn't imagine not spending our days with you!

Oh and around here, our motto is: "If all else fails, eat ice cream."

# PART

# IV

# OUTREACH

*By Paddy Moogan*

YOU CAN HAVE the best content on the web, but if no one ever reads it, it's useless. If you have a large, established website with an existing community or readership, it is possible that your content will be read and shared without much work from you. For the majority of websites, however, content will need to be promoted before anyone will read or share it. Content sometimes needs that push to give it the attention it deserves. This is where *outreach* comes in.

## WHY OUTREACH IS IMPORTANT

Outreach can help give your website the exposure that it needs in order to thrive. In an ideal world, your audience would just be able to find and engage with your content naturally, and you wouldn't need any outreach. This is certainly possible; there are many products and companies that have succeeded online without having to think about outreach. However, this seems to be the exception rather than the rule, particularly as the web is becoming more competitive every day. It can also take a long time for promotion to happen naturally if you do not give your site that push it needs or dedicate time to getting the word out yourself, and instead rely only on word of mouth referrals to drive traffic and links.

You need to spend some time thinking about whom you should be promoting your content to, and how you are going to get their attention. This is the very first stage of outreach—thinking about who might care enough about your content to share it with their audience.

You also need to spend time finding the right influencers for your content area, so that you don't end up wasting your time contacting people who are not interested in what you have to say.

Once you've done this, you can work on crafting your message to influencers and think about the best way to contact them. Email is the most common form of outreach for online content, but don't forget that phoning people can be very effective, too. Many higher-level links from magazines and newspapers will come when you pick up the phone and talk to the right people.

In this section of the book, we have included chapters that cover crafting your message and making sure that you give yourself the best chance possible of getting a positive reply. Don't underestimate the power of a good email or thoughtful phone call; it would be a shame for your best content to be lost because of bad messaging in your outreach communications.

## GOOD OUTREACH VERSUS BAD OUTREACH

Good outreach can help your content spread to a large, *relevant* audience who will engage with it. This can lead to social shares, links, bookmarks, and, ultimately—more traffic to your business, which is what we are all striving for.

As part of a good outreach campaign, you should make sure you're targeting people who have the ability to send you traffic that converts into revenue. When you do this, it ensures that your work generates more than links or social shares; that is, it ensures that it will lead to real customers.

Remember that you are contacting people in your industry who are influencers, and that you are working on behalf of your client. Bad outreach can damage more than your personal reputation. It can damage the reputation of the website you're representing, get your email blacklisted, and generally annoy a lot of people. Sometimes, bad outreach can get you results in the very short term, but it will never help you build long-term relationships that will help you succeed online.

This section of the book provides many examples of how to do good outreach, as well as some examples of what doesn't work. Keep these lessons in mind, but remember, every website owner is different. Each one will need to use a customized approach when building relationships with influencers and customers.

## HOW OUTREACH HAS CHANGED

Traditionally, many SEOs focused on *volume* of links rather than quality, which meant that outreach was mostly a numbers game. You could usually calculate that for every thousand emails you sent, you would get about ten links. With these numbers, you could then scale outreach in order to build more links. But when you scale anything, there is a danger that the quality will diminish. As the outreach scaled up, chances were that you would rely on a default template, rather than personalizing each email for the recipient. Many website owners are savvy enough to see through an email template, particularly if their website is a high-quality one that they care about. Still, this strategy used to work well.

However, things have changed. Emphasis on *high quality* links has never been greater, so the tactics of SEOs have changed to reflect this. In order to get these high quality links, you need to focus on *building relationships*. In recent years, outreach has become more about building relationships and providing content that is of real value. It has moved heavily away from automated emails and more towards what we'd expect PR consultants and general marketers to do.

Outreach today is much more focused on bloggers who have a large following on social media communities such as Facebook, Twitter, and Pinterest. This focus means that if your outreach is successful, you're not just getting a link to your content. You are also getting exposure to a large, established audience who is interested in your products. This aligns your goals much more with good marketing, rather than just adding up links.

Many SEOs are now also working closely with PR consultants who are able to tap into contacts they have at high-profile national media outlets. Some SEO companies have gone as far as hiring dedicated PR consultants who can get those hard-to-get links that may not be achievable via email outreach.

Essentially, this is what outreach is all about—building long-term relationships that will help you succeed and benefit others on the web. SEOs can sometimes forget that a relationship is a two-way thing. The person you're contacting needs to receive something of value in order to give you what you want.

## THE DANGERS OF BUYING LINKS

Some website owners will only link to you or share your content if you pay them. *Don't buy links.* This is strictly against Google's Webmaster Guidelines, and if you get caught buying links, your website can be penalized *or even banned* from Google's index.

Website owners and bloggers are also much more savvy than they used to be; they are not only aware of what SEO is, but are also aware of the value of a link. Therefore, it isn't a surprise when a blogger responds and wants to be paid to share your content. Don't let yourself be tempted to go down this route; it is an easy win, but it is still buying links, and is dangerous for both you and the blogger/seller.

When you offer website owners something of value, it shouldn't be anything that can get you into trouble with Google. Instead, offer something that is valuable to the audience of the website you're contacting. For example, you could offer a great piece of content, a tool they could really use, or an interview with someone they like. This strategy will not only increase the number of links you receive, but will build interest in your content and create goodwill for your clients.

## THE CHALLENGES OF OUTREACH

Outreach is usually identified by SEOs as one of the hardest parts of their job. Some of the major challenges of outreach include scaling without being spammy, crafting content that appeals to a wide range of people, and getting the attention of large influencers who can share your content with their audience.

While the content in this section will help you overcome many of these challenges, the one thing that I would advise keeping in mind is this—invest your time and resources properly, and don't take risky shortcuts. Good outreach is an investment, and investments take time. You will read a lot about link building that make it sound very easy, and while there are some low-hanging fruits that you can harvest easily, many parts of the outreach process are tough.

Each part of the outreach process is important and there are various things you can do to optimize each one, but there is one thing that makes the entire process go much more smoothly—exceptional content.

## THE IMPORTANCE OF EXCEPTIONAL CONTENT

An often overlooked part of outreach is the "hook" or "story" that provokes the interest of the person you're contacting. This is usually backed up with a piece of content—it might be a written article, an infographic, or data visualization. Without this, every other step in the process becomes much harder. It is much easier to be successful at outreach if you have something that is of genuine interest to your target market.

Many SEOs will start doing outreach and just expect the people they contact to care enough to take the time to link to them. In reality, a blogger doesn't wake up in the morning wanting to link to every person that emails him. In particular, popular bloggers with large followings will receive many outreach emails every day. You truly need to spend time thinking about why they should care about your content.

There has been a rise in the number of SEO companies who are now investing heavily in content creation. This means that more time and money is being spent very early in the outreach process on the story that will hopefully appeal to influencers. While this is the way that SEOs should be thinking, there is a challenge here in that it increases pressure on the people doing outreach to get results. A lot of time may have been spent already on the content creation, so to fail when it comes to getting shares, links, or traffic can mean that people lose faith in the whole process.

Don't let this happen to you. Read the chapters in this section to learn how to improve your outreach efforts, and then customize an outreach strategy and put in the time required to make it successful. Create and maintain mutually beneficial relationships with influencers in your target markets. As with networking offline, focus on how you can help others when networking online. Be genuine. And keep the faith.

# 16

# THROW AWAY YOUR FORM LETTERS (OR 5 PRINCIPLES TO BETTER OUTREACH LINK BUILDING)

*By Michael King*

*Editor's Note: Michael King shares five principles of effective outreach link building. When this post was originally published on <u>The Moz Blog</u> on Aug. 12, 2011, these principles were worth adhering to in order to dramatically improve the effectiveness of outreach emails. Two years later, in a post-Penguin world, these principles not only still work, but are essential for anyone using outreach emails as part of their link-building strategy. Their effectiveness will be likely be improved even further (and future-proofed) for those who suggest their content be shared, versus linked to.*

I'M SITTING ON an air mattress in my new, unfurnished Brooklyn apartment listening to the sounds of the city outside the window after a long day of client meetings. At one point, I was thinking, "Man I wish I had bought that ugly sofa from Ikea so I'd have something to sit on," and the next thing I knew, I was considering the Tao of Outreach Link Building.

I know, I know. Outreach link building is hard. It takes time. You send 1,000 emails and end up with seven links, but I believe that's largely because most search marketers approach link building the wrong way. In fact, I'm going to declare right now that link building should be the easiest and most fun part of SEO. Yep, I said it. Let me finish, though, before you head to the comments to tell me why I'm wrong.

First, let me say that I love where we are moving with link building as a community, especially with the stuff the King of Link Building, Justin Briggs (`http://justinbriggs.org`), has been giving us lately. In fact, what I have to offer for your consideration is very much an expansion on Dan Deceuster's new perspective on link building.

There is often a lot of talk about who to target and how to find them, but there isn't much said about how to get their attention, sustain it, close the deal, and maintain the relationship. Most recommendations revolve around building form letters and then tailoring them to your target.

In my experience, this is the least effective method to engage in outreach link building. The following are five principles of effective link building that have increased my link building success rate from about 20 to 80 percent.

**References**

> "Content-Based Outreach for Link Building" by Justin Briggs, *Outspoken Media* (`http://outspokenmedia.com/seo/content-based-outreach-for-link-building`)
>
> "A New Perspective on Link Building" by Dan Deceuster, *The Moz Blog* (`www.moz.org/blog/a-new-perspective-on-link-building`)

## 1. TALK TO PEOPLE LIKE PEOPLE (THROW OUT YOUR FORM LETTERS)

Search Marketers tend to think of link building as obtaining a link from a website. Link building is cast as a very impersonal process where we use various methods to identify link targets, write form letters, and then fire off emails—expecting the return to be so low that it doesn't make sense to spend much time on them.

Honestly, just reading that last sentence back to myself makes me think of how counterintuitive the process is. In truth, link building is speaking to a person and convincing them to take an action that is beneficial to you.

Everyone reading this post has been subject to some sort of email, Twitter, MySpace, or Facebook spam. Hell, even President Obama and his friends have been spamming me for five years now. Think for a second—how do you react to spam? You erase it or ignore it, of course.

As an owner of various sites, people often contact me to ask for links, offer me SEO services, and such—with form letters that never get opened.

People can usually sense a form letter immediately. Dare I say it? No, I'll let my homey Link from *Legend of Zelda* tell you.

I myself failed many times using the same approach to link building. Then one day, I realized that the link building strategies I was taught are counterintuitive to everything I've learned about building relationships with people through networking. So I developed my own link building style. Be warned, my approach requires a genuine interest in people. Here goes.

## OPENING

Link builders are typically very heavy-handed, and send emails that basically say, "Hey, I have this site. Will you link to me because of x,y,z?" The only thing that I attempt to accomplish with my first email is an engaged response. I never bring up the idea of wanting something from this person until later in the email or tweet thread; the same way I wouldn't walk up to a girl and say, "You're hot! Let's have sex because I'm cute, I drive a luxury car, and I have an apartment in a cool part of Brooklyn!" I keep my opening correspondence short, engaging, and relevant to something that person has tweeted about or written on their site/blog.

Quite simply, people love to know their work has been viewed, absorbed, and enjoyed, so actually take the time to read it and strike up a conversation about something you truly find interesting. As marketers, we are taught to optimize one message that appeals to many people; there is simply no place for that in effective outreach link building.

In the following example, I'm building links for the official *Transformers 3* movie site (not that this would ever happen because those sites are always powered by Paid Media).

**The Old Way of Link Building:**

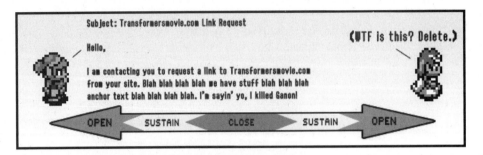

**Subject: Transformersmovie.com Link Request**

Hello,

I am contacting you to request a link to Transformersmovie.com from your site. We have trailers, downloads, exclusive video and a gallery. Visitors can also find information on movie times and buy tickets online.

I see that your blog talks about Transformers and I think visitors to your site will find this content very useful.

Please link to http://www.transformersmovie.com using the anchor text "Transformers," or use the following code: <A href="http://www.transformersmovie.com">Transformers</a>.

Please contact me if you have any questions.

Thank you for your time and careful consideration.

Transformers Web Team
www.transformersmovie.com

While I don't doubt that some link builders have some very spiffy form letters much better than this, most of the time they still come across just as sterile as this one. Now take a look at an alternative that shows the new way for link builders to build relationships:

**The New Way of Relationship Building:**

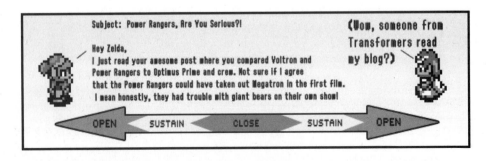

---

**Subject: Power Rangers, Are You Serious?!**

Hey Zelda,

I just read your awesome post where you compared Voltron and Power Rangers to Optimus Prime and crew. Not sure if I agree that the Power Rangers could have taken out Megatron in the first film. I mean honestly, they had trouble with giant bears on their own show!

Truthfully, I think Voltron would make short work of all of them. Speaking of Voltron, have you ever seen this hilarious live action spoof? http://www.youtube.com/watch?v=YtwX0nuqPOO

Anyway I'm curious to know what you think of the new Transformers film. Give me a shout when you get a chance!

-Link

Link of Hyrule
Transformers Web Outreach Team
mike@transformersmovie.com
www.transformersmovie.com

---

Option two is clearly stronger, and was even more fun to write. Creating context allows me to hit more touch points to elicit a response. Also, the engagement is all about opinion sharing, thus framing the conversation as just that—a conversation—rather than a link request.

## SUSTAINING

Sustaining is all about keeping the conversation going, building a rapport with this person and offering something of value. Most people will be tempted to jump the gun at this stage and just ask for the link right when the person responds. This is not the way to go because then your original correspondence will appear to be a thinly veiled link request (which it is, of course, but that is the mindset we are trying to eliminate).

In this stage, it is good to have some content to share that this person may be interested in. It could be related to the site you're trying to get a link for or not. The important point is that you demonstrate that you are a worthwhile resource of some sort, whether it be for entertainment or educational purposes. Not only does this build trust, but it establishes context. This phase can continue as long as it takes for you to actually develop a relationship.

*Let's just rename link building "relationship building."*

Continuing with our robot cartoon blogger example:

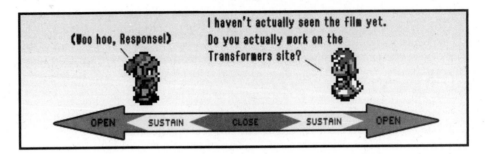

Hey Link,

LOL Link, that video was hilarious and thanks for reading my post but there is noooo way that Voltron could take out the combined power of the MegaZord!! I'm not even sure Voltron could take out the GoBots!

I haven't actually seen the film yet. Do you actually work on the Transformers site?

Best,

Princess Zelda

Princess Zelda,

The GoBots? Zelda, you're killing me! The GoBots were a cheap rip off of the Transformers; they should not be typed in the same email as Voltron! I bet you preferred Silverhawks over Thundercats too, didn't you? HA!

Anyway, yep I sure do work with the Transformers web team. Do you have any interest in seeing the film?

-Link

Link of Hyrule
Transformers Web Outreach Team
mike@transformersmovie.com
www.transformersmovie.com

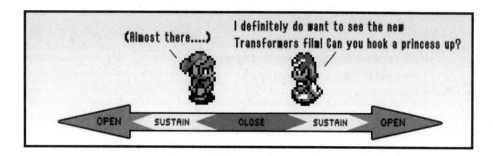

Hey Link,

LOL, you just keep making me laugh. Silverhawks?! I didn't think anyone remembered that cartoon. It was pure redux of Thundercats just as bird people!

I definitely do want to see the new Transformers film! Can you hook a princess up?

Best,

Princess Zelda

Notice how the suggestion of value (movie tickets) causes the link target to become further engaged, and sets up the link request as a natural progression of the conversation.

## CLOSING

The key thing in this phase is to only pull the trigger on asking for a link after context and value are established. The link request then becomes an aside to the correspondence, rather than the main subject of the correspondence.

At the end of our sustain phase, Zelda, our Robot Cartoon Blogger, has taken the bait, realizing that the link builder potentially has something of value to her. She then puts the link builder in a position to close the deal. The nature of the conversation puts Zelda in a position where she is comfortable enough to make the request so that when the link builder requests the link, it is natural for him to ask for something in return.

Princess Zelda,

Hmmm... well I don't make it a habit to do this, but since you have such good taste in cartoons....

Sure, I can get you two tickets to see the film in your local theater, but in return can you write a review or write another one of your great articles and link back to our site?

If that works just shoot me your closest theater and I will send you a Fandango confirmation code for your tickets.

Also, are you on Twitter? I'd love to keep up with the stuff you are posting on your blog!

-Link

Link of Hyrule
Transformers Web Outreach Team
mike@transformersmovie.com
www.transformersmovie.com

Just like that, we've built a link by talking about our favorite cartoons. The challenge—and the fun—is in finding something that interests both of you, and then using that information to build a relationship. The less you have to offer in the form of incentives, the more sustaining and rapport building you will need to do in order to build the link. Do not think that this method only works with incentives. Value can be established in many ways when building a relationship.

A caveat that I should offer here is that it is painfully obvious when this approach does not work because people will not reciprocate the engagement. Your email might result in a simple "thanks for reading" response. In this case, you can decide whether you want to do more research to identify a different touch point and try again, or to just move on to someone else. You'll get better at being able to spot a lost cause with a little experience.

## 2. STAND OUT IN THE INBOX

How do you feel about spam? Probably the same way you feel about telemarketers. When people can tell by their caller ID that a telemarketer is calling, they don't pick up the phone. By that same token, if they can tell an email is spam, they avoid it.

Never send an email with "Link Request" or something to that effect in the subject; those emails are doomed to never get opened. You want to take an indirect approach because you don't want the link target to dismiss your email before seeing what you have to say. This is the Trojan Horse approach to link building (Trojan Horse in the classic sense, not the virus).

Let's go back to the email I mentioned earlier in this post. On that day, my inbox was full of spam, and I only opened the one with the subject line "let's work together."

It was clear exactly what every other email was about. However, there was some mystery as to what the "let's work together" email was about. It appeared to be a naturally generated email, and it stood out to me because it looked like someone was requesting to collaborate with me in some way. The sender was a real name, and the subject was lowercased. It resembled the emails I receive from people that want to send me beats, or hire me to appear as a musical guest artist on their albums.

President Obama tricks me into clicking open his emails pretty often, too. I don't always look at who the emails are from when I get them, but most of my friends use short email subjects (like the ones in this image) that cause me to click through.

Even when I do look at the sender's name, it might be just a quick glimpse to make sure it's a person, not a company or www.something.com. It was my assumption that other people reacted this way when I started to apply these principles, and therefore the improvement in response rate is the only thing in the way of science I have to show for this.

However, what I can show you is a clear example of a subject fail.

---------- Forwarded message ----------
From: **1-800 CONTACTS** <info@email.1800contacts.com>
Date: Sat, Jul 16, 2011 at 11:26 AM
Subject: FIRSTNAME, re-ordering your ITEMNAME contacts from 1-800 CONTACTS is fast and easy!

1-800-Contacts clearly runs some sort of CRM software for these types of emails. Either someone was asleep at the wheel or they messed up the input fields. This could easily happen to you if you use a link building program like Link Assistant. Don't be that person. However, judging by the format of the sender and subject fields, it is highly unlikely that these emails will have an open rate worth talking about.

While I'm sure there are more comprehensive studies on email optimization, here's a quick summary:

**Tips for standing out in the inbox**

- Keep subjects short.
- Keep subjects natural.
- Do not use "Link Request."
- Send emails as a person (not as a company or "web team").
- Include a natural salutation (since the first line of the email will appear next to the subject).

## 3. DO YOUR RESEARCH

I don't want to encourage you to stalk your targets, so ... study your targets. Bloggers and webmasters are certainly not the most private people in the world; they have shared their personal thoughts, favorite music, films, travel plans and other endless minutia about themselves online for years. Use this publicly shared information to develop your context for the initial email.

User data drives models of people for targeting your broad messaging, so it only makes sense to use user data to create the context for your specific messaging.

Don't get caught up in the whole romantic comedy "OMG I manipulated you but it turns out I really love you and I wish I could take it all back" aspect of this. Think of it as a way to increase your odds of effectively relating to someone. Again, **Context is King**.

Choose something that relates back to the content that the person wrote about on their site. The subject should be something that you related to, can offer insight into, and speak about at length. So if I'm doing link building as illustrated in the example emails, I might check Zelda's Facebook, Twitter, and Last.Fm accounts, and then weave into a conversation how Voltron was actually created after Power Rangers, contrary to popular belief, as a reaction to the stance she takes in her blog post. Then I might end the email with something to the effect of "Wouldn't Radiohead be a great choice for the Voltron soundtrack?" Now we have a conversation that is still contextually relevant, if only tangentially so, to the topic at hand.

Researching your targets turns link building into a video game—with a strategy guide.

## 4. OFFER VALUE

We tend to think of link building in terms of "what can this site offer me?" rather than "what is it about my site that will be interesting or useful to this webmaster or blogger?" or "what of value can I introduce this person to?"

Depending on where you are contacting them from, simply the fact that you have reached out to this person can offer some value. If you are working for a client with a good reputation in the space you are building links for, it's important to obtain an email alias on their domain. For example, if you are doing link building for Moz, you should have a Moz email address. That way, if you are following up with a blogger who has written a review about Moz's software offerings, for instance, they will feel as though their voice has been heard by Moz.

In some cases, you may be link building for a client who has not established a reputation in the space, so it's important that you share something of tangible value with your link target. Perhaps you have a link to some content important to the niche that hasn't been seen by too many people—share it with your link target. Maybe an awesome video has just floated around your office and you are now having an active email conversation with your link target—toss it in there. Maybe you just have an interesting story that you can share. Failing all that, it's very important to include any client-provided incentives.

The bottom line is this: Approach your link target in the same manner you would when meeting one of your friend's friends, and your efforts will be more effective.

## 5. MAINTAIN THE RAPPORT

No one likes to be used. Therefore, it is important to maintain an active rapport with your new friends. If you only contact them when you need a new link, they will be less inclined to help you out. Twitter is the perfect place to maintain this rapport. Follow your newfound friends and encourage them to follow you. Be sure to retweet their links and engage with them from time to time so that you are in constant contact. This process continues to generate a shared context, so even if you faked your way this far (which won't be the case if you have a genuine interest in people), you can easily start the process again based on their latest tweets.

## CONCLUSION

Is this approach scalable? Well, it depends how much information you need to sift through to find a hook for the person you're reaching out to. Once you go through this process enough times, you'll be able to create shared context in little more than the time it takes to uncover a buried email address. However, outreach link building isn't the place you need to be looking for scalability to begin with.

The benefits of this approach are two-fold. First, your link building becomes more effective, and while you may not reach out to as many people, you will convert a lot more of the people that you do. Second, you are building a rapport with many people that you can then activate in social media as it becomes more of a ranking factor.

Link building is often viewed as an arduous task that no one really wants to engage in, but it really shouldn't be seen that way. Link building is really an opportunity to make friends throughout the web and social media. Perform your link building like a marksman, not a drive-by shooter, and you will see better results.

**Context is King. Link Building is Dead. Long Live Relationship Building.**

Also, you'll be happy to know that I now have a bed, a desk, a chair and a dresser in my apartment. Definitely give me a shout if you're ever in Brooklyn!

Oh, yes ... I almost forgot to include the infographic. Go easy on me, it's my first one!

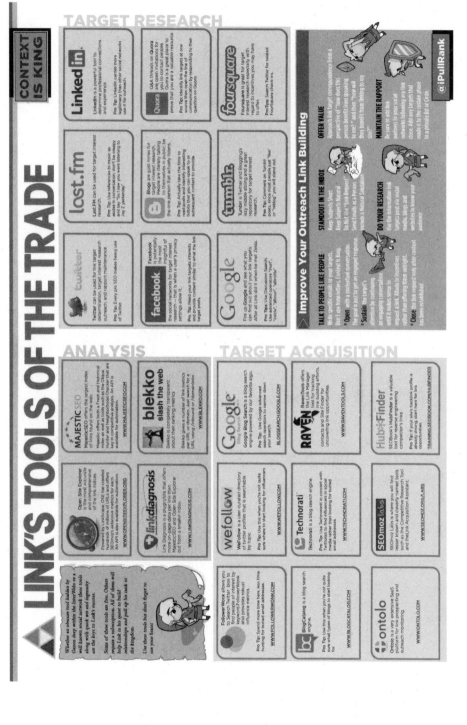

# 17

# A LINK BUILDER'S GMAIL PRODUCTIVITY SETUP (WITH OUTREACH EMAILS FROM 4 INDUSTRY LINK BUILDERS)

*By John Doherty*

---

*Editor's Note: Many of the email productivity tools that John discusses here were brand new (or even in beta) when this post was originally published on Jan. 15, 2012, on The Moz Blog. This post has been revised to reflect subsequent updates to those tools. Even though the game of link building changed dramatically in 2012, these tools are still incredibly useful for increasing outreach email productivity—and email productivity in general. Please note that the outreach email templates at the end of the post have been left in their original form.*

---

BECAUSE LINK BUILDING is hard, we all look for ways to make the process less painful and our outreach more successful. I constantly struggled with how to make my job more effective when working in-house, and since coming to Distilled (www.distilled.net), I have had to become even more of a productivity ninja in order to keep up with the fast pace of an agency.

The goal of this chapter is to teach you some link building ninja ways that will markedly speed up the outreach email process and increase your response rate.

*The tips I give you today apply to people who use Gmail as their email provider. There are probably similar tools available for other programs like Outlook. So take the principles applied here, tailor them to fit your needs, and then share the knowledge!*

## GMAIL TOOLS AND TIPS

Let's look at some Gmail tools, tips, and tricks that can improve your outreach email productivity.

### GMAIL SHORTCUTS

Gmail shortcuts are an email productivity ninja's best friend. Once you enable them, you have a whole wealth of shortcuts to use so that you never have to touch your mouse unless you need to edit text or do something like inserting a canned response. You'll find that shortcuts tend to eliminate many superfluous steps. When you use them in combination with the other tools mentioned, you can drastically speed up your email processing time.

*Editor's Note: To use Gmail shortcuts, you need a Standard 101/102-Key or Natural PS/2 Keyboard. To turn them on, log in to Gmail online. In the upper right-hand corner of your inbox (underneath the link to your Google+ profile, if you have one), you should see a gear icon. Click on it and then select General Settings. Finally, choose the option next to Keyboard shortcuts to turn them on. Gmail shortcuts are case-sensitive.*

The most important shortcuts are, in my opinion:

- c—compose a new message
- e—archive a message
- g then i—return to inbox from a message
- r—reply to a message
- a—reply all to a message
- f—forward the message
- j—when in your inbox, move to the next message
- k—when in your inbox, move to the previous message
- x—when in your inbox, mark an email. Most useful when processing out emails that don't require any attention (such as daily emails).

You should think about shortcuts as "recipes" of sorts. Use them in combination, like Tab+Enter for sending, j+x+e for archiving messages in your inbox, or r+Message+Tab+Enter for responding to a message. String them together, and you'll be more awesome.

For a complete list of Gmail shortcuts, visit `http://mz.cm/XD5ort`.

> *Pro tip: Combine these shortcuts with Send and Archive (mentioned below) to take your processing to the next level.*

## CANNED RESPONSES

Canned Responses are something that our New York Sales Exec Ron Garrett recently introduced me to. A Gmail Labs tool, it allows you to save email templates to use so that you are not constantly copying and pasting from one source to another, risking making a mistake.

To enable Canned Responses, click on the Labs tab in Gmail Settings. Enable "Canned Responses by Chad P", save your changes, and return to your Gmail inbox. As you can see in the image, the Canned Responses tool installs a "Canned responses" button right under the Subject field. You can use this to save drafts of canned responses for quick access.

> ***Editor's Note:*** *The process for setting up a Gmail canned response is slightly different if you are using the new Gmail Compose view. After you compose an email in a new email, click on the triangle on the right side of the compose window and select "Canned responses." Finally, click on "New canned response…."*

Here is how a canned email might look if I was sending an email to Tom Critchlow:

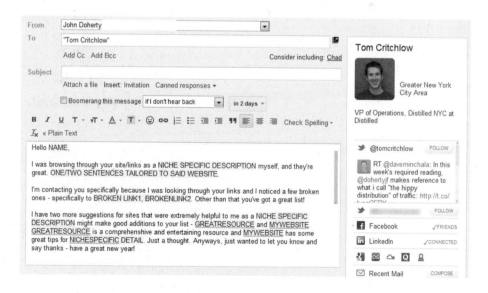

> *Pro tip: Highlight the text to change in yellow so that you make sure to insert all relevant information.*

Make sure you check out the example link building emails from some industry experts at the end of this chapter.

## RAPPORTIVE

Rapportive is a Gmail plugin that I've been hyping recently, because it's so freakin' awesome (see `www.johnfdoherty.com/rapportive-linkbuilding-tool`). The idea is simple, but the outcome is powerful.

After you download it from `Rapportive.com` and install into Gmail, the Rapportive box will appear on the right side of your screen when you go to compose a new email. The social features element is what makes this plugin so powerful for link building and connecting with others.

You can see many different ways for you to connect with, or build rapport with (see what I did there?), your email contact. You can even connect with them formally by sending a LinkedIn invitation directly from Rapportive.

BOOM.

Check out all the options I get when I go to email Ross:

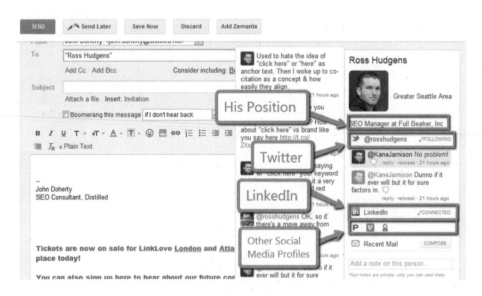

*Pro tip: Use Rapportive to help you find contact emails. If you are not sure of the combination of their company's email (john.doherty, john-doherty, jdoherty, dohertyj, for example), try different combinations. When you hit the right one, their information will appear :-)*

## BOOMERANG

Boomerang (www.boomeranggmail.com) is a Gmail plugin that I found via Napoleon Suarez. After you install it, a little boomerang icon will appear in your Gmail screen and a "Send Later" button will appear on every email you go to send. When expanded, it looks like this:

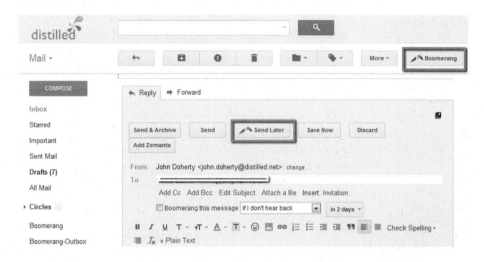

The really powerful features of Boomerang enable you to:

- Send emails at a designated time. (For example, you write an email at 2 a.m. on Saturday night. Set it to send at 9 a.m. on Monday so it doesn't look like you are working at 2 a.m. on Saturday night.)
- Send an email back to the top of your inbox at a later point in the day. (I do this with emails that I want to respond to at a designated email time later in the day.)
- Send the message back to yourself if you don't hear back within a set amount of time. (This is great for re-contacting people you emailed about links.)

I'd love to hear other ways you find to use Boomerang as well!

> *FYI—You receive a certain number of Gmail Boomerangs per month for free, and then it moves to a paid service. If I was doing more link outreach, I definitely think the paid service would be worth the money, but at this point I have never hit my max. Boomerang may also be purchased for Outlook (PC only) following a free trial period* (www.baydin.com/boomerang).

## UNDO SEND

Another awesome Gmail Labs tool that is handy to have around is Undo Send by Yuzo Fujishima, a Google engineer based in Tokyo. What it does is allow you a time buffer (about five seconds) to recall an email before it sends.

Once you send the email, you will be returned to your email but this little box will show up:

> *Pro tip: To avoid sending an email early, even with this tool, don't put the recipient's name in the To: field until you're done. After you've completed your email, use the Shift+tab combination twice to return to the To: field. Insert the email address, tab three times, and Send and Archive.*

## SEND AND ARCHIVE

The final Gmail productivity ninja tip I have for you is the Send & Archive Gmail feature. After you enable it by selecting the "Show 'Send & Archive' button in reply" in your Gmail Settings, a Send & Archive button will appear on your Reply screen. If you're an Inbox Zero nut (like most of Distilled), you're already excited to try this.

Here's a screenshot showing the button:

Now, when you have finished replying to an email and you are ready to send it, simply Tab from your message and press Enter.

Boom! Email sent and the message is now out of your inbox. You've just eliminated the step of archiving the message after the fact. Go and do something awesome.

> *Pro tip: Just enable and use it. Nothing more to be said.*

# LINK-BUILDING EMAIL TEMPLATES FROM INDUSTRY LINK BUILDERS

I emailed some friends to ask for some examples of actual link request emails that they have sent to prospective link partners. The following samples are those examples. Please note that these are drafts, and emails should always be as customized as possible for the recipient.

## BROKEN LINK BUILDING

Ross Hudgens is the SEO Manager at Full Beaker (`www.fullbeaker.com`), a lead-gen focused SEO company outside Seattle. Ross responded to my email with this gem of a broken link email that he sends to people when asking to be included on their list, but wants to provide them value by helping them out with some links broken on their site. Here's the email:

---

Hello NAME,

I was browsing through your site/links as a NICHE SPECIFIC DESCRIPTION myself, and they're great. ONE/TWO SENTENCES TAILORED TO SAID WEBSITE.

I'm contacting you specifically because I was looking through your links and I noticed a few broken ones—specifically to BROKEN LINK1, BROKENLINK2. Other than that you've got a great list!

I have two more suggestions for sites that were extremely helpful to me as a NICHE SPECIFIC DESCRIPTION might make good additions to your list - GREATRESOURCE and MYWEBSITE. GREATRESOURCE is a comprehensive and entertaining resource and MYWEBSITE has some great tips for NICHESPECIFIC DETAIL. Just a thought.

Anyways, just wanted to let you know and say thanks - have a great new year!

Regards,

EMAIL NAME

---

Notice how he has put information to change in CAPS so as not to forget to change a field. Boom!

> **Editor's Note:** Ross Hudgens left Full Beaker last year to found Siege Media (`http://siegemedia.com`), a digital marketing consultancy based in Los Angeles.

## GUEST POSTING

This email comes from Distilled SEO Geoff Kenyon, who works in our Seattle office. Geoff has been killing it for his clients for a while now, so I asked him for an example of what he sends to people. He came back with this example of a templated email sent to people for guest posts.

---

Hey NAME,

I saw that you're the THEIR POSITION over at THEIR COMPANY and I wanted to get in touch. I've seen guest contributions before on the TOPIC blog and wanted to know if you were open to any more guest contributions. I am looking to write about something related to NICHE and thought that the topics I had in mind may go well on the TOPIC blog.

I was thinking about the following subjects:

  IDEA 1

  IDEA 2

  IDEA 3

What do you think about these? If you're interested, I am happy to get something written up and sent over to you - or if you have another topic you'd like to see covered, I am more than happy to write on that.

Thanks,

NAME

---

*Do not mass email a ton of people your content ideas, but customize them to appeal to each recipient person. Also, just don't mass email. Send emails one at a time. It doesn't scale easily, but it's more effective. Finally, don't send template-based emails like this to high-level contacts. Those MUST be totally personalized.*

## PR

This next example comes from Paul May over at Buzzstream (www.buzzstream.com), a link building CRM tool that we use and love at Distilled. Paul sent me this example of an email that they sent out during their most recent launch. I think it shows a great mix of professional and personal tones, and like that it includes a lot of detail.

I especially love the "Pick your poison ;)" part!

Hi ,

Don't know if you remember me, but I've commented on a number of your blog posts and we've written a couple of posts on the (YOUR COMPANY) blog that continued discussions you'd started (I think the TOPIC post was the most recent one). I wanted to reach out to you about YOUR COMPANY, the PR/SEO startup I co-founded.

We're now preparing to launch (DATE) and I wanted to see if we could set up a time to brief you on it. QUICK BACKGROUND ABOUT YOUR COMPANY. WHY YOUR COMPANY IS GREAT.

Here's the gist. You can:

SELLING POINT 1
SELLING POINT 2
SELLING POINT 3

Launch is happening DATE. We'd love to find some time to show the thing to you. Are you comfortable with an embargo until TIME a.m. ET on DAY, DATE (i.e. late Monday night PT)? If so, here are some suggested times...pick your poison ;)

TIME OPTION 1
TIME OPTION 2
TIME OPTION 3

Thanks in advance.

Regards, NAME

## PUSH CONTENT

This final example comes from Mike Essex at Koozai (www.koozai.com) in the UK. Mike shared this example email that he sends to people when they are pushing out content that they have created, to help generate a buzz. In Mike's own words: "The first method I use is to find content that we have, which could be relevant to other websites and then I get in touch with them to ask them to link or continue to debate the issue. This works well as it gives them a reason to link, and an opportunity to add new content to their websites."

Here's the example:

---

Hi NAME,

ONE OR TWO SENTENCES ABOUT THE PURPOSE OF THE EMAIL AND WHY YOU CREATED THE CONTENT. ALSO, WHY THEY SHOULD CARE ABOUT THE CONTENT.

The guide can be found at LINK and I'd love if you could share this with your readers and help make them aware of THE POINT OF THE RESOURCE, and how they can help. If you need any further information please let me know.

NAME

---

## EXCHANGE FOR A LINK (BUT NOT A LINK EXCHANGE)

This next email comes from Allie Brown at SEER Interactive (www.seerinteractive.com). Link building used to be all about link exchanges. I give you a link, you give me a link, everyone's happy. Those days are over, so we either have to create content for people to link to, or offer someone something in return (that's not a link). That's what I like about this email from Allie.

---

Hi NAME,

My name is Allie and I work with [Client] online marketing team.

First, I have to thank you for repeatedly featuring [Client] on [your blog name]. The [client] team truly loves it when their customers share their favorite looks with others on their personal blogs.

Secondly, I wanted to see if you would be interested in linking to [Client] the next time you feature one of their products. I noticed that you often mention us in your [XYZ] posts and I want to propose an idea that I think we could both benefit from.

In exchange for linking to [Client], we'd like to post a Tweet about your blog sometime within the next week. As you may know, we have over [x] followers, so the opportunity for exposure is pretty grand. You'd also be helping our team out by sending your readers directly to our site when they see a product they like.

Let me know if you're interested in this idea, and hopefully we can find some way to work together!

Thanks again for all your support and Happy New Year!

---

## INCENTIVIZED REVIEWS FOR ECOMMERCE

This email template comes from Abbott Shea, also from SEER. This email proposes some free product in exchange for someone leaving a review. It provides a lot of detail and adds value to the recipient.

---

Subject: Merrrrrrry Christmas! Wait, too early....?

Body:

Hi [Name],

My name is Abbott, and I work with [client] web promotions team. I came across [blog name] and wanted to see if you were interested in working with us. Our site, [client] has over 48,000 custom [product] designs across 113 categories. We were inspired by [something about their site], and seeing as how you love the holidays just as much as we do we'd like to provide you with 5 free Christmas cards for a product review on [URL].

You can either design these cards yourself with your own photos and text or select one from our already pre-designed cards - regardless we'll be crediting you with free shipping. Please let me know if you are interested in this idea or if you have any suggestions of how we can collaborate on something else. I look forward to hearing from you!

Take care,

Abbott

---

I hope this post has been helpful to you, and that you will share any email productivity tips that you have with the Moz community, especially for people using Outlook as that has not been talked about much in this chapter. Cheers!

# 18

# PUTTING GUEST POST OUTREACH THEORIES TO THE TEST [WITH SOME REAL-WORLD DATA]

*By James Agate*

---

*Editor's Note:* *Almost three months after this post was originally published to* The Moz Blog *(on Feb. 9, 2012), Google rolled out the Penguin algorithm update. Penguin changed the game for link builders who previously relied on generic, mass-solicited guest blogging campaigns as their primary means of acquiring links.*

*Guest blogging is no longer an effective strategy for building links in and of itself, and quality and diversity of links matters much more than quantity does. Nevertheless, high-quality guest blogging it is still a valuable activity that can effectively supplement both comprehensive link building and content creation strategies that make use of diverse tactics, especially when it is approached on a personal level that is far more organic than scientific.*

---

I WANTED TO bring you all some data right from a few of our real-world campaigns. As a business, we systemize a great deal and monitor a lot of processes, so it made sense for me to put some of this data to use and try to prove/disprove any commonly held theories about outreach.

The following is based on a sample of 400 guest posts that we placed for clients over a three-month period (Nov. 2011 through Jan. 2012). While the data isn't conclusive, I feel it does provide some good starting points for you to explore in your own outreach campaigns. As with most things, the best strategy is for you to test it out for yourself in the industry you work in.

# THEORY #1: BEING A WOMAN WILL GET YOU MORE LINKS

Speak to nearly anyone who has been building links for a while, and they will have at least come across the theory that you are more likely to be successful approaching someone with an offer to guest post if you are a woman. I would think this stems from the widely held belief (right or wrong) that women are more trustworthy and well-meaning than men.

I wanted to investigate this theory in a little more depth. Quite by accident, of the 400 posts in our sample, it was roughly a 50/50 split, with a woman conducting the outreach 52 percent of the time.

- 790 potential sites were contacted.
- 411 were contacted by a woman.
- 379 were contacted by a man.

## BATTLE OF THE SEXES: WHO PERFORMED BETTER?

Here are the results of our outreach attempts:

- 437 positive responses were received. (Remember, there is a small attrition rate which has to be accounted for within the guest posting process where the link partner either doesn't accept the content or doesn't deliver on his/her end of the bargain.)
- 263 positive responses were received by a woman (64 percent positive response).
- 174 positive responses were received by a man (45.9 percent positive response).

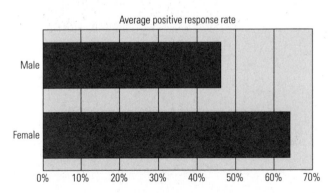

Average positive response rate

You might argue that this difference in performance between the genders could be attributed to a number of things:

- Some are better at outreach than others. While this might be true, all receive the same training, and any slight differences should be negated by the comparable training.
- Consultants have different methods. While some consultants may use slightly different methods to perform their outreach, we have systemized our process and continue to innovate, as a team, by sharing best practices. Therefore, any impact due to slightly different outreach methods is likely to be negated.
- Consultants contacted different websites. Again, there is a very real possibility that the difference in performance is attributable to the "leads" each consultant received. We do have different consultants who work and specialize in different industries, so this could potentially have an impact.

To really put this theory to the test, though, we had one of our female consultants get in touch with five potential link partners who had either declined the offer of a guest post or requested payment for a guest post from one of our male outreach consultants.

When a female consultant made contact, they managed to reduce the price of the paid placement (we didn't pay for it anyway), and we got a positive response from two of the potential link partners. To clarify, that was pitching exactly the same website and roughly the same content as before.

That's a pretty interesting find, I'm sure you'll agree.

## THEORY #2: JOB TITLE MATTERS

Depending on whether the client has a preference, we usually approach the link partner as either an agency employee or an individual/freelancer.

Some clients like us to contact link partners as if we are employees of their company, while others prefer that we disclose our agency connections. On the face of it, this may stir some ethical debate. However, in these situations we merely act as the facilitator between our freelance content team and the host blog, and since we strive to create win-win-win situations, I have no problem operating this way.

In all honesty, each of these approaches has its advantages and disadvantages. (While contacting as an agency employee might invoke more requests for payment, it does make the option of continuing the relationship and benefiting your other clients much more practical.) Let's put that aside for now, though, and focus purely on success rates.

- 790 potential sites were contacted.
- 297 were contacted by a freelancer.
- 373 were contacted by an agency employee.
- 120 were contacted by an in-house employee.

In cases where the partner was approached by a freelancer, a positive response was received 189 times (63.6 percent positive response). In cases where the partner was approached by an in-house employee, a positive response was received 78 times (65 percent positive). Finally, in cases where the partner was approached by an agency employee, we received positive responses 170 times (45.6 percent positive).

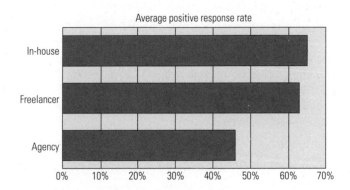

The results surprised me because one would think that an email from someone working directly for an organization that is going to benefit from the guest post would result in more declines, or at least more requests for some form of payment. Clearly though, trust is an important factor when it comes to largely unsolicited (albeit well researched and properly pitched) offers of guest posts.

## THEORY #3: TIMING IS IMPORTANT

I was really excited to pull together the data for this one because I was confident that timing really mattered, especially in regards to the introductory email.

While we don't actively record the precise time an email is sent, we do keep a note of the time of day (i.e., morning, afternoon, or evening) for the recipient. We're based in the UK, so running campaigns for our overseas clients requires rigorous planning and execution if we are to get the timing right.

In this case, I found the data inconclusive. This is because when you average the response rate out across industries and countries (as I did in this case), it is only logical that no correlation will be easily identifiable because no two prospects are the same—different industries, different time zones, and so on.

This doesn't mean you can't take advantage of timing, though:

- Recording when your prospect is at their most responsive is helpful for keeping the process moving, especially if they become a little wayward right before the agreed publish date.

■ Observing patterns in specific niches can be useful. For example, I have identified a responsiveness pattern across some of the sports blogs we work with (most, not all, respond in their late evening), which could be attributed to the fact they are hobby bloggers with full-time jobs and a family who sneak in a bit of "blog time" once the rest of the family has gone to bed.

# THEORY #4: PERSONALISATION IS WORTH IT (OR IS IT?)

We wanted to guarantee a quality standard with our outreach processes, so we approved templates that we tailor for each prospect.

In certain situations where we feel it will be beneficial, we will write emails completely from scratch.

In the course of our client campaigns, we don't actually send out any generic emails, but in order to compare the difference in outcomes between a personalized approach and a brute force (mass emailing) approach, we conducted a small experiment:

■ We sent 1,000 emails in total.

■ All were completely templated, offering no specific client website details.

■ Prospects were offered five relevant articles with non-specific explanations.

■ We were careful to ensure full CAN-SPAM compliance (`http://business.ftc. gov/documents/bus61-can-spam-act-compliance-guide-business`).

■ We focused on the Home Improvement/Interior Design niche.

We gathered the list using common guest post opportunity footprints, and ScrapeBox did all the heavy lifting. With two clicks we had many, many thousands of URLs, and the email harvester pulled together a list of contact details. We used two virtual assistants to do the emailing. They averaged around 125 emails an hour sending them one at a time—they were seriously efficient!

## THE RESULTS

I have to say, I was surprised by the results. Given the fact that it was a relatively small sample from just one niche, I would say additional data needs to be gathered before we can draw any final conclusions:

■ 36 agreed to take a guest post from us (a near 4 percent conversion rate).

■ 3 agreed to review a post.

■ 1 wanted payment. (I expected this number to be much higher.)

■ 12 wanted to unsubscribe.

■ 6 responded to say they weren't interested.

When the results first came in, I assumed that it would be a load of poor quality "www. this-is-my-interior-design-blog.info" style websites, but it wasn't. Many who accepted had a PageRank of 2 or 3 with somewhat relevant domain names.

## WHAT DID WE LEARN?

Well, we learned that the brute force approach does work to a certain degree.

You might be thinking, what's the problem then? Let's hire a virtual army, crank up the Scrapeboxing, and enjoy soaring above the competition.

In reality, though, this probably isn't the way to scale your guest posting campaigns. With this kind of practice you can easily blanket an entire industry in a few hours. Consequently, though, you may well burn your bridges and dismiss any hopes of guest posting on authoritative blogs in the space in the future.

In moderation, however, this method could be applied with some success, perhaps following a categorization of prospects—i.e., tailor outreach to the high-value prospects, and roll out a more templated approach for targeting mid-value prospects. This would assist in adding more volume (and likely improve the turnaround time) of your campaign.

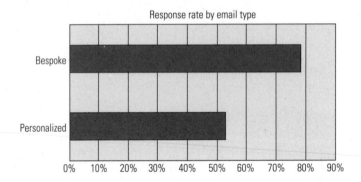

We make a note of whether the email sent was tailored or entirely bespoke (templated) and the results align with what you might expect. Completely bespoke emails generate a higher response rate, although the caveat to this is, of course, is that customizing every email just isn't possible if you want a campaign to be of a certain scale.

If you contacted 10 partners with a tailored email, you would get fewer positive responses, but similarly, try sending 100 completely from scratch emails. You need a lot of people and that costs money, which then impacts the ROI of a campaign.

The trade-off, and what I believe to be the happy medium, is a solid template that is tailored to each recipient. Be flexible with your templates, too, and allow them to evolve as you see certain elements working better than others. Innovate, then scale.

## THEORY #5: THE STYLE OF OUTREACH EMAIL HAS AN IMPACT

As mentioned, we have a number of base templates for our consultants to customize. We have one version which is very conversion focused, and another which is more soft-conversion—both variations are useful, just in different industries.

- **Template A** has very proactive wording that encourages moving to the next step, selecting one of the articles rather than asking whether they'll accept a guest post.
- **Template B** uses much softer wording that works well in industries where guest posting is less prevalent and where the prospect needs a bit more hand-holding.

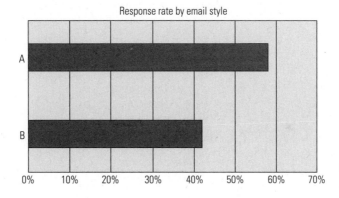

Response rate by email style

As you will note, the more proactive template A is more effective in terms of generating a response. However, given that these styles are effective in different industries, both templates will continue to have a place in our work. That being said, I found it useful and really interesting to compare their performance side by side.

## THEORY #6: PERSISTENCE PAYS OFF

I believe in creating win-win-win situations when it comes to guest posting, and because we go further to research and evaluate prospective websites, I see no issue in following up with the potential link partner three times before writing them off as unresponsive. If you categorize the responses received in relation to the number of times contacted, it becomes evident that persistence really does pay off.

You will note from the chart below that around 30 percent of positive responses received agreed only after the second or third email.

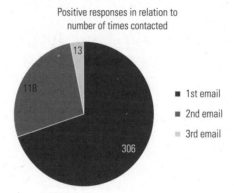

Positive responses in relation to
number of times contacted

■ 1st email
■ 2nd email
■ 3rd email

Had we not been persistent, we would have needed to find, research, and contact additional link partners, which would have greatly increased our workload.

Persistence is one thing, but relentless pestering is another. Follow up on leads, but be polite, and for the benefit of all of us in the industry, know when you should be taking no for an answer.

## WHAT'S THE PERFECT COMBINATION?

Is it best to be an in-house female link builder pitching content in the evening three times? No, not always. Different strokes for different folks. To summarize, it's important to test what works best in *your* industry.

Remember, this is a relatively small internal data sample, so it is by no means perfect. There are always multiple factors in play at any one given time. Despite this, I do feel the study is valid enough to be useful. Hopefully, it will act as a starting point for you to develop your own study or shape your initial guest post outreach strategy.

# V

# CONVERSION RATE OPTIMIZATION

*By Thomas Høgenhaven*

THE AIM OF conversion rate optimization (CRO) is to improve the performance of a landing page or website in terms of measurable actions users take that support business goals (that is, conversions). Depending on the particular business, desired conversions can be quite different from site to site, even within niche industries. Some of the most common conversions include:

- Purchases
- Form submissions (such as newsletter sign-ups or contest entries)
- Link clicks (such as affiliate links or email signature links)
- Social shares
- Downloads

Mastering CRO is crucial to succeeding in the online marketplace. Websites with high conversion rates are better at monetizing traffic than websites with low conversion rates. Their proven ROI allows them to invest more in marketing channels such as SEO and social media. Moreover, increased competition across online channels (both paid and organic) is driving down profit margins. As the cost of attracting website visitors continues to increase, conversion rates will become even more important in the future. A business' ability to convert the traffic it already has into paying customers can and will be the difference between growth and extinction.

There is little reason not to engage in CRO. Which leads to the next question: Is CRO hard to do? Is it really *that* difficult to tell the difference between high and low converting pages? It's probably harder than most of us think it is. According to Avinash Kaushik, "80% of the time you/we are wrong about what a customer wants/expects from our site experience." (See `www.kaushik.net/avinash/experimentation-and-testing-a-primer`.) Although an 80 percent failure rate sounds remarkably high, numbers from successful companies support this claim. Internal experiments at Microsoft show that only around 33 percent of all experiments produce an improvement, while another 33 percent have no significant change in performance, and the last 33 percent perform worse than before. Similarly, Netflix considers 90 percent of new features to be wrong. Amazon is more optimistic, assuming a success rate on new features of just under 50 percent. Even if we are better at guessing than these companies are, we will never be right often enough to make good business decisions based on gut feelings alone. This is why it is so important to conduct experiments before implementing new ideas.

> *Statistics from the preceding paragraph are from "Online Experimentation at Microsoft," by Ron Kohavi, Thomas Crook, and Roger Longbotham, 2009 (`www.exp-platform.com/Documents/ExP_DMCaseStudies.pdf`)*

## THE EVOLUTION OF CRO

Although CRO is a fairly new discipline, it has roots in ecommerce lead generation, which has been around since the early 2000s. In the early days of CRO, the aim was quite simple: to improve the performance of a signup form or sales page by tweaking design elements (e.g., buttons, headlines, copy, and images). The CRO process was isolated to particular landing pages and decoupled from the overall business strategy. The aim was to generate more leads and sales, not change or improve the overall business. The term "landing page optimization" describes this process well.

It quickly became clear that bigger changes have greater effects than small changes. Making big, bold changes can lead to vast improvements—and equally large failures. Some of the case studies examined in Chapter 21, "Lessons Learned from 21 Case Studies in Conversion Rate Optimization," are quite dramatic. On some pages, everything is changed. On others, the majority of the content is simply removed in order to reduce complexity.

Most highly successful CRO efforts result from big changes. But it is hard to make big changes when you are only working on a single landing page. Sure, you can change the presentation of the product, highlight different USPs, add great testimonials, and the like. But such changes only scratch the surface. Focusing on landing page optimization is too confining—too isolated—to create vast improvements. A broader perspective on CRO is needed, one that involves changing key benefits of products, creating engaging storytelling, improving customer service, nurturing community, and making binding commitments to customers (such as 30-day money back guarantees).

# TESTING AND CRO

CRO is more complex than it was just a few years ago. Today, most businesses need to optimize for multiple goals. Ecommerce websites not only want to optimize their sales funnels, they want to optimize their entire brand for user generated reviews, social shares, and links. This makes the tests more complicated.

As marketers, we are getting better at testing. But we still need to be smarter about *what* we test and *how* we test it. In order to figure out what to test, we need to collect qualitative and quantitative data, and then use it to formulate hypotheses about what we think will improve the conversion rate and why. We need to spend more time reflecting on why a certain change affects behavior, so that we can eventually understand (a) what makes some potential customers convert, and (b) what makes other potential customers *not* buy.

Equally important to carefully considering what we test is *how* we test it. Experimental methodology is crucial in the CRO process. In order to improve the conversion rate on a page, different variations are tested through A/B/n tests or multivariate tests (these are further examined in Chapter 22, "An Illustrated Guide to Web Experiments"). If we fail to run statistically valid experiments, we will make decisions based on highly dubious grounds. This is why it is important to understand the basic statistics behind experimentation. For example, when conducting a simple A/B test, we often notice very large differences between the two variations when data starts coming in. But over time, the differences will become smaller. Because there are only few data points early in the experiment, there is greater fluctuation in the results. This helps us understand why it is crucial not to get excited too early on, and to wait for statistically significant results before making any conclusions.

At this point, the CRO field is still influenced by persistent myths: red buttons convert better than green ones; having an arrow next to the call-to-action (CTA) improves conversion rate; short pages convert better than long ones. These claims are true in *some* contexts, but not all. These myths do not evolve out of thin air, after all. Some case studies (either from blog posts or conference presentations) document that red buttons outperform green buttons by a significant margin. But the lesson from such case studies is not in the substantive results (red button versus green button), but in the process that leads to the results. If you are going to follow best practices, test them in the specific context they are meant to be implemented in first.

Which leads us to the CRO blogger's dilemma: Many people want fast and easy ways to improve their conversion rates. Blog posts and presentations that focus on the long, cumbersome process that generates test results tend to be received with less enthusiasm than *quick wins* presentations and posts. So bloggers do their best to provide substantive knowledge, even though it is highly dubious to what degree the results are valid outside of the case study. This means that we tend to copy successful business *results* when we should be imitating their *processes*.

Two of the chapters in this Part, "The 12-Step Landing Page Rehab Program" and "An Illustrated Guide to Web Experiments," therefore focus on the CRO process rather than substantive findings. The first post provides a framework for inspiring and conducting tests, while the latter provides methodological insights into conducting scientifically valid experiments.

## THE FUTURE OF CRO

We will never be done improving and optimizing our landing pages and websites. While investments in CRO may have diminishing returns over time, it is very unlikely that you'll ever get to the optimal point. The web is too dynamic to reach this point. This makes it pretty safe to assume that there is a future for CRO. But how will it look? Optimizing conversion rates on a single page is good for a business. Optimizing the conversion rate on thousands of pages is much more valuable. This is why it is important to consider the degree to which CRO scales. There are at least two good ways to make CRO scale: hypothesis formulation and automation.

As mentioned above, hypotheses ought to be used to generate alternative variations that can be tested. Hypotheses also help us identify the boundaries of our experiments, which helps us to implement winning variations for similar situations without having to conduct near-identical tests. Understanding human psychology and social psychology helps us generate great hypotheses. Therefore, it is fitting that the first chapter in this Part is "An Illustrated Guide to the Science of Influence and Persuasion."

Many CRO activities can be automated. For example, *The Huffington Post* tests different headlines and images for the same story in order to optimize clicks and shares. The winning variation is automatically implemented. This makes it possible to conduct a large number of tests without going through the tedious work of reviewing each test and implementing the winning variation manually. This is especially important in industries where each page/product has a short life cycle.

*HuffPo* does not test random headlines, either. They use—you guessed it—hypotheses to generate alternative headlines: whether angle X or Y appeals more to the reader, or whether a person's name or his role appeals more to the reader (i.e., John Barrasso or GOP Senator).

We will never be done optimizing, whether it's optimizing for search engines or conversions. It is a circular process of research and testing. Sound hypotheses and automation will help us do it more efficiently.

Let the optimization begin.

# 19

# AN ILLUSTRATED GUIDE TO THE SCIENCE OF INFLUENCE AND PERSUASION

*By Rand Fishkin*

---

**Editor's Note:** *Ironically enough, the book that inspired Rand to create this visual reference in 2010, <u>Influence: Science & Practice</u>, was made into a graphic novel last year.*

---

CONVERSION RATE OPTIMIZATION, the practice of improving the number of visitors who take a desired action on your site, has been a hot topic the last couple of years. There's both an art and a science to the process of turning browsers into buyers, and drive-by readers into email subscribers, Facebook fans, and Twitter followers. In my opinion, no marketer should be engaging in this work without reading Robert Cialdini's seminal work *Influence: Science & Practice* (Pearson, 2008), now available in its fifth edition. I agree wholeheartedly with the assessment of Guy Kawasaki, currently founder and Managing Director at Garage Technologies Ventures and formerly Apple's Chief Evangelist.

> *"This book is the de facto standard to learn the psychology of persuasion. If you don't read it, I hope you enjoy pounding your head against the wall and throwing away marketing dollars."*
> —*Guy Kawasaki (*`www.amazon.com/Influence-Practice-Robert-B-Cialdini/dp/0205609996`*)*

The problem is, not every marketer will read the book, and that leaves a lot of head-shaped holes in a lot of walls. Thus, this chapter is here to help do the next best thing: explain the broad concepts of persuasion in a condensed, illustrated format.

The book covers six major "weapons of influence." I'm going to provide you with an illustration of each concept, followed by some tips and examples of how each can be used to increase online marketing conversions.

# #1 RECIPROCATION

Hold open a door, and you receive a "thank you" and a smile. Send a birthday present to a friend, and you're almost certain to get one in return. Pay for a co-worker's coffee, and she'll pick up the next one. As Cialdini painstakingly details in the book, there is no culture on Earth that does not have this unspoken, yet powerful rule of reciprocation.

Reciprocation in Action

The power of reciprocation relies on several conventions. The request must be "in-kind," which is to say, commensurate with the initial offering. The power is increased if the give-and-take happens in a short time frame. Reciprocity's influence increases with closer relationships, too. It's much harder to resist returning a favor to a friend than it is to refuse reciprocating one from an anonymous website.

**How You Can Leverage Reciprocity**

- Ask for permission to add the recipient to your email marketing lists in exchange for providing him free data and analysis tools.
- Tweet or blog about a prominent person or business in a positive fashion, and then email them to ask if they'll help spread the message.
- Email a site owner about a problem on her site and offer a solution/fix; she'll often follow up by asking how she can return the favor.
- Provide exemplary answers to questions posted in online forums. Leave a final note asking anyone who finds your answer valuable to consider visiting your site and sharing it with friends.
- Share great information on your blog, and ask your readers to subscribe to your feed.

# #2 COMMITMENT AND CONSISTENCY

As humans, we have an insatiable desire for consistency in behavior. It's why we abhor hypocrisy, and embrace leaders who "stick to their guns," sometimes to the point of foolishness. Our need for consistency can be observed through the effectiveness of political tactics like push polling, wherein a paid "surveyor" will call numbers and ask voters whether they'd cast a ballot for "a man who refused to say the Pledge of Allegiance," for instance. The purpose is to get a verbal commitment that will transfer into a vote come election day after the follow-on ad campaign alludes to precisely that inaction from the opposition candidate.

A case study from Cialdini's book illustrates this principle quite elegantly. Researchers on a New York City beach staged thefts to see if onlookers would risk personal harm to stop the "criminal." A research accomplice would listen to music on a blanket near their "test subjects" for several minutes, then stand up and stroll away, leaving behind a nice personal radio. A "thief" would then approach the scene, grab the radio, and attempt to hurry away with it. On average, only 4 in 20 bystanders intervened.

However, when the experiment was changed slightly, the results altered dramatically. In this second scenario, the research accomplice would ask the test subject to "watch my things" before strolling away. Now under the influence of consistency and commitment, 19 of 20 subjects became "virtual vigilantes, running after and stopping the thief, demanding an explanation, often restraining the thief physically or snatching the radio away."

Commitment and Consistency in Action

Commitment and consistency can't happen without that initial action of a response or promise. Cialdini notes that this power increases tremendously if the agreement is written, rather than merely verbal. (Last week, you told us you wanted XYZ ... Guess what? Here it is!)

### How You Can Leverage Commitment and Consistency

- Ask users to answer online questions about their habits and preferences, and then market to them based on their answers.

- Have website visitors sign an online pledge to take a certain action, and then email them at the specified time they have committed to act. The "Quit Facebook Day" movement used this technique. As a result, a number of "Internet famous" Facebook users deleted their personal accounts (see http://venturebeat.com/2010/05/31/quit-facebook-day-flops-as-only-1-in-15000-pledge-to-quit).

- Ask your users/members/fans to commit to doing something if a certain event occurs. For example, let's say that your startup is up for an award. You could ask your fans to offer support by emailing a friend about your service if you win the award. If/when you do win, email your fans an announcement, and request that they share it with their friends.

- Use a landing page plus a funnel process that defines users in a set number of ways based on their answers to multiple-choice questions. Then speak to how your product or service is the right choice for people like them.

# #3 SOCIAL PROOF

If you're walking along a street and see a crowd gathered, it's nearly impossible to resist the urge to go over and investigate for yourself what they are so interested in. If you're at a party and everyone else is drinking, the pressure for you to have a drink rises dramatically. We all hate the horrifyingly over-the-top laugh tracks on TV sitcoms, but TV producers keep using them because they know that the social signal of laughter makes us laugh along, too.

This same phenomenon applies when we judge exceptionally important life decisions like who we should date or marry, where we should go to school, and where we should work. The powerful influence of our peers can't be overlooked in the sphere of marketing.

Social Proof in Action

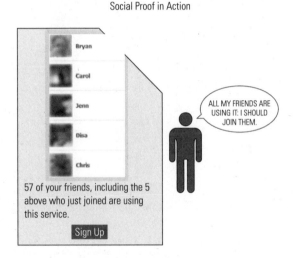

Social proof becomes more powerful when the numbers increase and (especially) when the action-takers become more like the targeted buyer. In other words, if you're selling games to rebellious teenagers, don't show testimonials from middle-aged parents. Show testimonials from rebellious teenagers.

**How You Can Leverage Social Proof**

- Let Facebook users see when their friends have engaged with your site using badges, like buttons, etc. (even more relevant social proof).
- Place testimonials on landing pages and in sales copy from customers that your readers will be able to relate to. Those that feature photos of the customers and their full names work best.
- Utilize the fast-growing and far-reaching online networks Facebook, Twitter, and LinkedIn.

# #4 LIKING

We've heard the phrase a thousand times: "People do business with people they know, like, and trust." It turns out, there's quite a bit of science to support this. Research confirms that factors like physical attractiveness (we like good-looking people), familiarity (we trust people we know), similarity (we like people like us), and compliments (we like people who say nice things about us) all factor into to the principle of "liking."

Liking in Action

It's hard to argue with the power "liking" has on us as consumers. When Will Critchlow (whom I like a lot, despite constantly losing presentation-off battles to him) recommends that I read a book or try a service, it's practically a guarantee I'll do it. (Note to Will: Please don't abuse this power.) Similarly, movie executives realize that asking Tom Hanks to go on the late-night circuit is a great way to drive viewership of a film, while sending Tom Cruise on a similar mission may have the opposite result.

**How You Can Leverage "Liking"**

- Start a blog, Twitter account, or email list. Share your personal thoughts with your audience in a personable, friendly way.
- Employ the power of celebrity in microcosms. If Seth Godin (`http://sethgodin. typepad.com`) wrote a blog post saying that Moz was a valuable resource, then that would likely drive many people who like Seth to take commensurate actions.
- Join in conversations on the web (on forums, in blog comments, on Twitter, via other social services) in ways that engender you positively to those community members. Follow up personally with community leaders and organizers to help spread the liking effect in a more scalable way.

# #5 AUTHORITY

A story from Cialdini's book illustrates this principle so well that I couldn't resist sharing it here:

> *Professors of pharmacy Michael Cohen and Neil Davis attribute much of the problem to the mindless deference given to the "boss" of a patient's case: the attending physician. According to Cohen, "in case after case, patients, nurses, pharmacists, and other physicians do not question the prescription." Take, for example, the strange case of the "rectal earache" reported by Cohen and Davis. A physician ordered ear drops to be administered to the right ear of a patient suffering pain and infection there. Instead of writing out completely the location "Right ear" on the prescription, the doctor abbreviated it so that the instructions read "place in R ear." Upon receiving the prescription, the duty nurse promptly put the required number of ear drops into the patient's anus.*
>
> *Obviously, rectal treatment of an earache made no sense, but neither the patient nor the nurse questioned it. The important lesson of this story is that in many situations in which a legitimate authority has spoken, what would otherwise make sense is irrelevant. In these instances, we don't consider the situation as a whole but attend and respond to only one aspect of it.*

The power of authority can come from a variety of sources. Here are a few examples:

- Clothes—Think of the movie *Catch Me if You Can,* in which Leonardo DiCaprio "becomes" a doctor or pilot simply by changing his attire.
- Titles and prefix/suffixes—Dr., Senator, President, C-level executive all carry weight.
- Context—The famous Milgram study (see http://www.cnr.berkeley.edu/ucce50/ag-labor/7article/article35.htm) in which ordinary people commit horrifying acts simply because they are told to do so by an authority figure.

Authority in Action

Photo of Anthony Bourdain courtesy of Corbis Entertainment

An authority is only influential when the target believes in the power and authenticity of that authority. The stronger the association the target has with the authority, the more powerful the impact. The reverse is also true. Not all authorities influence all people.

**How You Can Leverage Authority**

- Has a well-respected individual or organization endorsed your product/company? Make that a prominent feature when you request an action from your visitors.

- In some cases, the product itself can positively influence sales conversions by demonstrating its value in a concrete way. Software tools, for example, can provide a limited amount of free data to users. This develops trust and confidence in the product, ultimately converting into sales revenue from product/subscription upgrades that give users access to more of the data and features they become reliant on.

- Experts in your field can provide you with great testimonials and endorsements. They need not be recognizable, or even speak to social proof elements if they carry the credentials and weight that will your target audience will respond to.

# #6 SCARCITY

Ever notice that some shops seem to be perpetually running "going out of business" sales? It's no mistake. The power of potential loss is a remarkable influencer. The Rolling Stones' "last ever" tour, the final can of Crystal Pepsi, the limited edition collectors' keepsake (only 70 ever released!). All are examples of the scarcity principle at work.

As Cialdini notes:

> *The feeling of being in competition for scarce resources has powerful motivating properties. The ardor of an indifferent lover surges with the appearance of a rival. It is often for reasons of strategy, therefore, that romantic partners reveal (or invent) the attentions of a new admirer. Salespeople are taught to play the same game with indecisive customers. For example, a realtor who is trying to sell a house to a "fencesitting" prospect sometimes will call the prospect with news of another potential buyer who has seen the house, liked it, and is scheduled to return the following day to talk about terms. When wholly fabricated, the new bidder is commonly described as an outsider with plenty of money: "an out-of-state investor buying for tax purposes" and "a physician and his wife moving into town" are favorites. The tactic, called in some circles "goosing 'em off the fence," can work devastatingly well. The thought of losing out to a rival frequently turns a buyer from hesitant to zealous.*

Scarcity becomes more powerful when it's clear that the resource is finite (houses are great for this reason), and when immediacy is added to the scarcity (as in the case of another buyer on the horizon). Auction sites like eBay combine the power of these persuasion tactics with remarkable results.

**How You Can Leverage Scarcity**

- Offer a special version of your product for a limited time, in limited quantities.
- Feature messages like Expedia's "only two tickets left at this price" or Zappos' "only three pairs in this size in stock" next to search results and product pages to encourage timely sales conversions.
- Create an incentive for the first x number of visitors to take an action.
- Show the number of people viewing an item right on the product page (for example, "Six others currently on this page") to help create excitement and a feeling of immediacy. This works particularly well for one-of-a-kind or limited quantity products.

Individually, these principles are powerful instruments of persuasion. Together, they're a marketing force to be reckoned with. Let's try an experiment and see if I can effectively employ the six principles in relation to Moz. (Please note, I'm not normally this self-promotional, and this exercise is meant to be somewhat tongue-in-cheek.)

1. This blog post is the result of many hours of studying, writing and illustrating. If it's helped your business in some way, we hope you'll say thanks by sharing it through tweets, links, or an email to someone you think would appreciate the reference.

2. Are you the kind of SEO who bases her decisions on data or gut feeling? Close your eyes for a minute and think. If you said "data," I'd urge you to check out the new Keyword Difficulty tool (`http://pro.moz.org/tools/keyword-difficulty`). It will help you make decisions about where and how to compete from a much more data-driven perspective.

3. 2,426 search marketers on Facebook have become fans of Moz (www.facebook.com/moz). Won't you join them?

4. Danny Dover is impossible not to like. Make Danny happy by following him on Twitter - @DannyDover

5. The Search & Social Awards named Moz the best SEO Blog, top SEO community and favorite SEO tool suite this year.

6. This summer, we're throwing our annual conference, MozCon. Ticket prices will be lowest starting with Early Bird savings and will increase for PRO and non-PRO members when they sell out. There are only 400 Early Bird tickets available, so register now—before they're gone!

The next time you make a landing page or try to drive actions on the web, think about how you might leverage these principles of influence to improve your conversion rates.

# 20

# THE 12-STEP LANDING PAGE REHAB PROGRAM

*By Oli Gardner*

---

**Editor's Note:** *The premise that you can increase your conversion rates by improving your landing pages still holds water almost three years after Oli Gardner shared his process for doing just that in this blog post (originally published on the The Moz Blog on July 26, 2010).*

---

AS WITH THAT other program, the first and most critical step is admitting you actually have a problem. So go ahead. Shout it out loud so your coworkers can hear:

*"My name is Earl. My conversion rate sucks, and I can't stop sending expensive PPC traffic to my homepage."*

Feel better? You should.

You just passed the "unofficial" first test of landing page rehab, and now you're ready to take those 12 steps—with the help of your very own rehab sponsor—that'll lift you from that river in Egypt (denial?!?) to a higher place on the conversion charts. This is the intervention your landing pages have been crying out for, so take a deep breath … and let's get started.

Study the 12-step infographic to see where each step in the program should be applied to your conversion funnel. You can see a full-size version of the infographic at `http://unbounce.com/docs/12-step-conversion-rehab.png`.

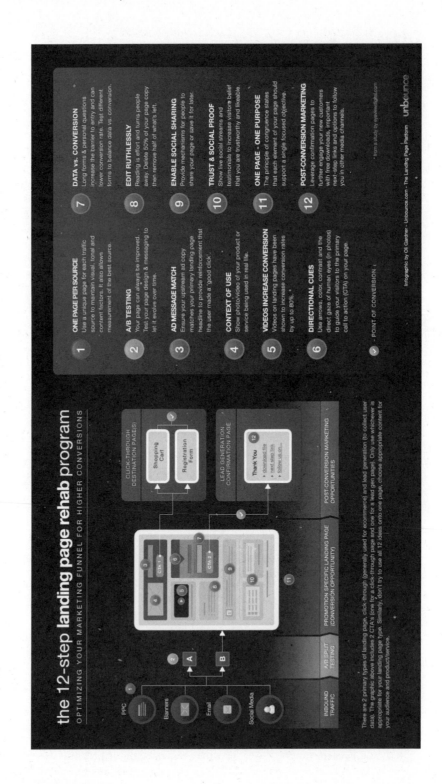

## ESTABLISHING A CONVERSION BASELINE— THE CONVERSION SCORECARD

Before we begin, we need a quick breathalyzer test to get some baseline metrics in place and measure how effective your treatment program is. The *conversion scorecard* (http://unbounce.com/docs/rehab-scorecard-full.png) can be used whether you're using a standalone landing page for your marketing campaigns, or sending traffic directly to a page on your website (home page, shopping cart or registration page)—although it is geared slightly more towards the standalone variety.

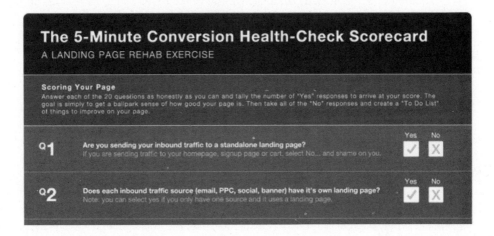

## SCORING YOUR PAGE

Answer each of the 20 questions as honestly as you can and tally the number of "Yes" responses to arrive at your score. The goal is simply to get a ballpark sense of how good your page is. Then take all of the "No" responses and create a "To Do List" of things to improve on your page. You'll find some guidance and tips for making these improvements as you follow the 12-step program outlined in this chapter.

Remember that after you leave the rehab clinic and have made some positive changes to your conversion funnel, you should revisit the scorecard to measure your improvements.

## STEP 1: USE A SEPARATE LANDING PAGE FOR EACH INBOUND TRAFFIC SOURCE

The principles of inbound marketing are founded on facilitating multiple streams of traffic. Examples include pay-per-click (PPC), email, banner ads, and social media. There are two key reasons why you should be using a separate landing page for each source:

- **With measurement comes accountability.** With separate funnel flows, you can measure the effectiveness of each inbound stream and focus your efforts on the one(s) that convert the best—and potentially stop spending time and money on channels that aren't working for a specific campaign or audience.

- **Each inbound medium has it's only unique style and limitations.** Using separate pages allows you to sync up the visual and tonal qualities with the source. Email for instance can contain a lot more information that a tweet, so the amount of extra information your landing page needs to communicate is inherently different. Imagine also that one of your inbound streams suddenly requires a different offer (perhaps a 20% discount for an affiliate). With only one landing page you would have to show this change to all sources. This is especially critical for PPC. Once you've established a good quality score and conversion rate, you don't want to change the page and risk an increase in cost-per-click or a drop in your quality score.

## SPONSOR'S ADVICE

This is where A/B testing becomes really useful. *Set up multiple versions of your form and test them to find where the balance lies.* Is it acceptable to remove a few questions in order to get more leads? Does your conversion rate even get affected by the addition of extra questions? Only testing with your target audience can answer these questions.

Start thinking of each inbound source as its own mini campaign. You want to have multiple rivers bringing boats to your port (rather than many tributaries feeding one river). Print out the ads for each inbound source (PPC, email, banners, social media) and spend time observing their differences—size, tone, language, and visual weight. This will help you design appropriate landing pages.

# STEP 2: A/B TEST YOUR LANDING PAGES

A/B testing is the process of splitting your traffic between a series of pages to see which performs the best. Anne Holland's WhichTestWon.com is a fun site that shows examples of A/B tests and lets you pick which version you think would produce the highest conversion rate.

On a corporate level, testing helps to remove conjecture and subjective argument from the boardroom and is a great way of understanding your customers (i.e., which messaging and design they respond to best). It should be done as an iterative process—think evolution versus revolution.

> *Fact: Your landing page can always be better. Just like a plant, it needs ongoing attention for best results.*

## SPONSOR'S ADVICE

Take the plunge and get a tool set up so you are at least able to start testing your landing pages. Then the fun part of trying new ideas and experimenting can come.

> **Tip:** *You can start a free trial Unbounce account at* `http://try.unbounce.com` *and start creating and A/B testing pages in minutes.*

## STEP 3: MATCH YOUR LANDING PAGE MESSAGE TO THE UPSTREAM AD

If the primary headline of your landing page doesn't match the copy on your ad, you'll be getting a lot of action on your browser's back button.

*Bad message match:*

Ad: Get 20% off a MacBook Pro
Landing page message: Welcome to Bobby's Computer Store

*Good message match:*

Ad: Get 20% off a MacBook Pro
Landing page message: Get 20% off a MacBook Pro at Bobby's Computer Store

Seems obvious, right? The problem is that most inbound traffic gets sent to company home pages, where the messaging is necessarily generic. *Using a targeted standalone landing page is key to reinforcing the customer's belief that they made a "good click."* You will also get a better quality score and thus a lower cost-per-click from Google AdWords if your message match is strong. (This extends to the entire content on the page, which should be congruent with the headline's message.)

> **Bonus tip:** *If you are driving social media traffic, you can enhance the "social message match" by including an appropriate social icon on your landing page to further reinforce the connection between the source and destination.*

## SPONSOR'S ADVICE

Learning to construct your campaigns in the right order can help you ensure good message match.

- Start with a concept based on communicating your product/service/offer to your target market.
- Come up with your promotional headline and landing page content.
- Work on a series of ads that closely match the headline.

If you do it the other way round (ad first), you are forced into building from what might be the wrong foundation.

## STEP 4: CONTEXT OF USE

They say a picture is worth a thousand words. A better picture is one where your product or service is shown being used in context. Salespeople will tell you to sell the fire, not the fire extinguisher—the point being that *you need to illustrate the need in order to develop desire for the solution.* Effective landing pages use photography and video to provide evidence of how your product or service solves a real problem.

A statement like "Our vacuum cleaner is so powerful it can suck up a bag of nails" beside a stock photo of the product against a white background is far less likely to convert than a video that allows customers to see and hear the vacuum cleaner actually doing its job.

An example using photography could show a fold-up ladder in two states: 1) being tucked into a small cupboard by its owner, and 2) extended to show the owner reaching onto high shelves to retrieve something. *Simply showing it in its intended context of use will improve your sales.*

Would you really have bought a ShamWow or Slap Chop without seeing it in action?

### SPONSOR'S ADVICE

Take your product or service and use it yourself. (You'd be surprised how many people haven't even used the item they're selling.) This will help you understand and visualize how it should be presented in your photography and videos. If it's an online tool, try observing someone else using it.

## STEP 5: USE VIDEOS TO INCREASE ENGAGEMENT AND CONVERSIONS

According to a study by eyeviewdigital.com, the use of video can increase your conversion rates by as much as 80 percent. By providing users with a passive engagement mechanism you can keep them on your page longer, allowing your brand message to seep into their subconscious.

If you're peddling a physical product, show people using it, as mentioned in Step 4. If it's an online tool, provide a demo of the primary features while narrating the benefits of its use. (Don't show every step, make it a highlight reel.)

If you offer a service, put yourself front and center. Communicate directly with your viewers.

Make eye contact for maximum engagement and *make use of directional cues to guide visitors to your intended conversion goal.* Great videos do this by having the host look and point outside the frame towards other elements on the page—bringing the whole page into the experience.

> **Bonus Tip:** *Usability best practices say to never auto-play a video, as the audio shock can make people hit the back button immediately, especially if they are in a sound sensitive environment—like most offices. However, this is something you should test on your visitors. If you really want the video to start automatically, my advice is to at least allow a short delay before it starts, and make the controls very obvious so that the user can easily mute or pause it.*

## SPONSOR'S ADVICE

If you don't use video yet, plan to start soon. For online product demos, try recording a screencast using software like Jing (`www.techsmith.com/download/jing/default.asp`). It's a really simple and cost-effective. Once you get a feel for it, you can upgrade to more elaborate tools with stronger editing and post-production features. Audio is a very important aspect of video production—write a script before you record so you're not bumbling your way through, and try to use an external mic for better quality.

# STEP 6: USE DIRECTIONAL CUES TO LEAD THE WAY

Imagine an airport without the expertly placed wayfinding signs and maps—it would be chaos. If you've visited the emergency room at a hospital, you might be familiar with the colored lines they paint on the floor to take you to different departments—follow the yellow brick road. These are examples of *directional cues.*

Directional cues are used on landing pages to guide the visitor to your call-to-action (CTA). Here are some examples of ways to do this:

- **Graphical arrows:** Take a look at the header area of the lead gen form on this landing page template from `http://templates.unbounce.com/lead-gen-message-in-banner`. When you add a lead gen form to your page, the call-to-action button is often pushed below the fold. Here, the arrow lets you know that the point of interaction can be found directly below that area.

- **Whitespace:** Don't cramp the style of your CTA. Resist the temptation to fill in every pixel of your page; instead give your buttons plenty of room to breathe.
- **Color:** Classic colors for buttons include blue and orange. At the end of the day, the most important thing is that it stands out clearly from the rest of the page. (For example, don't make your CTA button blue if your page has a blue color palette.)
- **Contrast:** This is essentially the same as the point about color, but thinking in terms of black and white or tonal range.
- **Eye direction:** Studies have shown that when using photos of people (or animals), you can improve conversions by having them look at your intended CTA. It makes sense. If you see someone looking up at the sky while you're walking down the street, the chances are you'll follow their gaze in case you're missing something important.
- **Interruption:** Surprise is an excellent way to get someone's attention. Breaking established design boundaries gives reason to pause and observe.
- **Encapsulation:** Think of binoculars or the viewfinder on a camera and how they focus your vision. You can construct similar experiences using shapes and contrast. Think about archways, holes, and windows for inspiration.
- **Pathways:** Roads or the earlier example from the hospital floor are examples of pathways. You can use background design elements (lines with arrows, generally) to walk someone round your page in the order you prefer.

For a more exhaustive study of the effects of directional cues, read "Designing for Conversion—8 Visual Design Techniques to Focus Attention on Your Landing Pages" (http://unbounce.

com/landing-page-design/designing-for-conversion-8-visual-design-techniques-to-focus-attention-on-your-landing-pages).

## SPONSOR'S ADVICE

*Learn to point.* It might be considered rude in some cultures, but in Conversion Land it's actively encouraged. Make the intended action of your page as obvious as possible—subtlety is for shy folks. Add at least one directional cue to an existing landing page. If your design is quite restrictive, you can try breaking the visual boundaries by placing an arrow outside of the page edge, pointing in towards your CTA—this disruptive visual tactic can be very effective at directing eyeballs.

# STEP 7: FIND THE OPTIMAL BALANCE OF DATA VERSUS CONVERSION RATE

Lead generation is about two things—the size of the barrier (how long, personal, or complicated the form is) and the size of the prize (what you are giving away in return for the data). *If these are out of proportion, you risk losing customers.*

It's a delicate balance to achieve. Make the form too long, and people walk away from the perceived effort. Make the questions off-topic, or too personal, and you wind up with false data. Conversely, if the form is too short, you can skew your leads towards those just seeking a freebie instead of real, determined, and relevant customers. It can also result in you not being able to qualify your leads accurately.

The other factor that complicates all of this is the giveaway you are offering. If your eBook, coupon, or webinar isn't good enough to warrant the information you are asking for, folks will bounce. For a webinar registration keep the info to a bare minimum—name, email, and maybe company and role if it's B2B. If you're giving away an eBook, it needs to be one of two things: significant in size or significant in its exclusive data content. Above all, quality is what counts.

You can tease people into completing your form to get your super awesome whitepaper, but if it turns out to be smoke and mirrors, you'll have a lead that's disappointed and likely to unsubscribe immediately.

## SPONSOR'S ADVICE

This is where A/B testing becomes really useful. *Set up multiple versions of your form and test them to find where the balance lies.* Is it acceptable to remove a few questions in order to get more leads? Does your conversion rate even get affected by the addition of extra questions? Only testing with your target audience can answer these questions.

## STEP 8: BE HONEST ABOUT YOUR WRITING AND EDIT RUTHLESSLY

*Never publish the first thing you write,* unless you are in the business of reportage poetry. (I may have just made that name up.) Campaigns and their associated messaging need to be refined over time through testing, but also through editing. Steve Krug, author of the classic usability book *Don't Make Me Think,* made the best observation on the subject I've heard: *Delete 50 percent of your page content, then throw away half of what's left.*

### SPONSOR'S ADVICE

Try removing two sentences from the main body of copy on your landing page. I bet it won't hurt as much as you think. If you have five bullet points, try going with the three most important ones.

Keep deleting extraneous words and redundant phrases until your copy is as tight as you can make it. Like everything you change on your pages, you should make your edits on a duplicate page and run an A/B test to verify if it produces higher conversions.

## STEP 9: MAKE IT DESIRABLE TO SHARE

The impulse to share content can be fleeting, so don't make people work for it. While not applicable to all landing pages, those with special offers or special content should have a simple way for people to spread the word for you.

There are two great ways to make this work:

- **Run a contest:** Then give people an extra entry by Tweeting about it (free marketing).
- **Produce exceptional content:** If you are giving away a great eBook, place sharing widgets such as retweet buttons on your pages. Better yet, put them on your confirmation page if you have one. (See Step 12 for more on this.)

### SPONSOR'S ADVICE

*Be relevant to your audience.* If you're driving Twitter traffic, retweet buttons are familiar and easy to use. The beauty of many social widgets is that they utilize AJAX-style interaction and don't take you away from the page. Similarly, if you are funneling Facebook traffic, add a Like button to the page. Most Facebookers are logged in all the time, and the button will add your landing page into their timeline with a single click.

## STEP 10: LEVERAGE SOCIAL PROOF AND TRUST DEVICES

Testimonials work, if they're real. Avoid stock photos and scripted hyperbole as most people can spot a fake testimonial a mile away. Try a mixture of testimonials that describe how your product or service has benefited someone's business—ideally with stats such as:

> *"Using your product, I was able to increase conversions by 20 percent, resulting in an additional $11,000 in revenue per month."*

To modernize your landing pages, *illustrate social proof by showing your standing in a relevant social network.* There are many widgets available that can show how many people like or follow you. Social capital and the herd mentality of network participants can help convince prospects to become customers. A word of caution, though: sometimes adding Tweet or Like buttons can be a distraction to your landing page's intended goal—and asking some to share an ebook landing page before they've completed the form is like asking for you-know-what before the first kiss.

As you'll learn in Step 12, there are other places you can place sharing components that remove distractions while maximizing the chance of them being used.

One of my favorite techniques is for webinar registration pages. By showing how many people have signed up, you can increase the importance of the event, making it more likely for others to register.

### SPONSOR'S ADVICE

Ask ten of your customers for a fresh testimonial and add the best to your landing page. Remember to state your usage intentions and ask for a photo if possible. If you have a decent social network presence, try adding a live feed widget based on a specific phrase or #hashtag search to show who is involved and how people are interacting with your brand.

## STEP 11: ONE PAGE, ONE PURPOSE

Imagine a web page that exhibits the same tendencies as a kid with ADD. If your content can't decide on one thing to communicate at a time, your visitors certainly won't want to take the time to figure it out.

The principal of congruence states that *each element on your page should support a single focused objective*. A good way of looking at this is to imagine a series of arrows all pointing to the center of a circle where there is a big button (your CTA). Each arrow represents a piece of content on your landing page, and you need to ensure that they are all in *conceptual alignment*.

Contrast this to those same arrows all pointing in different directions (conceptually).

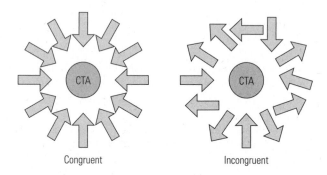

Congruent                    Incongruent

To maintain focus, don't talk about other products or services—you can use a different landing page and ad source for those. An exception to this is on an ecommerce product page that provides the ability to add extra products to the cart (in addition to your main conversion goal).

## SPONSOR'S ADVICE

Try this exercise: Explain the purpose of your campaign to a colleague by reading the content of your landing page out loud, and ask them to stop you if you veer away from the central purpose as previously stated. If this happens, *remove the offending content and start over*. You will learn a lot more about your communication style by saying it out loud.

For visual elements, try writing the goal of your campaign on a piece of paper, then print and cut out the images from your landing page and place them around the goal. *Remove or replace any images that don't seem to be in total agreement with this goal.*

# STEP 12: POST-CONVERSION MARKETING

*Post-conversion marketing* is probably the most overlooked stages of the conversion funnel. The confirmation page from your lead gen form, ecommerce checkout, or registration form is the perfect place to start capitalizing on the positive mood of a newly qualified customer.

To increase your engagement potential, tell people what to do next on your confirmation page. This amplifies your reach and makes sure you are heard, not forgotten.

Here are some common examples of effective post-conversion page elements:

- Follow us on Twitter (so they see regular updates)
- Like us on Facebook (so they see updates and become part of your community)
- Give away an extra free eBook to increase your "thought leadership" score
- Visit this page (send them to other content they may find interesting)
- Share this with your friends/colleagues (leverage *their* network)
- Bookmark us on Delicious

## SPONSOR'S ADVICE

Go beyond a simple "Thank you" on your confirmation pages. Start by adding one new link to the page and track how much extra traffic visits that target.

# WHAT NOW?

Now you have the tools and advice to break those bad conversion habits and rehabilitate your struggling marketing funnel. *Did you do the scorecard exercise?* Are you on the epic end of the scale or the "I did, like, 19 things wrong!" end of the scale?

The scorecard is there to provide you with a "to-do list" of conversion improvements. *Take every question you answered "no" to and create a personal task to fix it.* Then implement a new A/B test to see how well your new landing page fares.

Good luck with your rehab, and remember: *Your landing page can always be better.*

# 21

# LESSONS LEARNED FROM 21 CASE STUDIES IN CONVERSION RATE OPTIMIZATION

*By Paras Chopra*

---

**Editor's Note:** *Conversion rate optimization (CRO) must be tailored to support the specific goals of a website's business. After observing more than 1,000 split tests for landing pages, however, Paras Chopra identified a number of general patterns among the ones with the highest conversion rates. He shares them in this post, which was originally published Aug. 3, 2010, on The Moz Blog.*

---

CONVERSION RATE OPTIMIZATION (CRO) is the newest darling of Internet marketers. After all, what good is traffic if it doesn't convert? Unfortunately (or fortunately, depending how you look at it), unlike pay-per-click (PPC) marketing, CRO isn't a game of how much money you can throw. In fact, this field requires as much creativity as it requires monetary investment. That's what makes conversion rate optimization a fair arena. Your well-funded, bigger competitors can of course beat you at generating more traffic, but they can't beat you at the conversion rate game (unless you allow them to).

Every website has unique conversion goals, so the best approach to CRO is unique for every website. You should not expect to follow tips from a "best-practices" article and boost your conversion rates instantly. Chances are high that what worked for others may not work for you. So, the biggest step in increasing conversion rates is coming up with creative ideas and designs that can work

Even though CRO is a highly customized process for every website, over the course of the last couple of years (and the course of more than 1,000 split tests), I have observed a few general patterns that yielded great results. Different ideas for increasing conversion rates are worth discussing because they become a great source of input for coming up with your own ideas. In this chapter, I discuss a variety of ideas for CRO, detailed through different case studies. Four main elements that influence conversion rates are as follows:

- Design
- Social proof
- Headline and copy
- Call-to-action (CTA)

Let's start by discussing the role design plays in increasing conversion rates.

## THE ROLE OF DESIGN

From a conversion perspective, the design of a website is the most important aspect among all variables involved. The difference between a more successful converting design and a less successful converting design usually boils down to making it clear to the visitor what he is expected to do on a page. Take a look at the following examples, showing the old and new site design for Basecamp.

What made the new design convert 14 percent more visitors? A clean design. The new design clearly guides a visitor towards the Plans and Pricing button, while the old design presented a whole lot of choices.

Old Design

New Design

Basecamp home page design: 14 percent increase in conversions

Need more proof that having fewer choices on the page can increase conversion rates? Have a look at the following case study results (http://mz.cm/166nB5h).

Gyminee home page redesign: 20 percent increase in conversion rate

You can check out other similar case studies where design played a key role in optimizing conversion rates at the following links:

- How we increased the conversion rate of Voices.com by over 400 percent (www.conversion-rate-experts.com/voices-case-study/)
- Skype home page redesign (http://mz.cm/XR21hy)
- Official Vancouver 2010 Olympic Store home page redesign (www.getelastic.com/ab-test-case-study-homepage)
- Performance Based Design—Web Design Book: 131.2 percent improvement on landing page (www.abtests.com/test/83001/landing-for-performance-based-design-web-design-book)

## THE ROLE OF SOCIAL PROOF

In addition to reducing the number of choices for the visitor, having a design that demonstrates you are a professional and trustworthy company can also increase conversions. Take a look at the following case study, where the redesigned sales page has various trust elements (seal, money back guarantee, testimonials) and the design has various little tweaks (color scheme, buttons instead of links for download, layout, etc.) which made it look professional (see http://visualwebsiteoptimizer.com/split-testing-blog/how-aquasoft-increased-their-sales-by-20-doing-ab-split-tests-in-multiple-phases).

Note that sales (not just conversions) increased by 20 percent when the design was changed. No additional products, no additional traffic, pure CRO.

Old Design

New Design

AquaSoft sales page redesign: 20 percent increase in sales

Or take another case study, where simply replacing a "Never Beaten on Price" image with an "Authorized Seller Site" increased sales by 107 percent. The conversion rate increased from 1.81 percent to 3.76 percent, effectively doubling Express Watch's business (http://visualwebsiteoptimizer.com/split-testing-blog/increase-in-sales).

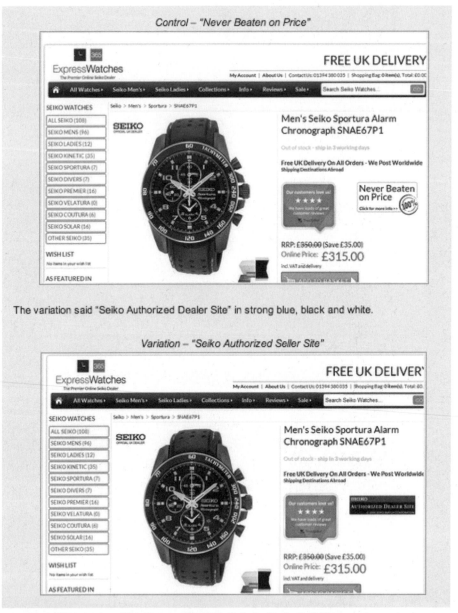

Express Watches replaces "Never Beaten on Price" with "Authorized Dealer Site": 107 percent increase in sales

Social proof has shown to increase conversions on repeated occasions. `Wikijobs.co.uk` had one goal when they decided to A/B test how customer testimonials affect conversions: to increase sales (`http://visualwebsiteoptimizer.com/split-testing-blog/customer-testimonials-increase-sales`).

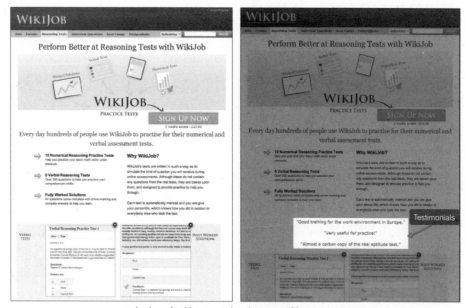

Wikijob.co.uk add testimonials: sales increased by 34 percent

Adding customer testimonials increased sales by 34 percent in spite of the testimonials being very sober, versus the overly enthusiastic ones you usually see in marketing collateral.

Check out some of the following links on how social proof affects conversions:

- Harvard Business School study finds one-star increase in Yelp rating increases revenue 5-7 percent (`www.hbs.edu/research/pdf/12-016.pdf`)
- Trust Badge on website results in 32 percent increase in conversions (`http://visualwebsiteoptimizer.com/split-testing-blog/do-trust-badges-on-websites-work-oh-yes-32-increase-in-conversions`)
- Check out page A/B testing: three dead simple changes increase sales by 15 percent (`http://visualwebsiteoptimizer.com/split-testing-blog/checkout-page-ab-testing-increase-sales`)

## THE ROLE OF HEADLINE AND COPY

When you receive an email, it's the name of the sender and the subject line that influence your decision to open it right way, or to postpone it. Similarly, when a visitor arrives on your website, it's the design/brand name AND the headline of the page that influence his decision to engage with your page or not. Visitors' attention is the most valuable commodity on the Internet, and your page's headline is where it goes right after arriving on your page.

Take a look at the case study at `http://37signals.com/svn/posts/1525-writing-decisions-headline-tests-on-the-highrise-signup-page`, where 37Signals tested different kinds of headlines (and the winning one boosted the conversion rate by 30 percent).

Highrise headline test: 30 percent increase in conversions

The winning variation said "30-day Free Trial on All Accounts," and the worst performing variation said "Start a Highrise Account." Note that the clear, no-nonsense headline won. If you think about it, if a visitor is on signup page, he obviously knows that he is signing up for a Highrise account. The winning headline clearly convinces the already interested visitor that there is nothing to lose, as they offer a 30-day free trial.

Here's another example of how much headlines matter: CityCliq, a startup in the local marketing industry, split tested the positioning of their product (`http://mz.cm/XR4nNt`).

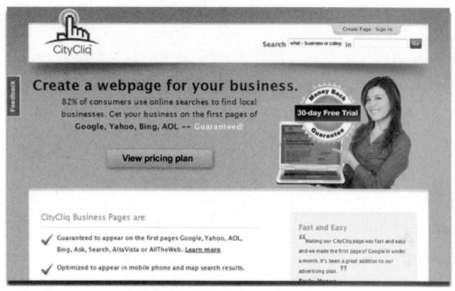

CityCliq headline test: 90 percent increase in conversions

Here are the headlines CityCliq tested:

- Businesses grow faster online! (*too fuzzy, and so what if they do?*)
- Get found faster! (*found where?*)
- Online advertising that works! (*too generic*)
- Create a webpage for your business. (*clear, concise, and to-the-point*)

The winning headline "*Create a webpage for your business*" tells the visitor exactly what CityCliq does. No wonder it increased conversions by 90 percent. As they say, don't make your visitors think.

Right after looking at a headline, if his interest is piqued, a visitor looks at the (text/video) copy on the page. That's why a combined optimization of headline and copy proves to be effective, as it did for Moz (`www.conversion-rate-experts.com/seomoz-case-study`).

Conversion Rate Experts' "How we made $1 million for Moz" strategy

They tested a variety of headlines and copy elements on the landing page for a Pro subscription. In the end, they found out that a headline that piqued interest, and copy that laid out what exactly constitutes a Pro subscription won.

Check out some other case studies where headline and copy mattered:

- Dustin Curtis' "You should follow me on Twitter here" experiment—12.8 percent increase in conversions (http://dustincurtis.com/you_should_follow_me_on_twitter.html)
- Marketing Experiments Response Capture case study—a triple-digit increase in conversions (www.marketingexperiments.com/blog/research-topics/response-capture-case-study.html)
- Landing Page case studies from SiteTuners (www.sitetuners.com/landing-page-case-study.html)

## THE ROLE OF CALL-TO-ACTION

So, you optimized your design, your headlines, and your page copy. You got the visitor interested and motivated to try whatever you are offering. There is still one last hurdle before you can throw a success party for your CRO project. Yes, the call-to-action (CTA) is the last hurdle for you to cross. Even though the CTA may be considered as minutiae for CRO (www.moz.org/blog/dont-fall-into-the-trap-of-ab-testing-minutiae), the following case studies demonstrate that even simple A/B testing of CTAs can result in great improvements.

A highly motivated visitor will sniff out even the poorest of all CTA buttons. So while optimizing this aspect of your page, make note that you are optimizing for the busy, semi-interested visitor. If he can't immediately see how to try out whatever you are offering, he will hit the back button. (And in CRO, the back button is the greatest enemy of all.)

37Signals' call-to-action: signups increased by 200 percent

The now-omnipresent "See Plans and Pricing" button increased signups for Highrise by 200 percent (`http://thinkvitamin.com/business/how-to-increase-sign-ups-by-200-percent`). I have included this case study not to convince you to replace all your buttons with this text (it may not actually work for you). Rather, the point is to convince you that even small changes in the CTA can have a dramatic impact on conversion rates. And the best thing about CTAs is that they are so easy to test. It literally takes five minutes to get such a test up and running.

Another oft-repeated test is to see which color works best for a CTA. (Unsurprisingly, a bright color such as red mostly works better; this may be because bright colors are eye-catching and drive visitor's attention towards them.) As an example, along with testing "Sign up for free" versus "Get Started Now" buttons, Dmix also tested green versus red buttons—and found out that red works better (`http://dmix.ca/2010/05/how-we-increased-our-conversion-rate-by-72`).

Dmix case study: 72 percent increase in conversions

To repeat my earlier point, with CTAs, sometimes surprisingly trivial changes can produce significant results. Take a look at the following case study on Soocial's home page (`http://visualwebsiteoptimizer.com/split-testing-blog/ab-test-case-study-how-two-magical-words-increased-conversion-rate-by-28`).

Soocial's home page: 28 percent increase in conversions

Notice that all they did was to add "It's free" alongside "Sign up now" to boost the conversion rate. This is definitely a trivial change. And why wouldn't you test such trivial changes if it doesn't take much effort and has the potential to fatten your bottom line?

Here are some other case studies where tweaking the CTA helped increase the conversion rate:

- Get Feedback v/s Respond Now—13 percent increase in conversion rate (`http://rypple.com/blog/give-feedback-vs-respond-now`)
- RIPT Apparel's Buy Now button test—6.3 percent increase in sales (`http://visualwebsiteoptimizer.com/split-testing-blog/how-ript-apparel-increased-their-sales-by-6-3-ab-testing-case-study`)
- Firefox Download button test—3 percent increase in downloads (`http://blog.mozilla.com/metrics/2008/11/21/changing-the-firefox-download-button`)

## YOUR ROLE

The framework of optimizing the design, headline, copy, and CTA of each conversion page should provide you with a good starting point for creating your own CRO strategy. What matters in increasing conversions are two factors: not making your visitor think too hard about what you are offering, and showing them how to actually try that offering. Try to make everything obvious and simple, guiding your visitor from headline to copy to CTA like a smooth-flowing river.

However, no matter how many case studies you read, in the end, your conversion rate optimization program will turn out to be unique because your website is unique, your audience is unique, and your goals are unique. The real key to increasing conversion rates is to keep experimenting and testing what works for you.

# 22

# AN ILLUSTRATED GUIDE TO WEB EXPERIMENTS

*By Thomas Høgenhaven*

**Editor's Note:** *Experimentation is an essential conversion rate optimization (CRO) activity. However, the statistics that form the foundation of running web experiments can intimidate inbound marketers who are new to CRO. The author created this illustrated guide to conducting web experiments with this in mind. It was originally published March 26, 2012, on The Moz Blog.*

WEB EXPERIMENTATION IS a great methodology to improve most things on the web. It can be used to make adjustments to existing products such as increasing user engagement and conversion rate. But it can also be used to guide entire business decisions, as suggested by Eric Ries (http://theleanstartup.com). The primary strength of controlled web experiments is the possibility to isolate variables, and thus examine causality between different metrics such as tagline and conversion rate (see www.moz.org/blog/correlation-vs-causation-mathographic).

Much of the literature on experimental design has its roots in statistics and can be quite intimidating. To make it more accessible, I created this illustrated guide to web experiments.

> **Author's Note:** *Special thanks to Andreas Høgenhaven, who kindly made the illustrations for this guide.*

Before getting started on the experiment, you need to get the basics right: Test metrics that align with your long-term business goals (see www.kaushik.net/avinash/rules-choosing-web-analytics-key-performance-indicators). Test big changes, not small (see http://blog.hubspot.com/blog/tabid/6307/bid/20569/Why-Marketers-A-B-Testing-Shouldn-t-Be-Limited-to-Small-Changes.aspx). And remember that the test winner is not the optimal performance, but only the best known variation. It doesn't mean that you have found the all-time optimal performing variation. You can (almost) always do better in another test.

## A/B OR MVT

One of the first things to consider is the experimental design. An A/B test design is usually preferable when one or two factors are tested, while a multivariate test (MVT) design is used when two or more independent factors are tested. However, it is worth noting that more than two factors can be tested with A/B/…/n tests or with sequential A/B tests. The downside of using A/B test for several factors is that it does not capture interaction effects.

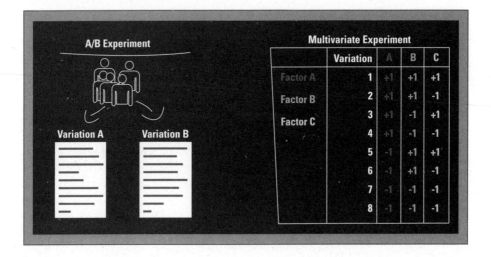

| | Variation | A | B | C |
|---|---|---|---|---|
| Factor A | 1 | +1 | +1 | +1 |
| Factor B | 2 | +1 | +1 | -1 |
| Factor C | 3 | +1 | -1 | +1 |
| | 4 | +1 | -1 | -1 |
| | 5 | -1 | +1 | +1 |
| | 6 | -1 | +1 | -1 |
| | 7 | -1 | -1 | -1 |
| | 8 | -1 | -1 | -1 |

# MVT FACE-OFF: FULL FACTORIAL VERSUS FRACTIONAL FACTORIAL

So you want to go multivariate, huh? Wait a second. There are different kinds of multivariate tests. If you have ever visited `WhichMVT.com`, you probably came across terms such as *full factorial*, *fractional factorial*, and *modified Taguchi*. Before getting into these wicked words, let's get our multivariate test down to earth with an example. In this example we have three different factors, and each factor has two conditions.

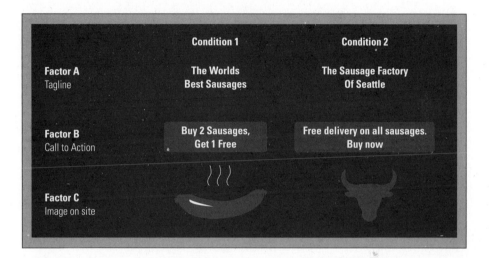

This example has three factors, each with two conditions, giving a total of $2^3 = 8$ groups. In the full factorial design, all possible combinations are tested. This means eight variations are created, and users are split among these. To get 100 users for each condition, a total of 800 users are needed. In the following table, +1 Indicates condition 1, while -1 indicates condition 2.

**Full Factorial Experiment**

|  | Variation | A | B | C |
|---|---|---|---|---|
| Factor A | 1 | +1 | +1 | +1 |
| Factor B | 2 | +1 | +1 | -1 |
| Factor C | 3 | +1 | -1 | +1 |
|  | 4 | +1 | -1 | -1 |
|  | 5 | -1 | +1 | +1 |
|  | 6 | -1 | +1 | -1 |
|  | 7 | -1 | -1 | -1 |
|  | 8 | -1 | -1 | -1 |

**Fractional Factorial Experiment**

|  | Variation | A | B | C |
|---|---|---|---|---|
| Factor A | 1 | +1 | +1 | +1 |
| Factor B | 2 | -1 | -1 | +1 |
| Factor C | 3 | -1 | +1 | -1 |
|  | 4 | +1 | +1 | -1 |

This design is not too bad when you have three factors with two conditions in each. But if you want to test four factors each comprising four conditions, you will have $4^4 = 256$ groups. This means we would need 25,600 users to get 100 users into each group! Or if you want to test 10 different factors with two conditions in each, you will end up with $2^{10} = 1,024$ groups, requiring a lot of subjects to detect any significant effect of the factors. This is not a problem if you are Google or Twitter, but it is a problem if you are selling sausages in the wider Seattle area.

> **Author's Note:** *You can calculate the test duration time with VisualWebsiteOptimizers Calculator (`http://visualwebsiteoptimizer.com/split-testing-blog/ab-test-duration-calculator`). The output of this calculator does, however, come with great uncertainty because the change in the conversion rate is unknown. That is kind of the point of the test.*

Enter fractional factorial design. The fractional factorial design was popularized by Genichi Taguchi and is sometimes called the Taguchi design. In a fractional factorial design, only a fraction of the total number of combinations are included in the experiment (hence the name). Instead of testing all possible combinations, the fractional factorial design tests only enough combinations to calculate the conversion rate of all possible combinations.

In the previous example, comprising three factors each with two conditions, it is sufficient to run four different combinations, and use the interaction between included factors to calculate combinations of factors not included in the experiment. The four groups included are ABC; A + (BC); B + (CA); C + (BA).

Instead of testing Factor A three times, this factor is only tested once while holding B and C constant. Similarly, Factor B is tested once while holding A and C constant, and Factor C tested once while holding A and B constant. I'll not dive too deeply into the statistics here, as the experimental software does the math for us anyway.

The fractional factorial test assumes that the factors are independent of one another. If there are interactions between factors (for example, image and headline), that would affect the validity of the test. One caveat of the fractional factorial design is that one factor (e.g., A) might be confounded with two-factor interactions (e.g., BC). This means that there is a risk that you end up not knowing if the variance is caused by A or by the interaction BC. Thus, if you have enough time and visitors, full factorial design is often preferable to fractional factorial design.

## TESTING THE TEST ENVIRONMENT WITH THE A/A TEST

Most inbound marketers are quite familiar with A/B tests. But what is less well known is the A/A test. The A/A test is useful as a test of the experimental environment, and is worth running before starting A/B or MVT tests. The A/A test shows whether the users are split correctly, and whether there are any potential misleading biases in the test environment.

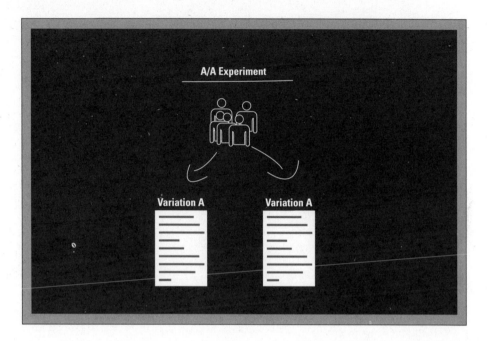

In the A/A design, users are split up like they are in an A/B or MVT test, but all groups see the same variation. You want the test results to be non-significant, and thus find no difference between the groups. If the test is significant something is wrong with the test environment, and subsequent tests are likely to be flawed. But as discussed in the following section, an A/A test is likely to be significant sometimes, due to random error/noise.

The A/A test is also a good way to show co-workers, bosses, and clients how data fluctuate, and that they should not get too excited when seeing an increase in conversion rate with 80 percent confidence. Let's call it a sanity check—especially in the early phases of experiments.

## STATISTICAL SIGNIFICANCE

In the ideal experiment, all variables are held constant except the independent variable (the thing you want to investigate, such as the tagline, call-to-action, or images). But in the real world, many variables are not constant. For example, when conducting an A/B test, the users are split between two groups. As people are different, the two groups will never consist of identical individuals. This is not a problem as long as the other variables are randomized. It does, however, inflict noise in the data. This is why we use statistical tests.

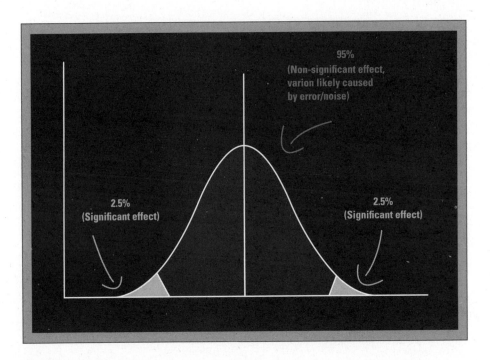

We conclude that a result is statistically significant when there is only a low probability that the difference between groups is caused by random error. In other words, the purpose of statistical tests is to examine the likelihood that the two samples of scores were drawn from populations with the same mean, meaning there is no "true" difference between the groups, and all variation is caused by noise.

In most experiments and experimental software, 95 percent confidence is used as the threshold of significance, although this number is somewhat arbitrary. If the difference between two group means is significant at 98 percent probability, we accept it as significant even though there is a 2 percent probability that the difference is caused by chance. Thus, statistical tests show us how confident we can be that difference in result are not caused by chance/random error. In Google Website Optimizer, this probability is called *chance to beat original.*

## PRO TIP: RAMP UP TRAFFIC TO EXPERIMENTAL CONDITIONS GRADUALLY

One last tip I really like is ramping up the percentage of traffic sent to experimental condition(s) slowly. If you start out sending 50 percent of the visitors to the control condition, and 50 percent to the experimental condition, you might have a problem if something in the experimental condition is broken. A better approach is to start sending only 5 percent of the users to the experimental condition(s). If everything is fine, go to 10 percent, then 25 percent, and, finally, 50 percent. This will help you discover critical errors before too many users do it.

PART

# VI ANALYTICS

*By Annie Cushing*

THE THRUST OF analytics isn't data; it's improvement. Improvement just starts with data because you can't improve what you don't measure.

But measurement alone isn't going to lead to improvement—or any action at all. The road to business hell is paved with good data.

The key is marrying sound measurement methodologies with thorough analysis and tying all of that glorious data and those keen insights back to an organization's business objectives.

So Part VI focuses on both prongs of that fork: setting up reporting systems that will collect the data for analysis at a later juncture, and honing in on the truly actionable insights.

Having started off college as a biochemistry major, I still have a strong inclination toward scientific processes. So what we're going to do in this intro is look at a handful of marketing conundrums currently being mulled over by entirely fictional people and businesses. Hey, it's the closest I could come to forming a hypothesis to test in a Petri dish! We'll dissect the process of how to separate the signal from the noise in data sets accessible to marketers.

# ECOMMERCE BUDGET ALLOCATION DECISION

Anita has an ecommerce shoe store and a handful of trusted drop-shipping companies that keep her supplied with the latest fashions. Her cousin Monica took a social media strategies class in college, and at Monica's urging, she signed the store up for Facebook, Twitter, and Pinterest and has hired a couple of college students to work on building up a following for the store. She's experienced moderate success and has just over 3,000 followers on Twitter, just under 700 Facebook likes, and 88 Pinterest followers (but has only been pinning a few months). Anita also has a well-vetted email list that she uses to announce her weekly specials.

Monica says that email is dying, and that Anita needs to invest more time and effort into social media or her shoe store will eventually die. Her argument is that no one under 40 uses email for shopping. She's a judgmental little juggernaut of persuasion, huh?

## BURNING QUESTION

Anita wants to know if she's focusing too much on email and if she could make more money by shifting her priorities from email production and distribution to social media.

## DATA NEEDS

Anita hawks over the metrics she gets from MailChimp like it's her job (because, well, it kinda is). She also has lists segmented and stays on top of keeping them scrubbed. Her problem is she doesn't know what those visitors do when they get to the site, although she's tried to figure that out using Google Analytics (GA). But, from what she can tell, social media doesn't seem to be generating much revenue for her.

## ANALYSIS

Well, for starters, Anita doesn't have the data she needs to make any decisions at this time about social media or email. She would need to start tagging her emails with campaign parameters (covered in this Part of the book). But then she also needs to understand that GA, by default, uses last-click attribution in crediting conversions, so the ecommerce reports she's been down-loading from GA are only giving her part of the story. It's kind of like writing a movie review for *The Sixth Sense* without getting to the end. Sort of. Okay, not really. But wow, what a movie!

Furthermore, upon further investigation, we realize that Anita is only including referrals from twitter.com, facebook.com, and pinterest.com in the social media report she created and has emailed to herself every week. We need to inform her that Twitter traffic especially comes from many sources, not just twitter.com, and introduce her to GA's robust social reports.

Finally, because she's not tagging links in her emails that point back to her site, much of her traffic from email is getting dumped into the direct bucket. She doesn't know that desktop email apps, like Outlook and Mac Mail, don't pass referral data. As long as we're talking about depressing GA limitations, webmail providers that use a secure (https) server by default, like Gmail, don't pass referral data either.

Go ahead. Kick something, Anita. You'll feel better.

That said, Anita *definitely* needs to read Part VI before making decisions that could hurt her profit margins.

# PAUL'S GRIEF OVER HIS LACK OF BLOGGING SUCCESS

Paul runs a pet loss blog. He has a counseling degree and enjoys helping people who have experienced the loss of a beloved pet. In conjunction with his blogging, he's very active on Twitter, with 12,400 followers. He follows everyone except for bots back because he wants people to feel comfortable DMing him with questions.

Paul uses bitly to shorten his URLs and he monitors clicks. About twice a week, he has tweets that go viral, but he hasn't been able to figure out the secret sauce of what makes one tweet more retweetable and reply-worthy the others.

But Paul's real pain point is that he feels like a failure as a blogger. He's read that bounce rate is the golden metric (hat tip to Avinash Kaushik for that one!). Like a good Avinash disciple, he monitors his bounce rate very closely, along with visits. But his bounce rate is consistently north of 60 percent. He's tried everything to get it under control: videos, a couple of infographics, a "related post" WordPress plugin . . . all to no avail.

Convinced that he just can't cut muster as a blogger, he's considering selling the pet loss blog and starting a blog about his other passion: kiteboarding.

## BURNING QUESTION

Paul wants to know what more he could do to make his blog "stickier" so people will stick around longer. Secondarily, he wants to know if he's being strategic enough in his use of Twitter.

## DATA NEEDS

Paul wants to know if there are GA reports he can use to diagnose his fatal unattraction. He also is at a loss for how to quantify his own Twitter trends to figure out what captures the attention and curiosity of his followers.

## ANALYSIS

Oh boy . . . There's just so much wrong with this picture. First of all, Paul is making a mistake that's very common among bloggers: obsessing over a single metric to measure his success. It just so happens that for his case, he couldn't have chosen a worse one to obsess over.

Bounce rate may be the golden metric in many cases—because it helps you identify pages on your site that visitors just don't grok on— but it's a terrible metric to measure the success of a blog. There are a couple of reasons for that:

- Blogs are notorious for high bounce rates. People typically land on a blog post to read that post. If your site offers more than just a blog, you can craft a strategic call-to-action on your blog posts that may woo readers deeper into the site. But Paul's site is just a blog—a place for people to read insights about dealing with the loss of a pet and share their stories. Paul needs to understand this phenomenon about blogs and not hawk over this metric.

- Even if a visitor comes to your blog and reads for 20 minutes, when s/he leaves it will be considered a bounce. And, to add insult to injury, that visit won't add to the average time on site because a visitor has to click on a second page to register how long the time on page (and on site) is. You could get fancy with event tracking and trigger events based on time on page—and even time on a page in the front tab of a browser using the Visibility.js library—but that's way beyond the scope of this book. In Paul's reports, every bounce is going to show up as 0 seconds time on page/site and skew those metrics as well.

Applying the "Non-Bounce Visits" advanced segment that comes baked into GA will help Paul cut down some of the weeds, but there are some other metrics he should be focusing on to round out his perspective anyway. For example, Paul should monitor the number of comments he gets per post to measure engagement. He could track this in GA by attaching an `onSubmit` event to the form in his comments.php file since an enterprise tracking system like Radian6 is out of range for him. An analytics aficionado would be able to help him set this up.

Another suggestion I'd make to Paul is that he should measure "microconversions" like newsletter signups and downloads of his eBook using event tracking and goal conversion tracking.

And since he gets a decent number of shares and likes and because GA can now track social interactions, I'd recommend that he use either the AddThis or ShareThis plugin on his site.

Finally, I'd recommend that Paul take a look at his Twitter use and try to ascertain what makes some of his tweets go more viral than others. Is it the length? Subject matter? Resources shared in the tweets (he shares a lot with his followers)? Rand Fishkin shares some great techniques for how you can use the Twitter and bitly APIs to get this data in Part VI.

You'll learn a lot about how to set some of these things up in this section. Half the battle is nailing down the proper metrics and key performance indicators (KPIs) to monitor.

## NAOKI'S OBSESSION WITH BEING #1

Naoki runs a popular sushi bar in Philadelphia. He's hired an SEO consultant to help him get to the first position in Google for *sushi* in local searches but to no avail. He thinks his consultant is a snake oil salesman because it's been nine months (and eight days), and all he's been able to accomplish is getting Naoki listed in the seven pack of local results. But Naoki has to scroll to even see the local results when he searches for *sushi*. And freaking Wikipedia is at the top. Because people want to know the history of sushi when they search, I'm sure. Pfft.

## BURNING QUESTION

Can he justify paying his SEO consultant when he can't get him to the top of Google Page 1?

## DATA NEEDS

Naoki needs perspective. And new KPIs. At minimum, he should create a custom report to track visits from Philadelphia (and some of its surrounding metro areas, if applicable) that's filtered by 'Medium' Matches exactly 'organic'.

## ANALYSIS

First of all, Dr. Pete did an interesting eye tracking study (included in this section) that shows that visitors tended to gravitate toward the local one box, even when it was farther down the page. If someone's searching for sushi because he's hungry and totally jonesing for a California roll, he's not going to click on the results at the top of the page that lean more informational in intent. He's also not going to care about images of other people enjoying sushi. He's going to make a beeline for the local box and focus most on the result at the top of that listing and/or the restaurant that's closest to his growling tummy.

I'd encourage Naoki to set up some custom alerts in GA for when organic visits increase or decrease by more than 10 percent (or whatever threshold he wants to set).

Furthermore, Naoki really needs to connect his Google Webmaster Tools account with his GA account to monitor impressions for the main keywords he's tracking (covered in this section). He can also use his Google Places Dashboard to monitor the queries his site is showing up for.

And before jumping to conclusions at the first sign of a dip, I'd encourage Naoki to check Google Insights for Search (now Google Trends . . . again) to see if the ebb and flow he sees in impressions correlates with the natural cyclical pattern of searches for sushi-related terms. He'll learn interesting things, like people just aren't as into sushi in May and November. Who knew?

At the end of the day, if Naoki's consultant took him from invisible to prominently placed in a local box, he should be thrilled. He may not be able to track conversions without some call tracking in place (which is an expense most small businesses don't assume), but he can certainly take these insights and reassess if he's getting enough value for the money he's spending on SEO.

# TO SHOOT OR NOT TO SHOOT; THAT IS THE QUESTION

Amy has a wine glass painting business that has really taken off. She started teaching classes locally, in her San Francisco shop, on Sunday evenings after it closes. Most of her revenue comes from online orders, so she figured she'd connect with her community by teaching them something she enjoys doing anyway. But she's been encouraged by some of her Facebook fans to create videos that she can post on her site. Being an artist and a perfectionist, she can't bring herself to just have her husband record her painting wine glasses on his phone. She wants professional-quality videos on her site.

## BURNING QUESTION

Can the cost of creating videos be justified?

## DATA NEEDS

Amy needs to see data that will give her some assurance that creating and hosting videos on her site will bring her increased traffic and conversions.

## ANALYSIS

This is a tough one, because without creating and hosting at least one video, she has no data to suggest whether adding these videos to her site will increase her traffic and conversions. However, there is anecdotal evidence that Amy could use to help her inch her way closer to a decision.

For starters, in Dr. Pete's eye-tracking study (see Chapter 24), he showed that video-rich snippets are hotspots. That should be a focal point for Amy's cost-benefit analysis. How can she increase her chances of getting the highly coveted rich snippet for the queries she decides to target, if she were to move forward with this?

There are keywords she can optimize for that may increase her chances of getting a rich snippet like *how to, tutorial,* and *video.* She could also use a third-party video hosting service, like Wistia, for even higher chances of getting the snippet. Google shows preferential treatment toward YouTube pages over pages that merely have a YouTube video embedded in them.

She would also want to create dedicated landing pages for each of her videos, and track them in GA to see what kind of love they get over time. If she put all of these pages in a specific directory, creating a segment for these pages would be a piece of cake.

She would also benefit from multi-channel funnels to see if visits from her Facebook fans are resulting in conversions at some point. The cookie only lives for 30 days, so these reports are hamstrung by that limitation. But she could gain some valuable insights about the impact of her Facebook sharing. Multi-channel funnels are covered more (you guessed it) in Part VI.

Hopefully, as you read this Part—and all the great ideas and insights contained herein—you'll think about how real people with real businesses and projects can apply these strategies to garner real results!

# 23

# 11 GOOGLE ANALYTICS TRICKS TO USE FOR YOUR WEBSITE

*By Eugen Oprea*

---

**Editor's Note:** *Google Analytics offers a wealth of valuable data to anyone managing a website, and is loaded with options. You don't need to know how to use all the features Google Analytics offers you, though—just the ones that will present you the data you need to track in way that is meaningful for your business. In this post, originally published March 1, 2012 on The Moz Blog, Eugen Oprea introduces 11 of Google Analytics' most accessible features.*

---

THE MOST COMMON question that I am asked every day through social media networks, forums and email is "How do I get insights about my Google Analytics data?" People approach me saying that they have had a Google Analytics (GA) account for years, but they look only at page views or the number of visitors they get. This is wrong, so wrong, when they have powerful, free web analytics tools—tools that they could leverage to gather insights about their visitors, and then use those insights to better serve their visitors.

That's why in this chapter I will teach you some GA tricks that you should use for your website.

> *You can also sign up for my free Google Analytics course, which covers the basics, at* http://www.eugenoprea.com/google-analytics, *or pick up advanced Google Analytics tips at* www.moz.org/blog/advanced-google-analytics-tips-and-tricks.

## 1. SET UP YOUR ANALYTICS GOALS

After you install the tracking code on your website, you need to *set up goals* in GA (http://mz.cm/169fJQq). The goals you set up for your website will be the foundation of your website analysis. Your website goals are, ultimately, your business goals.

If you are wondering what goals you need to set up, start by asking yourself what the purpose of your website is. Is it to sell tangible goods as an ecommerce site? Is it to become a popular blog that earns revenue from ads? Is to promote your business' offline services? Is it to become a leading educational resource in your field? Once you figure out what the main purpose of your site is, you can start setting up goals based on your business objectives.

If this is still unclear for you, here are some examples of analysis goals to give you some traction:

- **Product purchases**—Enable ecommerce tracking (http://mz.cm/XTqvH2) to track the sales cycle for your products, from product viewed, to item placed in shopping cart, to final purchase.
- **Visitor engagement**—Track the number of people who spend more than one minute on your site.
- **Free Downloads**—Use event tracking (more on this later in this chapter) to measure calls-to-action (CTA) like downloading your eBook.
- **ROI on Ads**—Again, use event tracking to measure your best-performing ads.
- **Subscriptions**—Use analytics to track the number of email subscriptions on your site and related data.

Later, these goals will help you track conversion rates and get insights about what traffic sources convert best on your site, what keyword searches send you the most customers, which landing pages have the most sign-ups for your newsletter, what are your most engaging content pages, etc.

Use these examples to get started, but please note that every website is unique and will have customized goals.

## 2. CONNECT YOUR GOOGLE WEBMASTER TOOLS ACCOUNT

Google Webmaster Tools (GWT) is another free product from Google which helps you see data about your website, such as the number of impressions for your search queries and their position in Google, the number of links to your site, or diagnosis information reported by Google after crawling your website.

Additionally, you can check +1 metrics, your site performance, or submit a sitemap for Google to index.

But the really interesting thing is that you can connect your GWT with your GA account to access to the new Search Engine Optimization reports (`www.moz.org/blog/ seo-reports-google-analytics`). Once you do that, you will be able to see three new reports in your GA account: Queries, Landing Pages, and Geographical Summary. These reports will help you learn more about your top performing search queries (keywords) and landing pages. Then, you can use that data to identify the following:

- Keywords with a low click-through rate, but a good average position. Once you know them, you can change the meta title and description of your page to improve their click-through rate.
- Landing pages with a good click-through rate, but a low average position. These pages can be easily run through an on-page optimization process that will improve their rankings.
- The home countries of your organic visitors, which you can compare against your target market(s).

To connect your GWT and GA accounts, go to the Traffic Sources section of GA, select Search Engine Optimization and then choose one of the three reports.

At this stage, you will see a page that explains the benefits of linking your accounts, as well as a button labeled Set Up Webmaster Tools Data Sharing. Click that button, and then click Edit in your settings for GWT. You will be redirected to your GWT, where you can connect them with GA.

## 3. LEVERAGE SITE SPEED REPORTING

Site Speed reporting is also a neat feature of GA. It lets you see the load time of your pages (`www.moz.org/blog/google-analytics-now-tracks-page-load-speed`). This will help you check which pages need your attention, and enable you to look for ways to speed up your page load times.

If you wonder why this is important, I can tell you that the load speed of your pages can significantly improve your visitors' experience on your site, which will increase conversions, and is a minor ranking factor in Google search. (`http://www.moz.org/blog/ site-speed-are-you-fast-does-it-matter`). So a good load speed can make your visitors happy, increase conversions, and possibly give you a little boost in the SERPs as well.

*Editor's Note: The Shortcut link pictured in the screenshot is now a standard feature of the top navigation bar, and DOM Timings has been added as a subtab of the Explorer tab (next to the Site Usage and Technical subtabs).*

Along with the number of page views and bounce rate, you can see the average page load time (in seconds), and the number of visits that have been used as a sample for every page on your website.

Additionally, if you click on the Performance tab, you can check different buckets of your page load time and see the average load speed of individual pages.

Primary Dimension: Page Load Time Bucket (sec)

| | Page Load Time Bucket (sec) | Page Load Sample | Percentage of total |
|---|---|---|---|
| ⊞ | 0 - 1 | 23 | 3.47% |
| ⊞ | 1 - 3 | 130 | 19.61% |
| ⊞ | 3 - 7 | 207 | 31.22% |
| ⊞ | 7 - 13 | 151 | 22.78% |
| ⊞ | 13 - 21 | 64 | 9.65% |
| ⊞ | 21 - 35 | 44 | 6.64% |
| ⊞ | 35 - 60 | 22 | 3.32% |
| | 60+ | 22 | 3.32% |

The Map Overlay tab will show you the load speed for different countries or territories, cities, continents, and sub-continent regions.

## 4. ENABLE SITE SEARCH

It's a fact that visitors who use the search box on a site are more likely to convert than the ones who don't. This is because they are more engaged with your website.

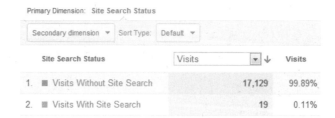

The beautiful thing about site search is that it lets you discover the exact keywords that people use to search for your products, so you can take this a step further and use them in your search engine optimization campaigns. You can use the most important keywords that people use to search on your site to optimize your pages and drive more targeted traffic to your website. Additionally, visitors might look for products or services that you do not have on your offer. Because people are already looking for them, you now know that adding them to your site will increase sales.

If you have a blog, site search is a great way to see what your readers are looking for and get a ton of article ideas.

If you would like to enable Site Search in GA, first make sure that you have a search form on your site, then customize your GA tracking code for Site Search (`http://mz.cm/ZopPrd`) and install (or re-install) it (`http://mz.cm/XS0Jml`).

## 5. TRACK EVENTS

Event tracking is a powerful feature in GA (`www.moz.org/blog/google-analytics-event-tracking-to-monitor-calls-to-action`). It can help you track the following items, among others:

- How many people download your eBook
- What ads are performing better and who clicks on your ads
- Which signup form converts better (sidebar, below the post, about page)
- Who pauses, fast forwards, or stops a video
- What errors a visitor encounters during checkout

But that's not all. Using the latest version of GA, you are also able to set these events as goals, which can help you see the performance of your events based on different metrics.

Enabling event tracking is not a difficult process. All you have to do is add the following code next to the URL of your link, before you replace the default values:

```
onClick="_gaq.push(['_trackEvent', 'category', 'action',
  'opt_label', 'opt_value']);"
```

These default values will help you identify your events. Here's what they represent:

- **Category (required)**—You can use this element to identify what you want to track: eBook, video, signup form, or ads.
- **Action (required)**—This element can be used to define the interaction of your visitor. The choices are click, button, play, and stop. Personally, I use it to specify the place of my button/signup form/ad.
- **Label (optional)**—Use this to identify the type of event that is tracked.
- **Value (optional)**—This element helps you specify a value for your event that can be used when you set up a goal for your event.
- **Non-Interaction (optional)**—This element, when set to `true`, identifies that the event will not be used in bounce-rate calculation.

If you would like to see a working example, here's what I used to track a link to my new product, where `Ads` is the category of my link, `Sidebar` is the place where I added the link, and `WAB` is the label.

```
<a href="http://www.webanalyticsblueprint.com/"
onClick="_gaq.push(['_trackEvent',
  'Ads', 'Sidebar', 'WAB']);">Start Free Trial</a>
```

Once you have set up your links, you will see event tracking data. All you have to do is set up that event as a goal using the category, action, label, and value conditions you have set up for your event (`http://www.blastam.com/blog/index.php/2011/03/how-to-use-events-goals-google-analytics`). You will also see data appearing in Event Tracking Reports, which can be found under Content and in the Events Flow reports.

## 6. REAL-TIME REPORTING

Google has taken analytics one step further with Real-Time reporting, which allows you to see how many visitors are on your website in that moment, where they are on your website, how they found you (keywords and referrals), and where they live.

*Editor's Note: Top Social Traffic data is now available in Real-Time's Overview report as well.*

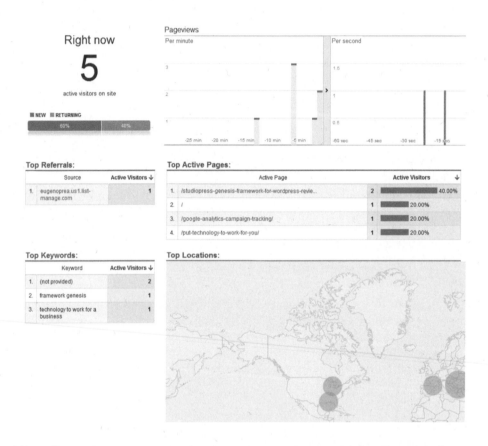

Additionally, you have access to another three reports with more insights about their location, how they arrived on your website (including Social sources), and what pages they visit.

To access this feature, select Real-Time from the Standard Reports tab.

The Locations report provides information about the number of visitors currently on your site, and as well as the cities and countries where they are located. You can even check their locations on a map.

Traffic Sources displays information about where they come from to reach your site. You will see the medium and source along with the total number of your visitors.

The Content report shows you what are the active pages that your visitors read and how many active visitors are on each of the pages displayed on your report.

## 7. MULTI-CHANNEL FUNNELS

With Multi-Channel Funnels, GA provides even more value for users who are passionate about conversion rates.

If before you were able to track the last source that the visitor used to convert, with Multi-Channel Funnels you are now also able to track other sources (ads, referrals, social media, organic) that the visitor used to reach your website from.

Say, for example, that your visitor (Cindy) landed for the first time on your website from Twitter and subscribed to your RSS feed. On her next visit, Cindy used the feed reader to come and read your new articles. Ultimately, she was looking for advice on blogging and found your eBook using a search engine. Now, because she knows your site already, she will buy it and become a customer.

Using this example, in the old version of GA, the search engine was credited for the conversion; but now, with Multi-Channel Funnels, you can see the whole path that Cindy took to convert: Social Network→Referral →Search Engine.

To check the Multi-Channel Funnels reports, go to the Conversions section.

> *Watch the video at* `http://mz.cm/XRMZak` *learn more about using Multi-Channel Funnels in Google Analytics.*

## 8. USE CUSTOM CAMPAIGN TRACKING

Tracking online marketing campaigns will help you get past that large number of direct visits that come from URL shorteners like bitly (`http://bitly.com`), or apps like TweetDeck (`http://tweetdeck.com`). Additionally, it will help you track the effectiveness of your campaign activities more accurately.

To use custom campaign tracking in GA, you need to tag your URLs with special parameters. Those parameters can be added to your links using the Google's URL Builder tool (`http://mz.cm/XTMmxV`).

Once you tag your URLs with the mandatory parameters, you can use them as they are, or use a URL shortener when sharing them. Then check the Campaigns report, under Traffic Sources→Sources, to get insights about your online marketing campaigns.

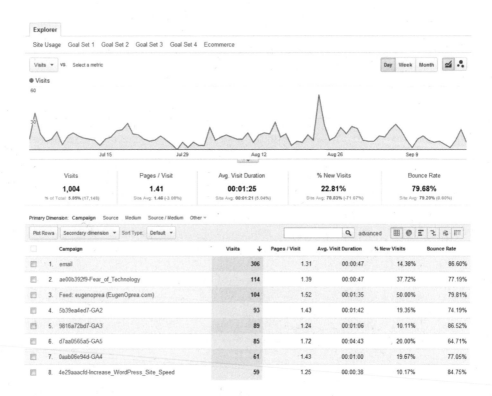

To see step-by-step instructions for using custom campaign reports in GA, visit `www.eugenoprea.com/google-analytics-campaign-tracking`.

## 9. PLOT ROWS

Plot Rows allows you to create instant segments of your data in tabular reports. If you usually look at standard reports, you can use Plot Rows to get more insights from your metrics.

To use this feature, you need to select two rows from any tabular report and then click the Plot Rows button from the bottom of the table. Once you do that, you will see that the chart has changed, and you are able to see additional information there about the items that you have selected.

Use this feature to check how your main keywords, referrals, or pages compare with each other and with the overall site metrics. Make sure, however, that you select items that do not have a big difference between their metrics. (For example, don't compare a keyword with 2,340 visits with one that has 154.)

## 10. CUSTOM DASHBOARDS

In the old version of GA, you had only one dashboard available to you. Now you can create up to 20 dashboards and customize them to meet your needs.

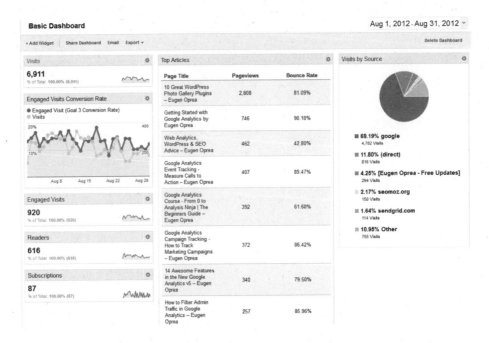

To create a custom dashboard, go to the Home menu→Dashboards and select +New Dashboard. You will need to choose whether you will want to start from scratch with a blank canvas or use the Starter Dashboard. Then you can add slick widgets to it that create custom metrics, pie charts, timelines, or tables.

For more information on creating custom dashboards, check out my *YouMoz* post "5 Insightful Google Analytics Dashboards" (www.moz.org/ugc/5-insightful-google-analytics-dashboards).

## 11. FLOW VISUALIZATION

Flow Visualization definitely deserves its own article. For now, I'll give you a brief introduction to its benefits.

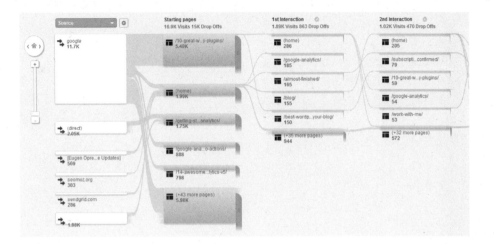

## VISITORS FLOW

GA rolled out two reports, Visitors Flow, under the Audience section, and Goal Flow, under the Conversion section. The Visitors Flow report displays the path your visitors used to navigate through your website. Selecting a dimension such as country source or keyword lets you see the exact path your visitors took and where they stopped to read your content.

On hover, the report displays additional details for each page like the total number of visits, how many visitors moved to a different page, and how many of them dropped out of the funnel and left. If you click on a page, you can explore all kinds of information about its traffic by highlighting it.

## GOAL FLOW

The Goal Flow report is essentially a better representation of the Funnel Visualization report, and contains the same dimensions as the Visitors Flow report. The main difference between the two is that the Goal Flow report doesn't show data from all pages, and focuses on the steps you configured in the conversion funnel.

Additionally, you can use advanced segments to filter your data and gain additional insights into it from the Visitors Flow and Goal Flow reports.

# CONCLUSION

I hope that the GA tools I've presented you with here will give you better insight into how your visitors use your website. Hopefully, you will be able to use this data to give your visitors more of what they want, which will give you more of what you want—increased conversions.

# 24

# EYE-TRACKING GOOGLE SERPS— 5 TALES OF PIZZA

*By Dr. Peter Meyers*

---

**Editor's Note:** *For years, SEOs vied for the top three spots of search results, as they have traditionally enjoyed the highest click-through rates. With the advent of Universal search, plain text listings now compete with a variety of attention-grabbing visuals, including review ratings, expanded site links, product images, videos, and maps (to name a few). Predicting the highest-converting spots on a SERP has become much harder. Eye-tracking equipment, however, can be used to figure out where a person's attention is drawn when looking at a SERP. In this post, Moz's Chief Marketing Scientist, "Dr. Pete," shares the custom eye-tracking data he obtained firsthand in his study of five different Google SERPs for pizza queries. Originally published on <u>The Moz Blog</u> on Oct. 5, 2011, this post is more relevant today than ever.*

---

A WHILE BACK, we got an offer we couldn't refuse. The good folks at Mirametrix (http://mirametrix.com), an eye-tracking hardware and software company, asked if we were interested in custom eye-tracking data (which traditionally costs a small fortune) for any Google searches. Um, does Matt Cutts like cats?

Since I once worked down the hall from an eye-tracking lab, I was the obvious choice to lead this shopping spree at the nerd candy store. So, we picked five different Google search engine results pages (SERPs), representing the diversity Google has created in the past couple of years, including expanded site-links. This is the story of those SERPs. They're all about pizza, because I'm from Chicago and was apparently hungry when I made the list.

## THE EQUIPMENT AND METHODOLOGY

First, a little bit of background. Mirametrix produces affordable, portable eye-tracking systems for researchers. Our data was collected using an S2 Eye Tracker, which looks a little bit like an Xbox Kinect. Each SERP was shown to eight subjects between the ages of 18 and 30 for 30 seconds. Subjects were told the search term of interest and were then allowed to view the full-screen SERP freely. All SERPs were de-personalized and localized to Chicago, IL.

Heat maps were created by aggregating the subject data. Subjects saw the full-screen SERP, but I've cropped each image below the point that activity trails off. I should note that this is actual eye-tracking data, which should not be confused with "click maps" or heat maps created from mouse movements. These patterns come from people's direct visual interaction with the SERPs as captured by the S2 Eye Tracker.

## LOCAL #1: "BEST PIZZA IN CHICAGO"

I'll start with a query for "best pizza in Chicago," because the results are probably closest to what you would expect. I picked this particular SERP because it had strongly integrated Local results, along with maps on the right. The eye-tracking data is shown in the figure.

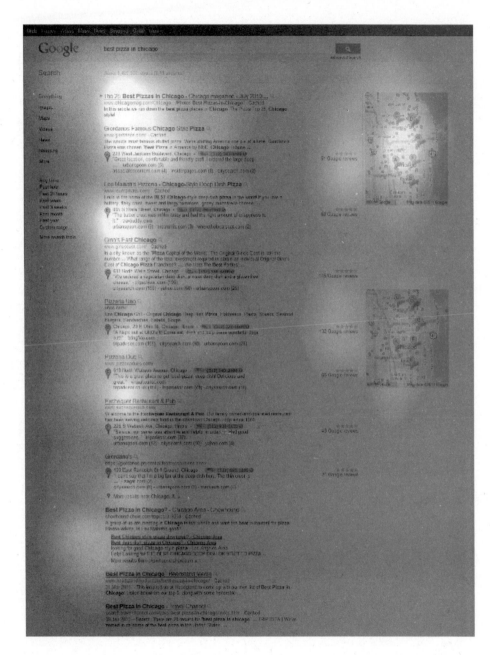

You can see a modified "F-shaped" pattern here, with most activity centering on the top results and some eye movement toward the map. As you might expect, the top listings attracted the most attention.

# LOCAL #2: "PIZZA"

Next up was a local search for "pizza." These results were more varied, with a couple of organic results followed by an integrated 7-pack that more clearly separated Local results. This data got a bit more interesting.

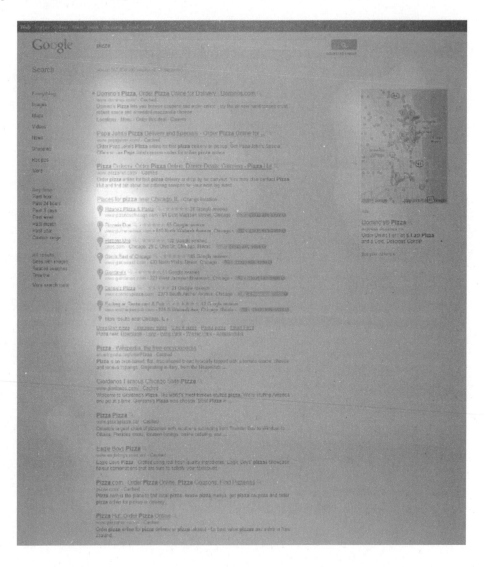

The impact of the Local 7-pack appears to be very powerful, drawing attention from the top three organic listings. Even map fixations appear to be toned down from the first SERP. Whether this is because people were familiar with Google's local results format or were attracted to the distinct formatting, it's clear that they were biased toward this part of the page.

## VIDEO THUMBNAILS: "HOW TO MAKE A PIZZA"

This one was a special request from our CEO. Rand was interested in the impact of video thumbnails in organic SERPs. I found that the query "how to make a pizza" brought up video thumbnails for the #2 and #3 spots. Here's what the data had to say.

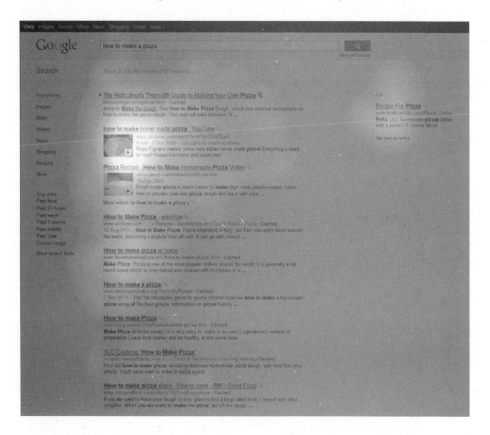

Although individual results are a bit hard to separate, it does appear that subjects' eye movements focused on the first video thumbnail, possibly even at the expense of the #1 organic result. Especially with something as visual as a pizza (who doesn't love pizza?), the attraction of an image could really tip the click-through scales.

## PRODUCT IMAGES: "PIZZA CUTTERS"

The next search was for "pizza cutters." This brought up brand and store searches at the top, along with images for shopping results after the third organic listing. The eye-tracking data looked like this:

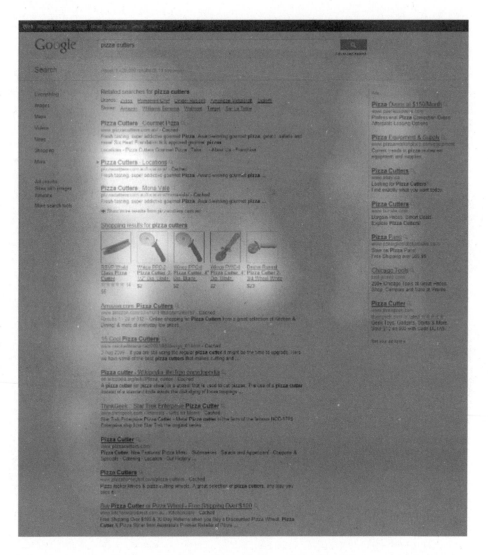

There's definitely some pull toward the product images, although the top organic results still do fairly well. The "Related Searches" seem to get relatively little attention, even though they appear where the first organic result would usually be.

## EXPANDED SITE LINKS: "PIZZA HUT"

Finally, we decided to test-drive the new site links. A search for "Pizza Hut" brought up six expanded site links. Not surprisingly, this search also triggered some local results. Here's the visual:

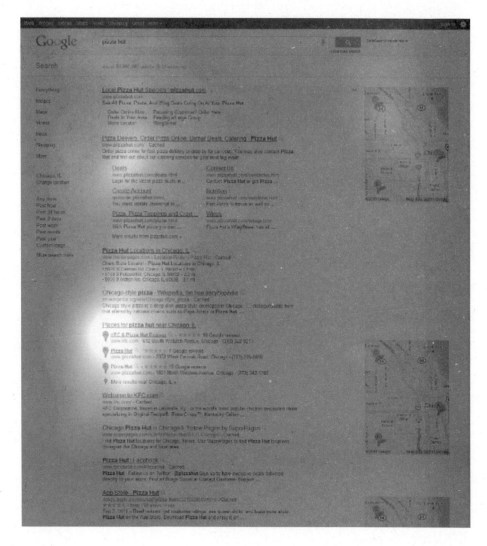

Although the Pizza Hut listing gets some fixation, there seems to be a strong pull towards the local listings. Even with a full pack of expanded site links, the main Pizza Hut site got much less attention than I would have expected. When you want pizza, you want pizza, not a corporate history.

## SOME GENERAL IMPLICATIONS

I think the first and most obvious implication is that as Google moves away from ten plain listings for more and more searches, it is definitely having an impact on search users. You need to be familiar with your competitive space and take advantage of SERP enhancements, like video thumbnails. Ranking #1 might not be pulling the weight it used to if your competitors down the page have more visually interesting results.

These results also suggest that the in-page Local results are having a strong impact, even if they fall in the middle of the page. In these limited cases, they seemed to pull attention away from the top organic spots. If your query has a local flavor, you need to be aware of how your Google+ Local page is competing.

Of course, these are exploratory results, and more data would be needed to back up any given finding, but I hope the general observations are interesting. I'd like to thank Ben Yoskovitz for setting up this opportunity, and Anton and Amineh at Mirametrix for managing and running the eye-tracking studies.

# 25 CALCULATING AND IMPROVING YOUR TWITTER CLICK-THROUGH RATE

*By Rand Fishkin*

---

**Editor's Note:** *Seeking to improve the click-through rate of tweet links, Rand walks readers of* The Moz Blog *through a manual process for analyzing Twitter data. He notes that while the process is interesting, it is not scalable, and challenges readers to create a robust "Twitter Optimizer" tool. That was November 2010. Flash forward to today. Marketers now have a dizzying array of Twitter Optimizers to choose from, including Buffer, HootSuite, Sprout Social, Social Bro, and Raven Tools, to name a few. Moz has even acquired a Twitter Optimizer of its own, Followerwonk, which helps you increase your Twitter ROI by analyzing your social graph. Who would have thunk?*

---

AS MARKETERS, MANY of us leverage Twitter as a direct traffic tool. We use the service to share URLs to increase brand awareness, help increase site visits, and possibly drive some direct actions (for example, sign-ups, sales, or subscriptions). From what I've seen and experienced, not many of us spend time thinking about how to improve the click-through rate (CTR) of the links we tweet.

Given that I have 21K+ followers, but most of the links I tweet generate 150-250 clicks, my CTR is only averaging 1.34 percent.

As analytics junkies, we're well aware that we can only improve things that we measure, analyze, and test. So let's look at a process for measuring our tweets, analyzing the data, and testing our hypotheses about how we could improve our CTR. If we do it right, we could make Twitter a more valuable marketing and traffic channel for our brands.

First off, we're going to need some data sets that include each of the following:

**Profile Data**

> # of followers
>
> # following
>
> # tweets
>
> Avg # tweets per day

**Tweet Data**

# clicks

# retweets

Time of day

Tweet structure (e.g., text, URL, text vs. URL, text VS text, URL vs. text, URL hash tags)

*Editor's Note: Tweet Data only applies to tweets containing a unique, trackable URL such as those produced by the URL shortening service bitly—see* `http://bitly.com.`

This data can be time-consuming to grab. If you know how to use Twitter and Bitly's APIs, though, you can make an automated system to monitor it. Once you have your data, you'll want to build a spreadsheet that looks something like this:

| Tweet | Content | Date | Format | # of Words | # of Chars | Tweeted URL | # of Clicks | CTR |
|---|---|---|---|---|---|---|---|---|
| http://twitter.com/#!/ | 18 Steps to Launching a New Site for Marketing + Metrics Success: http://seomz.me/b8cbwq | 11/9/2010 | 1 | 12 | 88 | http://seomz.me | 375 | 1.77% |
| http://twitter.com/#!/ | Working hard on an in-depth post for SEOmoz. Might not finish tonight, but did get this up earlier - http://seomz.me/9g5J7k | 11/9/2010 | 1 | 20 | 123 | http://seomz.me | 168 | 0.79% |
| http://twitter.com/#!/ | An update on LDA - http://seomz.me/dlYSwc - be sure to watch the video! | 11/8/2010 | 3 | 13 | 71 | http://seomz.me | 216 | 1.02% |
| http://twitter.com/#!/ | Vegas' dark underbelly - http://seomz.me/93yNAj - photoessay on 100s of people living in tunnels under "The Strip" | 11/8/2010 | 3 | 17 | 114 | http://seomz.me | 276 | 1.31% |
| http://twitter.com/#!/ | If you fly + go through security, read http://seomz.me/d8V0AV (analysis, stories + pics re: the new body scanners) | 11/8/2010 | 3 | 16 | 114 | http://seomz.me | 181 | 0.86% |
| http://twitter.com/#!/ | "Only in hindsight will people-you included– romanticize struggle, say success was always assured & imbue glory." via http://seomz.me/bMFiDW | 11/7/2010 | 1 | 17 | 139 | http://seomz.me | 51 | 0.24% |
| http://twitter.com/#!/ | A deeper explanation of LDA: http://seomz.me/cKtj6b w/ great visuals + graphics from the @webpronews team | 11/4/2010 | 3 | 14 | 105 | http://seomz.me | 193 | 0.91% |
| http://twitter.com/#!/ | Photos from the @SEOmoz meetup in Sofia, Bulgaria - http://seomz.me/c7ZkmH - including my handstand :-) | 11/3/2010 | 3 | 15 | 103 | http://seomz.me | 156 | 0.74% |
| http://twitter.com/#!/ | Good research on the influence of customer reviews on sales: http://seomz.me/cq4mDd from the crew @eMarketer | 11/2/2010 | 3 | 15 | 108 | http://seomz.me | 138 | 0.65% |
| http://twitter.com/#!/ | Smart suggestion from @wilreynolds for finding high-conversion keywords: http://seomz.me/9gTtKq | 11/2/2010 | 1 | 9 | 95 | http://seomz.me | 208 | 0.98% |

I've made the version I created for my own stats public on Google docs (see `http://mz.cm/ZETblg`).

With the help of my Twitter history page and Bitly, I constructed a chart of my last 25 tweets containing links that I personally created. (I did not include retweets, nor tweets containing links created by others in this chart, as they were irrelevant to this particular exercise.)

Using this data, I can find the answers to some very interesting questions, discussed in the following sections.

# Q: DO MY WORDIER TWEETS EARN HIGHER CTR?

To answer this question, I merely need to compare the number of words per tweet against CTR, and build a graph to visually illustrate the data.

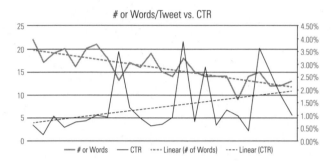

The trend lines (the straight, dashed lines) are showing me that there's a slight pattern, and Excel's correlation function returns a value of -0.262, suggesting that there's a very subtle correlation between shorter tweets and more clicks. I might try testing this in the future with particularly short tweets, since my average word count is 15.88 with a standard deviation of only 3.88 (i.e., most of my tweets are consistently lengthy).

# Q: DO MY SHORTER TWEETS PERFORM BETTER?

Let's look at the raw length of the tweet. According to HubSpot's data, shorter tweets are more likely to be retweeted (see http://www.slideshare.net/danzarrella/ the-science-of-twitter).

Does a similar relationship between shorter tweets and CTR exist?

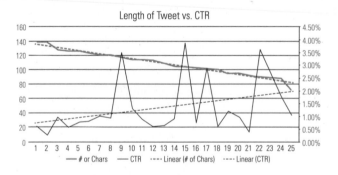

According to my analysis, the results are similar. The relationship is actually a little stronger here. The correlation is -0.335. This again, suggests that shorter tweets might be getting higher CTRs. My average tweet is 108.92 characters in length with a standard deviation of 16.94. Given this extra data point, I'm certainly tempted to focus a bit more on brevity when composing my tweets.

## Q: DO ON/OFF-TOPIC TWEETS AFFECT MY CTR?

In order to find out whether the topic focus of my tweets has an impact on the CTR, I had to assign a numerical value to each degree of "on-topicness," and then map them each URL accordingly. My Twitter profile says that I tweet about SEO, startups, and technology. Since I'm in the SEO field, and the majority of my tweets are about these subjects, I created this scale:

0 - Completely unrelated topic

1 - Topic subtly related to marketing, technology, startups, and SEO

2 – Topic is strongly related to marketing, technology, startups, and SEO

3 – Topic is specifically about SEO

I then made the following chart to compare topic focus against CTR:

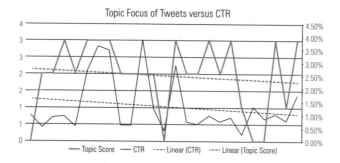

The correlation function is a bit higher, 0.43. This suggests that when I tweet about the topics people expect to hear from me about, the CTR is higher. That's not unexpected. In fact, I would have predicted a higher correlation. And who knows? Across a larger dataset, it might have been stronger.

# Q: IS MY CTR IMPROVING OVER TIME?

This is a pretty simple question to answer.

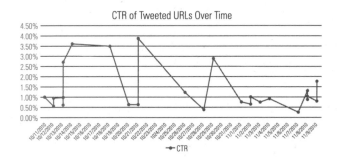

Sadly, that answer is no. I hit my CTR peak in early October with a few choice tweets, and haven't had many in the high ranges since that time. This is a good lesson for me. It shows me why it's important for me to be monitoring, testing, and working to improve my performance.

On a broader scale, we also recently analyzed 20+ Twitter accounts containing hundreds of tweeted URLs. Our raw dataset contains about 250 tweeted URLs with data for CTR and several other metrics (see `https://spreadsheets.google.com/pub?key=0AjlLl1 iDXp81dDU4VDVVT0pmSGUtZjlyMmtHVzVkUmc&hl=en&output=html`). Our hope was to see whether any of the metrics could help predict a higher versus lower CTR.

The following chart illustrates the findings.

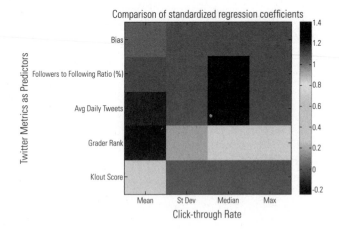

Overall, no single metric was particularly predictive of higher CTR, with the exception of Twitter Grader Rank. However, in this case, a higher numeric rank (meaning a "worse" rank) had a higher correlation to CTR, suggesting an awkwardly inverse relationship. I was also bummed to see that Klout scores, which I had hoped would be predictive of CTR, barely correlated.

One interesting thing I found was that the average CTR for all 250+ tweets was only 1.17% (with a 0.024 standard deviation.) Therefore, I shouldn't feel too bad that my average CTR is 1.34%.

The research, unfortunately, didn't lead to any great conclusions. The full report is available for download at `http://mz.cm/ZETsVj`.

While this type of analysis can be interesting, it's not a scalable or practical solution for most marketers. What we need is a tool that can analyze our Twitter accounts using more metrics in an automated fashion. That tool doesn't exist … yet.

P.S. Special thanks to Ray Illian for compiling the research and report discussed in this chapter.

# VII

# CONCLUSION

*By Rand Fishkin and Thomas Høgenhaven*

IN THE PRECEDING pages, you learned a lot about search engine optimization, content, social media, outreach, conversion rate optimization, and analytics. We hope those 25 chapters have inspired you to think about the many ways you can use inbound marketing and SEO to help your business become more successful.

This leaves one final question: Where to start? This final chapter provides you with a step-by-step plan so you can get moving. Whether you are launching a new website or want to enhance your existing business, these 18 steps will guide you through the process.

# 26

# LAUNCHING A NEW WEBSITE: 18 STEPS TO SUCCESSFUL METRICS AND MARKETING

*By Rand Fishkin*

---

**Editor's Note:** *The process of launching a new website for the first time is often intimidating—even fearful—for many entrepreneurs, bloggers, and business owners. Getting started (or even knowing where to start) can be the hardest part. In this post (originally published over two years ago and updated for 2013), Rand Fishkin shares an 18-step plan for launching a new website. The plan not only helps new website owners figure out where to start the launch process, but ensures they cover all the basics as well—both on- and off-site.*

---

THE PROCESS OF launching a new website is often an uncertain and scary prospect. This is typically due to lack of knowledge. In this chapter, I give my best recommendations for launching a new site from a marketing and analytics perspective. You'll learn not only how to improve your new website's SEO, but its accessibility and ability to generate traffic as well. You can also learn how to measure and improve just about everything regarding your site.

## #1: INSTALL VISITOR ANALYTICS

*Nothing can be improved that is not tracked.* Keeping these immortal words of wisdom in mind, get your pages firing analytics code before your first visitor arrives. Google Analytics (GA) (`http://google.com/analytics`) is the obvious choice, and customization options abound. For most sites, I'd highly recommend at least using first-touch attribution. While GA tracks last-touch attribution out of the box, you can configure your website and GA to pull first-touch attribution data for you. (See Will Critchlow's blog post for Distilled for the how-to: `www.distilled.net/blog/seo/first-touch-tracking-in-google-analytics`.) This way, you'll be able to track not only the interactions on your site that lead to conversions, but see how users find your site in the first place.

Tracking code for Google analytics, or any other analytics package (such as `Piwik.org` or `Clicky.org`) needs to be placed on every page of your site and verified. Google offers step-by-step instructions on how to do this at `https://developers.google.com/analytics/devguides/collection/gajs/asyncTracking`).

## #2: SET UP GOOGLE AND BING WEBMASTER TOOLS ACCOUNTS

Both Google (`http://google.com/webmasters`) and Bing (`http://bing.com/webmasters`) have webmaster tools programs that monitor and report on data about your site. This is the heartbeat of your site, from the search engines' perspective. For that reason alone, it's wise to stay on top of the data they share with you.

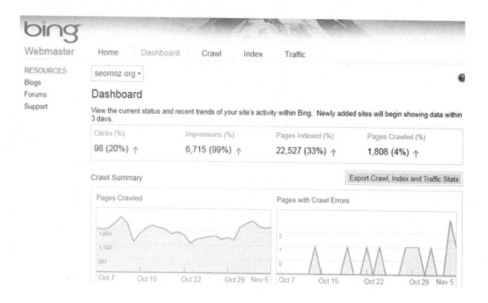

*Editor's Note: This screenshot of Bing Webmaster Tools was taken in November of 2010, when this post was originally penned for The Moz Blog.*

And while many webmasters did indeed sign up for GWT for that reason, and that reason alone, as the data was often flawed and features limited, GWT made some drastic improvements in 2012, and Bing is right there with them. GWT now provides data and insights you can't get anywhere else. Here are just a few things you can do with both GWT and Bing:

- Download your latest links.
- Preview how your rich snippets/structured data will appear in search results.
- Disavow inbound links not trusted by your site.
- Receive messages about issues with your site (such as malware detected or crawl errors).

It is also worth noting that you can view GWT data within your GA account. To learn how to do this (and why you might want to), see Chapter 23.

*Author's Note: For more information on what you can do with GWT, read "An Updated Guide to Google Webmaster Tools" on The Moz Blog at* `www.moz.org/blog/an-updated-guide-to-google-webmaster-tools.`

## #3: RUN A CRAWL SIMULATION OF YOUR SITE

No matter how perfectly you plan your launch, there will be problems when you roll out your site such as broken links, improper redirects, missing titles, pages lacking `rel=canonical` tags, and files blocked by `robots.txt`.

> *Author's Note: To learn why we recommend implementing the* `rel=canonical` *tag, and the danger of implementing it improperly, see* `www.moz.org/blog/` `catastrophic-canonicalization`.

By running a crawl test with a free tool like Xenu (`http://home.snafu.de/tilman/` `xenulink.html`), or leveraging a paid tool like Screaming Frog (`www.screamingfrog.` `co.uk/seo-spider`) or Moz Analytics (`www.moz.com/products`), you can check your site's accessibility and ensure that visitors and search engines can reach pages successfully in the ways you want. If you launch first, you'll often find that critical errors are left to rot because the priority list fills up so quickly with other demands on development time. Crawl tests are also a great way to verify contractor or outsourced development work.

## #4: TEST YOUR DESIGN WITH BROWSER EMULATORS

In addition to testing for search engine and visitor accessibility, you'll want to make sure the gorgeous graphics and layout you've carefully prepared checks out in a variety of browsers. My rule is to test anything that has higher than a 2 percent market share, which currently means Internet Explorer, Firefox, Chrome, and Safari for desktop, according to ZDNet (`http://mz.cm/15KUh2Z`). There's a great list of cross-browser testing options compiled by DesignModo at `http://designmodo.com/bcross-browser-compatibility`, so I'll just add that in-person testing, on your own devices, is also a highly recommended use of an hour.

> *Editor's Note: Don't forget to test how your site renders on mobile devices! BrowserStack (`www.browserstack.com`) offers live, online testing for a variety of browsers and devices (desktops, too), while MobileMoxie's toolset is dedicated to cross-browser testing for mobile (`http://www.mobilemoxie.com/s/register`). To find out what the hottest browsers, OS, and devices are for mobile are in various markets, create a custom report at NetMarketShare (`www.netmarketshare.com`).*

## #5: SET UP RSS FEED ANALYTICS

Virtually every site will have some form of structured data being pushed out through an RSS feed. And, just like visitor analytics, if you want to improve the reach and quality of the feed, you'll need to leverage data.

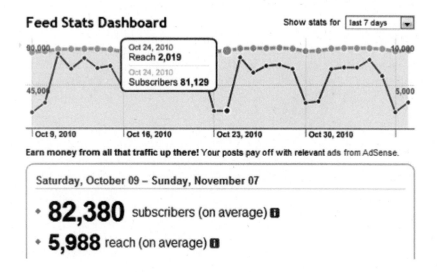

Feedburner (`feedburner.google.com`) is the de facto software of choice, and it's very solid. Getting your feed and the analytics to track and measure it is typically a very easy process because there's nothing to verify—you can create and promote any feed you want with just a few button clicks. It is also almost that easy to track Feedburner activity in Google Analytics, as well. That said, Google has shut down its API for Feedburner and stopped showing ads, so it would be wise to back up your subscriber list, or consider using an alternative service such as Feedblitz (`feedblitz.com`).

One important recommendation: don't initially use the counter "chicklet."

**Your Chicklet:**

It has a bad psychological impact to see that no one has subscribed to your new RSS feed. Instead, just provide a standard link or graphic. After you've amassed a few hundred (or thousands of) readers, use the chicklet counter to provide additional social proof for your site.

## #6: TAG THE ACTIONS THAT MATTER

No matter what your site is, there are actions you're hoping visitors will take, from tweeting a link to your post and leaving a comment, to buying a product and subscribing to an email list. Whatever those actions might be, you need to record the visits that make them through your analytics tool. The documentation for GA provides step-by-step directions on how to set up event tracking (see `http://mz.cm/15MDvAE`).

Once action tracking is in place, you can segment traffic sources and visitor paths by actions taken. This will give you insight into what your most valuable traffic sources are. If you're pouring hours each day into Twitter, but seeing no desired actions taken on your site (i.e., conversions), you might try investing more of your time and efforts in a different channel (even if the traffic volume from Twitter is high).

## #7: CONDUCT AN ONLINE USABILITY/BRANDING TEST

Before a formal launch, it can be extremely helpful to get a sense of what users see, experience, and remember when they browse to your site or start to take an action. There's some fantastic software to help with this, including Clue App (`clueapp.com`), shown in this screenshot from 2011.

I set up a Clue App test for Moz's homepage in 30 seconds and tweeted a link to the test. The tweet garnered 158 kind responses with words and concepts people remembered from visiting the home page. This type of raw testing isn't perfect, but it can give you some insight into the minds of your visitors. If they are not taking away the messages you intended, it may be critical for you to tweak your site.

In addition to Clue, dozens of other easy usability and user-testing apps are on the market, including Crazy Egg (`crazyegg.com`) and Click Tale (`clicktale.com`).

## #8: ESTABLISH A KPI DASHBOARD

No matter what your website does, you live and die by your key metrics. If you're starting out as a blogger, your RSS subscribers, unique visits, page views and key social stats (tweets, links, Facebook shares, etc.) are your lifeblood. If you're in ecommerce, it's all of the above plus the number of customers, sales, sales volume, returning versus. new buyers, etc.

| Day | Date | Gross Cash Revenue | Daily Cash Refunds | Net Cash Revenue | New PRO | New PRO Plus | New PRO Elite | New SignUps Total | downgrades |
|-----|------|-------------------|--------------------|------------------|---------|--------------|---------------|-------------------|------------|
| FRI | 3/5/2010 | $23,653 | | $23,653 | 25 | 3 | 0 | 28 | |
| SAT | 3/6/2010 | $13,985 | | $13,985 | 15 | 2 | 0 | 17 | |
| SUN | 3/7/2010 | $10,171 | | $10,171 | 11 | 2 | 0 | 13 | |
| MON | 3/8/2010 | $12,857 | | $12,857 | 11 | 2 | 0 | 13 | |
| TUES | 3/9/2010 | $15,229 | -$948 | $14,281 | 15 | 2 | 1 | 18 | |
| WED | 3/10/2010 | $15,458 | -$30 | $15,428 | 25 | 3 | 1 | 29 | |
| THU | 3/11/2010 | $14,945 | | $14,945 | 21 | 4 | 0 | 25 | |
| FRI | 3/12/2010 | $15,120 | -$158 | $14,962 | 21 | 6 | 1 | 28 | |
| SAT | 3/13/2010 | $11,758 | -$79 | $11,679 | 7 | 2 | 0 | 9 | |
| SUN | 3/14/2010 | $10,298 | | $10,298 | 9 | 1 | 0 | 10 | |

Whatever your particular key metrics might be, you need a single place—often just a basic spreadsheet—where these important numbers are tracked on a daily or weekly basis. Setting this up before you launch will save you a ton of pain later on, and give you consistent statistics that you can use as a baseline and as a resource for identifying trends in the future.

## #9: BUILD AN EMAIL LIST OF FRIENDS AND BUSINESS CONTACTS FOR LAUNCH

It's shocking how a friendly email blast to just a few dozen of your close contacts can help set the stage for a much more successful website launch. Start by building a list of the people who owe you favors, who have helped out in the past, and who you know you can always rely on. If you're feeling a bit more aggressive, you can go one circle beyond that to include casual business partners and acquaintances.

Once you have the list, you'll need to craft an email. I highly recommend being transparent, requesting feedback and offering to return the favor. You should also use BCC and make yourself the recipient. No one wants to be on a huge, visible email list to folks they may not know (and get the resulting reply-all messages).

## #10: CREATE YOUR GOOGLE ALERTS

The Google Alerts service certainly isn't perfect—but it's free, ubiquitous, and can give you a heads up when your brand is mentioned or your site is linked to (see www.google.com/alerts).

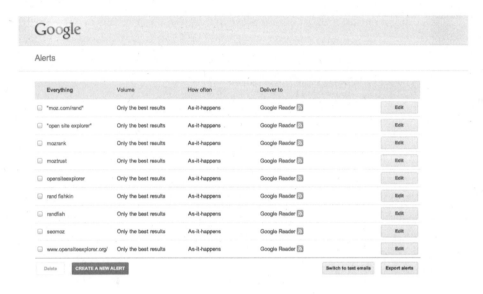

*Editor's Note: Google Reader retired in April 2013. When this screenshot was taken (in March of 2013), users had the choice of having Google Alerts sent to their Google Reader as an RSS Feed, or to their inbox as emails .*

Unfortunately, the service sends through a lot of false positives—spam, scraper sites and low quality junk. It also tends to miss a lot of good, relevant mentions and links, which is why the next recommendation's on the list.

## #11: BOOKMARK BRAND TRACKING QUERIES

In order to keep track of your progress and identify the sites and pages that mention or link to your new site, you'll want to set up a series of queries that you can run on a regular basis. These include a number of searches at Google and Twitter.

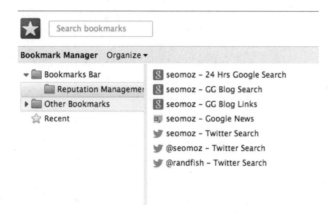

The queries should use your brand name in combination with specific searches, like the example below (using "seomoz" and "seomoz.org"):

- Google Blog Search mentions (`http://mz.cm/16s8rXY`)
- Google Blog Search links (`http://mz.cm/16s8mn9`)
- Google Web mentions, past 24 hours (`http://mz.cm/15MIUHP`)
- Google News mentions (`http://mz.cm/16s84gh`)
- Twitter Search (`http://search.twitter.com/search?q=seomoz`)

You can add more to this list if you find them valuable/worthwhile, but these basics should take you most of the way on knowing where your site has been mentioned or referenced on the web.

> **Editor's Note:** *Right before this book was published, Moz released a new beta product, Fresh Web Explorer (FWE). This tool makes it easy to keep track of all your new links, social mentions, and web citations in one place. In addition to monitoring your brand, you can also use FWE for competitive analysis, content strategy, and link building.*
>
> *To learn more about FWE, check out this blog post by Matthew Brown, Head of Special Projects at Moz:* `www.moz.org/blog/announcing-fresh-web-explorer;` *or try FWE yourself at* `http://freshwebexplorer.moz.com.`

## #12: MAKE EMAIL SIGNUP/SUBSCRIPTION AVAILABLE

Capturing the email addresses of your potential customers/audience can be a huge win for the influence you're able to wield later to promote new content, products or offerings. Before you launch, you'll want to carefully consider how and where you can offer something in exchange for permission to build an email list.

One of the most common ways to build good lists is to offer a whitepaper, eBook, video, or other exclusive content piece for download in exchange for an email address. You can also collect emails from comment registrations (which tend to be of lower overall quality), through email newsletter sign-ups (which tend to be of very high quality), or via RSS subscription. Services like MailChimp (`mailchimp.com`), Constant Contact (`constantcontact.com`), and iContact (`icontact.com`) are all good, affordable options for managing your email marketing campaigns.

> *Author's Note: If you collect emails from RSS subscribers, you'll need to self-manage your feed in order to have full access to those emails.*

## #13: CREATE YOUR SITE/BRAND'S SOCIAL ACCOUNTS

Social media has become popular and powerful enough that any new site should be taking advantage of it. At a minimum, I'd recommend creating accounts on the following networks:

- Twitter (`twitter.com`)
- Facebook for Business (`www.facebook.com/business`)
- LinkedIn (`linkedin.com`)
- Google+ for Business (`www.google.com/+/business`)
- YouTube (`youtube.com`)

And if you have more time or energy to devote, I'd also invest in these:

- Pinterest for Business (`business.pinterest.com`)—visuals
- Instagram for Business (`http://help.instagram.com/454502981253053`)—photos & other images
- Flickr (`flicker.com`)—photos
- Quora (`quora.com`)—Q&A
- SlideShare (`slideshare.net`)—presentations
- Scribd (`scribd.com`)—digital documents
- StumbleUpon (`stumbleupon.com`)
- Reddit (`reddit.com`)
- Any industry specific social portals (e.g., in software, this might include places like StackOverflow, Github, and Hacker News—`news.ycombinator.com`).

Setting up these accounts properly is important. Don't just reuse the same short bio or descriptive snippet over and over. Spend the time fleshing out profiles and networking to help build up your authority on the site. The effort is worth the reward. Empty, unloved social accounts do virtually nothing, but active ones can drive traffic, citations, awareness, and value.

Depending on the size and structure of your site, you may also want to consider creating profiles on company-tracking sites like CrunchBase and Businessweek, and Google+ Local.

## #14: CONNECT YOUR SOCIAL ACCOUNTS

If you've just set up your social account, you've likely added your new site as a reference point already; but if not, you should take the time to visit your various social profiles and make sure they link back to the site you're launching.

This is what Rand's own Twitter profile looked like a couple of months before launching Moz. com. He has since updated it to promote the new website.

Not all of these links will provide direct SEO value (as many of them are "nofollowed"), but the brand value and relationships you build on these social sites may prove to be invaluable. It's also a great way to leverage your existing branding and engagement, increase referral traffic to your new site, and send social signals to the search engines, which may increase your rankings in the SERPs.

## #15: MAKE A LIST OF OUTREACH CONTACTS

Depending on your niche, you may have traditional media outlets, bloggers, industry luminaries, academics, Twitter personalities, powerful offline sources, or others that could provide your new site with visibility and value. Don't just hope that these folks find you, though; create a targeted list of the sites, accounts, and individuals you want to connect with, and form a strategy to reach the low-hanging fruit first.

The list should include as much contact information as you can gather about each target, including Twitter account name, email, and physical mailing address. You can leverage all of these to reach out to these folks at launch (or have your PR company do it if you have one). If you tell the right story and have a compelling site, chances are good that you'll get at least a few of your targets to help you promote your site.

## #16: BUILD A LIST OF KEYWORDS TO TARGET IN SEARCH ENGINES

This is SEO basics 101, but every new site should keep in mind that search engines get lots of queries for virtually everything under the sun. If there are keywords and phrases you know you want to rank for, these should be in a list that you can measure progress against. Chances are that you won't even be targeting many of these searches with specific pages when you launch your site; but if you build the list now, you'll have the goal to create these pages and work on ranking for those terms already established.

As you're doing this, don't just choose the highest traffic keywords possible. Go for those that are balanced; moderate to high in volume, highly relevant in terms of what the searcher wants versus what your page/site offers, and relatively low in difficulty (www.moz.org/keyword-difficulty).

## #17: SET TARGETS FOR THE NEXT 12 MONTHS

Without goals and targets, there's no way to know whether you're meeting, beating, or failing your expectations. Nearly every endeavor, from running a marathon to cooking a meal, will fail if there aren't clear expectations set at the start. If you're relatively small and just starting out, I'd set goals for the following metrics:

- Average weekly visits (via analytics)
- Average page views (via analytics)
- Number of new posts/pages/content pieces produced per month
- Number of target contacts (from item #15) that you've reached
- Social media metrics (depending on your heaviest use platform, e.g., # of Twitter followers if you're a heavy Tweeter)
- Any of the key items from #8 on this list (your KPI dashboard)

And each of these metrics should have 3-, 6-, and 12-month targets. Don't be too aggressive, as this may leave you discouraged or, worse, not taking your own targets seriously. Likewise, don't cut yourself short by setting goals that you can easily achieve—stretch a little.

Every three to six months, you should reevaluate these and create new goals, possibly adding new metrics if you've taken new paths (RSS subscribers, video views, emails collected, etc.).

## #18: PLUG INTO MOZ ANALYTICS

I know this one's a bit self-serving, but I'd like to think I'd add Moz Analytics here even if it wasn't made by my company. (I recently set up my own personal blog—see `http://moz.com/rand`—and found the crawling, rank tracking, and GA integration features pretty awesome for monitoring the growth of the new site.)

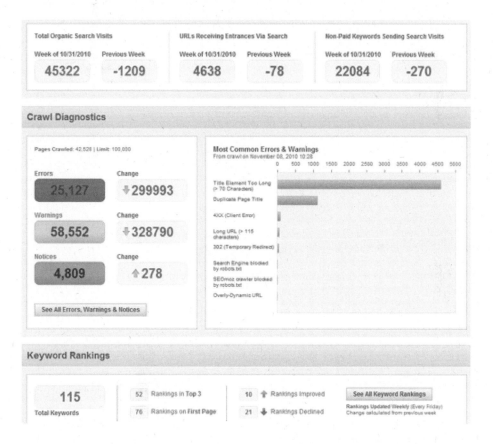

Moz Analytics (`www.moz.com/products`), shown here in a screenshot from 2010, has a number of cool tracking and monitoring features, as well as recommendations for optimizing pages targeting keywords, that make it valuable for new sites that are launching. The crawl system can serve to help with #3 on this list at the outset, but ongoing, it continues to crawl pages and show you your site's growth and any errors or missed opportunities. Tracking rankings can let you follow progress against item #16, even if that progress is moving from ranking in the 40s to the 20s (where very little search traffic will be coming in, even if you're making progress). And the GA integration features show the quantity of pages, keywords, and visits from search engines to track progress from an SEO standpoint.

> *Moz Analytics has recently been updated, and now offers even more features that can help you ensure the success of your new website.*

Using this list, you should be able to set up a new site for launch and feel confident that your marketing and metrics priorities are in place.

# MEET THE AUTHORS

**James Agate** is the founder of Skyrocket SEO, a link building and content marketing agency working with agency partners and large companies across the world. James is a regular contributor to *Moz* and other blogs, and an avid Tweeter. You can follow James on Twitter - @jamesagate.

**Craig Bradford** is an SEO Consultant for Distilled London, and a global associate of Moz. Craig has worked with clients of all shapes and sizes; from agile startups to multi-nationals. He is a regular contributor to the *Distilled* and *Moz* blogs; his interests include technical SEO and conversion rate optimization. Craig is on Twitter - @CraigBradford.

**Ruth Burr** is an SEO and data-driven marketer living in Seattle, WA. She is Lead SEO at Moz, where she builds and executes the SEO strategy for Moz.org and its related properties. Ruth has been working in agency-side and in-house SEO and PPC since 2006, and is passionate about technical SEO, content planning, SEO evangelism, karaoke, and grilled cheese sandwiches. You can find her tweeting from her personal account, @ruthburr.

**Paras Chopra** is the founder of Visual Website Optimizer, the world's easiest A/B split-testing software. Thousands of companies and agencies have been able to increase sales and conversions up to 90 percent within the first few days of using the tool. You can follow the company on Twitter - @wingify.

**Tom Critchlow** worked for online marketing agency Distilled for five years, helping to grow the company as it spread across the pond from London to Seattle, and then to New York. During that time, he consulted for some of the world's biggest brands, including Fortune 500 companies and small startups. In 2012, he left Distilled to join Google working for the Creative Lab, a small startup-like marketing group working across all Google products. He lives in Brooklyn, and can be found online at `tomcritchlow.com` and Twitter - `@tomcritchlow`.

**Will Critchlow** founded Distilled with Duncan Morris in 2005. Since then, he has consulted with some of the world's largest organizations and most famous websites, spoken at most major industry events, and regularly appeared in local and national press. In addition to consulting, Will spends a lot of time on R&D and content strategy, resulting in the most effective marketing Distilled has ever done. His academic background is in mathematics. He holds a degree from the University of Cambridge (St. John's College) and has written a graduate thesis on auction theory. Will's Twitter account is `@willcritchlow`.

**Stephen Croome** is a competitive digital marketer with a love for startups and music. With a B.S. in Biology and an M.A. in Social Media, he loves applying natural network theory to digital networks. He enjoys public speaking, and continuously fails to stay on-topic on Twitter - `@firstconversion`.

**Annie Cushing** is an SEO and analytics consultant based out of Cherry Hill, NJ. She started doing SEO in 2003, originally focusing on usability. She has since worked both in-house and for agencies. You can find her blog at `annielytics.com`, her data visualization posts on *Search Engine Land*, and her tweets at `@AnnieCushing`.

**John Doherty** is a New York City-based search marketer with Distilled. A web developer and technical writer by trade, he loves working with clients to make their websites friendly to both search engines and users. He has been a blogger for ten years, and currently writes for `johnfdoherty.com`, `distilled.net/blog`, and `moz.org/blog`. You can find John at Twitter - `@dohertyjf`.

**Rand Fishkin** is the CEO of SEO software company Moz. He co-authored *The Art of SEO* from O'Reilly Media, co-founded `Inbound.org`, and was named on *Puget Sound Business Journal's* "40 Under 40" list and *Businessweek's* "30 Best Tech Entrepreneurs Under 30." Rand is an addict of all things content and social on the web, from his blog on entrepreneurship (`Moz.com/rand`), to Twitter, Google+, Facebook, LinkedIn, and FourSquare. In his minuscule spare time, Rand enjoys the company of his amazing wife, Geraldine, whose serendipitous travel blog, *The Everywhereist*, chronicles their journeys (`www.everywhereist.com`). Follow Rand on Twitter - `@randfish`.

**Oli Gardner** is Co-Founder and Creative Director at Unbounce, The DIY Landing Page Platform. He is an opinionated writer, primarily on the subjects of landing pages and conversion rate optimization. You should follow him on Twitter - `@OliGardner`.

**Thomas Høgenhaven** is a Ph.D. Fellow at Copenhagen Business School focusing on online experimental methodology and online communities. He is Chief Strategy Officer at Better Collective, where he is in charge of product development and marketing. You can find him blogging at thogenhaven.com or on Twitter - @thogenhaven.

**Michael King** is an SEO engineer by trade and inbound marketer by evolution. He works as Director of Inbound Marketing for leading content marketing agency iAcquire. He has a background in software and web development, and has a proclivity for finding creative solutions. Mike is also a contributor to leading industry blogs such as *Moz, Unbounce,* and *Distilled;* and has spoken at conferences such as SearchLove NYC, Seattle Interactive, SMX Israel, SES New York, LinkLove London, and MozCon. You should follow him on Twitter - @iPullRank.

**Jennifer Lopez** is Director of Community at Moz. With a background in SEO, web development, and journalism, she spends her time supporting the Moz community both internally and externally. She blogs frequently on Moz, and shares her love for TAGFEE at speaking events all over the world. In her spare time, you can find her traveling, hunting down the best cupcake in Seattle, and spending time with her husband, Rudy, and daughter, Eva. Follow her on Twitter - @jennita.

**Dr. Peter J. Meyers ("Dr. Pete")** is a cognitive psychologist, former Internet start-up executive, and accidental entrepreneur. He discovered the *Moz* blog in 2006, after a client encouraged him to attend SES Chicago, and it's been his second home ever since. You can find Dr. Pete on Twitter - @dr_pete.

**Paddy Moogan** is an SEO Consultant for Distilled and works in its London office. He is also the author of *The Link Building Book,* and has written for numerous SEO and online marketing blogs. Paddy has been doing SEO professionally for over five years, and learned about it when he was meant to be studying for his law degree at Coventry University. Paddy tweets from @paddymoogan.

**Eugen Oprea** is an online entrepreneur who blogs about web analytics, SEO and WordPress at EugenOprea.com. You can get his Google Analytics course for free on his website, or check out his flagship product, the Web Analytics Blueprint. He also helps people build profitable businesses online by providing WordPress advice and services with WPBackpack.com. You should follow Eugen on Twitter - @eugenoprea.

**Cyrus Shepard** is an SEO and online marketing strategist. He's worked with several startups to help build their online presence, including Moz (a very happy time in his life). His website is cyrusshepard.com, and you can often find him tweeting at @cyrusshepard.

# INDEX